Only People

Make

Their Own

History

SAMIR AMIN

Only People

Make

Their Own

History

Writings on Capitalism, Imperialism, and Revolution

Introduction by AIJAZ AHMAD

MONTHLY REVIEW PRESS
New York

Library of Congress Cataloging-in-Publication data
available from the publisher.

ISBN paperback: 978-1-58367-769-8
ISBN cloth: 978-1-58367-770-4

First published in November 2018 by LeftWord Books, India

Monthly Review Press, New York
monthlyreview.org

5 4 3 2 1

CONTENTS

INTRODUCTION

Aijaz Ahmad

> To be a 'Marxist' is to continue the work that Marx merely began,
> even though that beginning was of unequalled power. It is not
> to stop at Marx, but to start from him . . . Marx is *boundless*,
> because the radical critique that he initiates is itself boundless,
> always incomplete, and must always be the object of its own
> critique ('Marxism as formulated at a particular moment has to
> undergo a Marxist critique.').
>
> – Samir Amin, *The Law of Worldwide Value*

Samir Amin (1931–2018) was one of the grand intellectuals of our
time.[1] A distinguished theoretician, his life of political activism
spanned well over six decades. A socialist from an early age and
trained as an economist, he insisted that laws of the economic
science, including the law of value, were operationally subject to
the laws of historical materialism. Trained also as a mathematician,
he avoided too great a mathematization of his concepts and kept
algebraic formulae to a minimum in even the most technical of his
writings. The ambition always was to retain theoretical rigour while
also communicating with the largest possible number of readers—
and activists in particular—through exposition in relatively direct
prose. His readership, like his own political activism, was spread
across countries and continents.

Amin came of age in the 1950s, when the wave of socialist
revolutions seemed to be very much on the ascendant and

---

[1] I have tried to keep the main text of this Introduction smooth and free of
digressions as much as possible. Some of the substantive points have been
jettisoned therefore to the footnotes. Hence the number of footnotes as well
as the fact that quite a few of them are quite lengthy.

the old colonial empires were being dismantled across Asia and Africa. Communist parties and socialist movements had emerged in these continents, more in Asia than in Africa, even before the Second World War. Onset of the postwar period witnessed immense expansion of revolutionary activity—the Chinese revolution, Korea, the onset of revolutionary liberation movements in Indochina and so on. With the notable exception of China, however, most countries in these continents had produced relatively little original work in the field of Marxist theoretical knowledge. Study of any sort of Marxism largely meant explication and/or translation of texts produced elsewhere, and that too was confined to the very brief texts or extracts from the Marxist classics or exegeses done in Britain, France or the Soviet Union. This now began to change, in several notable ways. First, we witness the rise of a new generation of Marxist scholar-activists across Asia and Africa over the very years when the colonial empires were getting dismantled. Second, a number of these new intellectuals, often associated with communist parties or national liberation movements, bring into their work increasingly sophisticated knowledge of the more fundamental of the classics: the major works of Marx, Lenin, Luxemburg, Bukharin, Kautsky and others. Third, attention shifts to extended, rigorous analyses of (1) the historical development, modes of production and class structures not so much of Europe as of Asian and African countries, and (2) the very elaborate mechanisms involved in the exploitation of the imperialized countries, i.e., the process whereby values produced in the colonies were appropriated for accumulation in imperialist centres.

Mention of a few dates should clarify this. Thus, for example, Amin submitted his 629-page doctoral dissertation to the University of Paris in 1957 and published it much later as the two-volume *Accumulation on a World Scale* (French edition 1970; English translation 1974). In the course of roughly those same years, India witnessed the publication of three books that were foundational in the making of Indian Marxist historiography: D.D. Kosambi's *An Introduction to the Study of Indian History* (1956), Irfan Habib's *The Agrarian System of Mughal India* (1963) and R.S. Sharma's *Indian Feudalism* (1965). Across the oceans, in Latin America, all the founding texts of Dependency theorists— Theotonio Dos Santos, Celso Furtado, Ruy Mauro Marini, Andre Gunder Frank, and others—also appeared in the 1960s and early '70s.[2] Theoretically, Amin was much closer to Paul Baran who published *The Political Economy of Growth* in 1957, the year Amin submitted his mammoth dissertation. The great classic of Marxist political economy that Baran co-authored with Sweezy, *Monopoly Capital*, followed soon thereafter, in 1966. Anatomies of imperialism had thus arrived at the very centre of new Marxist thinking across the world, and Marxism itself had become a powerful tool for independent thought and research across the Tricontinent. On both these counts, Amin's dissertation would appear to be among the first texts re-fashioning the contours of postwar Marxism in a very particular way, as we shall argue below.

Amin was proficient in several languages but wrote primarily in French. He was a stunningly prolific writer, producing books and articles with great speed until death itself silenced that fertile mind. Not all his work is available in English. Some of the translations have appeared elsewhere but, on the whole, Monthly Review Press has been by far the most devoted publisher of his

[2] Dependency theorists were of course more *marxisant* than Marxist. Like Amin, they too had borrowed Raúl Prebisch's conception of the world system as a bipolar structure of unequal exchange between the centre ('developed') and periphery ('underdeveloped'). For Prebisch, though, this was a distortion that could be corrected through fairer terms of trade, supplemented with protectionism and import substitution industrialization in the peripheries. For the *dependentistas*, as for Amin, this 'underdevelopment' was, however, not an inheritance from the precolonial past but a product of imperialism itself. The sharing of this premise would later bring Amin closer to them, particularly to Frank, and to the World System theorists, Wallerstein and Arrighi.

work in English translation. This collection brings together eleven of Amin's essays that the magazine has published since 2000. There are others that appeared in *MR* during this period.[3] The objective here is to assemble a not too cumbersome a collection of his essays that would elucidate some of the most fundamental coordinates of Amin's thought in the closing years of his life. The introduction here is designed not to *explicate* those texts but to *situate* them in the larger fabric of his life in which the personal, the political and the theoretical were meshed together in a tight weave.

I

Samir Amin published two books of reflections on his own life. In *Re-Reading the Postwar Period*, he offers his own reconstruction of his political views and theoretical positions as they evolved from one decade to the next, up to the beginning of the 1990s.[4] The fact that he arrived in Paris to start college in 1947, the year India got its independence, reminds us that his adult life coincided with exactly the period he reviews in that book. He was a young communist and a student activist in France during the great, bitter wars of liberation in the French colonies of Vietnam and Algeria. Dismantling of the British and French colonial empires were the epochal events of his youth. The overlap between colonialism, postcolonial imperialism and capitalist accumulation logically became the central occupation in his intellectual life as well as in his political activism for the rest of his life. In *Capital* and related works, Marx had shaped the science of the capitalist mode of

---

[3] For instance, 'Africa: Living on the Fringe', *Monthly Review*, March 2002; 'India: A Great Power?', February 2005; '"Market Economy" or Oligopoly-Finance Capital', April 2008; 'The Surplus in Monopoly Capitalism & the Imperialist Rent', July–August 2012; 'The Kurdish Question Then & Now', October 2016.

[4] Samir Amin, *Re-Reading the Postwar Period: An Intellectual Itinerary*, Monthly Review Press, 1994.

production as it had evolved in Europe, Britain in particular, up to his own time. In other texts, such as the *Grundrisse* and the much later *Ethnographic Notebooks*, Marx said much about the world outside Europe but mostly about *precapitalist* formations. He wrote extensively and often very perceptively about colonialism but mostly at the level of factual description and political denunciation, with only a few scattered remarks of lasting theoretical import. For Marx, a compulsive globalizing tendency was inherent in the very mode of functioning of capital itself. However, aside from this repeated prediction, the actual corpus of his work did not encompass, nor was the third quarter of the 19th century a propitious time to produce, a *theory* of a the capitalism that was to become a fully globalized mode of production—not only of appropriation, extraction and circulation—in the form, first, of colonizing imperialism and, then, even more strongly after the dissolution of the old colonial empires. Amin's distinctive undertaking in his doctoral dissertation that was later published as *Accumulation on a World Scale* was to apply the theoretical categories of *Capital* to the study of the capitalist mode as it unfolds globally through the agency of colonialism, putting in place structures of exploitation and accumulation that were to greatly outlast the colonial era *per se*.[5] For him, as for very few other Marxists, the end of the colonial period marked a decisive turning point in the history of human freedom that opened up new avenues for liberation struggles for peoples of the Tricontinent— but *not* a fundamental break in histories either of capitalism or of imperialism *per se*. This historical ambiguity of that conjuncture is

---

[5] This was somewhat analogous to Harry Magdoff's undertaking in his *Age of Imperialism* (1969) to elucidate the functioning of imperialism in his own time in terms of the basic categories that Lenin had established in his famous pamphlet. Amin, however, was more interested in comprehending the *structural changes* that the capitalist mode itself undergoes in the age of empire and monopoly capital, as it expands out of its initial European enclaves to become a world system of exploitative inequality between classes as well as nations of the world.

best witnessed in the fact that the quarter century, 1945 to 1970, in which those colonial empires were largely dissolved, has also gone down in history as the Golden Age of Capital.[6] This intent to read Marx rigorously but creatively in light of the later evolution of the capitalist mode remained a major thread in Amin's work all his life, up to *The Law of Worldwide Value* (2010) and beyond.[7] We shall return to this presently.

Re-Reading the Postwar Period recounts the stages of his own intellectual development in relation to the main features and events of that period. The latter portions of the other memoir, *A Life Looking Forward*, reconstruct that same politico-intellectual itinerary in more personal terms but it is in the earlier sections of the book that we get a vivid narrative of his growing up in a rather unique family and his early orientation toward revolutionary politics, so that all of his life, beginning to end, seems to cohere into an integral whole.[8] This more personal memoir opens with a simple sentence: 'Ancestors do matter.' This then is followed in the same opening paragraph with: 'Certainly my own family, on both my mother's and father's side, reminded me from time to time that the education they were giving me was a 'legacy' to which they were firmly attached.' With an Egyptian father and a French mother, this 'legacy' had two sides to it: '. . . my parents had actually met in Strasbourg as medical students in the 1920s. It was a happy meeting between the line of French Jacobinism and Egyptian national democracy—in my view, the best traditions of the two countries.'[9]

The father's side was Coptic upper class, part of a cosmopolitan

---

[6] Among countless studies of the phenomenon, one might just look at Stephen A. Marglin and Juliet B. Schor (eds), *The Golden Age of Capitalism: Reinterpreting the Postwar Experience*, Clarendon, 1990.

[7] This is a revised and expanded version of his book of 1978, *The Law of Value and Historical Materialism*.

[8] Samir Amin, *A Life Looking Forward: Memoirs of an Independent Marxist*, Zed Books, 2006.

[9] *A Life Looking Forward*, p. 5 (henceforth *A Life*).

mini-world of Christian and Muslim Egyptians, Greeks, Armenians, Maltese as well as French and British émigré residents sprinkled all over Cairo but spread more widely over Alexandria, Port Said and more generally across the region where the fertile Nile delta of Lower Egypt meets the country's Mediterranean coast. The family, which included well-known publishers and writers of the 19th century, was part of a larger milieu that valued secular democratic convictions, higher learning, professional standing, and a sort of liberal bourgeois enlightenment that looked down on all sorts of feudalism and conservatism. His father, a doctor by profession and a bourgeois with social conscience, was opposed both to British colonialism and to monarchy, and he preferred communists to demagogic nationalists, including Nasser. On the other side of the family, Amin quotes his maternal grandfather, a freemason and a socialist, as once explaining to him, 'we Alsatians helped to make the [French] Revolution and we know the meaning and price of liberty'. As for the maternal grandmother, she, 'born soon after the Paris Commune in 1874 . . . was one of the descendants of the French revolutionary Jean-Baptiste Drouet, who played a role in the arrest of Louis XVI at Varennes in 1791 . . . My grandmother was quite proud of this ancestor, who was also active in the Babeuf movement. . . . As for my grandmother's name, Zelie, this was quite fashionable in the 19th century, but she told me she had been given it in homage to the Communard Zelie Camelinat'. This grandmother disliked religion and preferred to revive the Enlightenment slogan 'No God, no masters', which 19th century Anarchists like Bakunin shared at the time with Marx.

Democratic Wafdism, left-oriented anti-colonialism, and anti-monarchism on one side; family memory of Republican and revolutionary regicide, Babeuf-style communism and the Paris Commune on the other side: a pleasing and formidable 'legacy' indeed! Amin grew up in this loving, happy, sprawling and well-integrated family with clear-cut political views and historical moorings, and he went to school during the Second World War when Britain was still a colonial presence and a master of the Egyptian monarchy while a German advance through the whole region was at one point a distinct possibility. His secondary school, a French Lycée, was not immune to various political currents in Egyptian society: monarchists and anti-monarchists, nationalists of various stripes, and of course communists. Amin writes of being firmly in the communist group of students. Upon finishing secondary education he officially joined the Egyptian communist party. When Andre Gunder Frank asked Amin's mother as to when in her opinion her son had become a communist, the mother good-humouredly recounted a childhood anecdote and conjectured that it was perhaps at the age of six.

The ten years that elapsed between 1947 when Amin first arrived in Paris for post-secondary education—joining the French Communist Party quite swiftly, having joined the Egyptian communist party upon finishing secondary education—and 1957 when he submitted his doctoral dissertation were of course the years of the great wars of liberation in the French colonies of Indochina and Algeria, as mentioned earlier, leading to bitter polarizations within French society between pro-war and anti-war segments of activists, intellectuals, university faculties and students, and the general population itself. That was also the last decade of the French Communist Party's (PSF) very formidable role in French politics, before the decline began, and of Marxism as the central issue in French intellectual life (indicated, for instance, by Sartre making his passage from Existentialism to Marxism[10] and Merleau-Ponty's contrasting renunciation of Marxism in favour of a left-liberal position). France was also home to substantial enclaves of immigrant working class drawn from its North African colonies, Algeria in particular. Paris itself had been a major intellectual centre for anti-colonial students, activists,

[10] From *Being and Nothingness* to *Critique of Dialectical Reason*, so to speak.

writers and intellectuals from the African and Caribbean colonies since the 1930s, when luminaries such as Senghor and the two Césaires (Aimé and Suzanne) were among the group that invented Negritude, a literary movement deeply marked by political and philosophical positions of the left and often combining a Pan-African ideology with Surrealist poetics.[11] Fanon (a student of Aimé Césaire) arrived in 1946 from yet another French colony, Martinique, to study psychiatry in Lyon, in an institution where Merleau-Ponty, a key influence on Fanon, was teaching philosophy. Amin arrived in Paris a year later, in 1947, and Alioune Diop founded the legendary journal *Présence Africaine* that same year, going on then to establish the equally legendary publishing house, *Editions Présence Africaine*, two years later in 1949. In 1956, the year before Amin completed his doctorate, the publishing house— by then the world's foremost publisher of writers of African origin (writers of the Black Atlantic, we might now say)—organized the first International Congress of Black Writers and Artists (for which Picasso designed the poster). That ten-year period witnessed the publication of four classics of anti-colonial literature that were centred very largely on the broader African experience: Fanon's two texts, *Black Skin, White Masks* (1952) and *The Wretched of the Earth* (1961), Aimé Césaire's *Discourse on Colonialism* (1961) and Albert Memmi's *The Colonizer and the Colonized* (1957).[12] Those

---

[11] On the Arab side of these émigré equations in Paris, the rather maverick career of the illustrious Messali Hadj, the many turns in his convictions from the Marxist to the Arabo-Islamist, and the various organizations he spawned, is a good illustration of the complex connections between the migrant workers and political currents in their home countries.

[12] Sartre wrote introductions to two of those books: Memmi's, and Fanon's later (last) book. In this trio of authors, Albert Memmi was different both in origin and later orientation. He was the son of Tunisian Jews, spoke a variant of Sephardic Arabic and French, became a well-known novelist in French who then left Tunisia after Independence and settled in France, eventually drifting into Zionism. In the book, though, Memmi's positions are closer to the other two, especially to Fanonian positions, but he also reflects on his own contradictory position as a Jew of North African origin whose milieu in

are not books of political economy but what they shared with Amin's dissertation which he submitted right in the middle of that anti-colonial intellectual ferment was the shared conviction, stated and documented at great length, that colonialism had produced a binary world—literally a *world*—that just could not be rectified through any kind of reform or reconciliation but had to be *destroyed* and then rebuilt on altogether different, revolutionary foundations. Amin and Césaire were of course communists at that point in their lives. Fanon had moved in communist circles in his student days, had studied Marxism as assiduously as he read existentialism and Nietzsche, was brought into the Algerian liberation movement by the leader of its left wing, Abane Ramdane, and toward the end of his life he would lecture to select groups of that movement on Sartre's *Critique of Dialectical Reason*, virtually the last great (and unfinished) philosophical work in Western Marxism. Samir Amin was very much product and part of that ferment. His difference and distinctive achievement, however, was that unlike others who did such distinguished work in literature and aesthetics, political theory, psycho-sexual anthropology or philosophical dialectics of a materialist kind, he was to strive for a rigorous Marxist theory of the political economy of this fundamental division between the colonizer and the colonized in terms of a structure of global capitalism resting on a Centre-Periphery relation that could not be rectified except through complete overturning of capitalism itself.

These few details are offered here to indicate the textures and dispositions of the social world in which Amin's intellectual and political formation was grounded. In his personal life, he was

....

its culture and economic status was closer to that of Muslim North Africans but who had been taught by the colonizer to identify with the French and was given some privileges denied to the Muslim. 'I was a half-breed of colonization,' Memmi says in the Preface, as he identified with each side of this unbridgeable Colonizer-Colonized divide with different parts of his consciousness; the 'double consciousness' that Du Bois speaks of in his *The Souls of Black Folk*.

possibly even more attached to his mother's family than to his father's, and he thought of the French Revolution as the singularly seminal event in modern world history. Yet his identification with Egypt and more generally with Africa was strong. After submitting his dissertation he left for Egypt at a time when Nasser was at the apex of his popularity after nationalizing the Suez Canal in July 1956 and steering Egypt safely through the Tripartite invasion later that year (mounted jointly by the U.K., Israel and France).[13] Amin took up a position in Nasser's Economic Development Administration which he resigned three years later in 1960 thanks partly to the frustrations he encountered at work and partly because of Nasser's accelerated persecution of communists. He then moved to the newly independent Mali where he worked in the Ministry of Planning for the next three years. After receiving appointment as professor of Economics in France he chose to teach at the universities of Poitiers, Vincennes and Dakar. From 1970 onwards he served as Director of the UN's African Institute of Economic Planning in Senegal. Later, he was to occupy a host of other positions including those of the director in the Africa office of the Third World Forum and president of the World Forum for Alternatives, while Dakar remained a major base for his work even as he travelled the world and maintained a residence in Paris. Between submitting his dissertation in 1957 and re-writing it for publication in book form as the two-volume *Accumulation on a World Scale* in 1970, he published seven books, all, significantly, on various countries and regions of Africa: Mali, Guinea, Ghana, Ivory Coast and Senegal, two on the Maghreb and one—*Class Struggle*

---

[13] The invasion began at the end of October. A rare joint Soviet-American resolution at the Security Council halted the war, with the Soviet Union threatening use of nuclear weapons to protect Egypt and the U.S. President threatening to impose economic sanctions on his allies if they did not end the invasion and withdrew from Egypt. France and the U.K. complied faster, withdrawing in December that year but Israel held on until March 1957. Amin arrived in Cairo later that year.

in Africa (1969)—with reference points across the continent.[14] That was all in addition to his practical participation in a number of political movements in various African countries. No wonder that in Africa Amin was always seen as much more of an African intellectual than an Arab one.

II

The great colonial empires of the past were dismantled during the thirty years after the Second World War, with the process reaching its grand closure with the liberation of Vietnam in 1975 and the 470-year old Portuguese rule over its African colonies ending the same year. That, alas, was only one side in the historical constitution of that period. For, those same years witnessed the making of a far more powerful and historically unprecedented empire of worldwide proportions. I have written elsewhere that two world wars were fought to determine whether Germany or the United States would inherit the earth if and when the older colonial empires were to expire. In the event, the United States achieved swiftly what the Nazis had only dreamed of: world domination, economically, militarily, politically, even culturally. Only the socialist countries remained outside this dominion for some time but in a state of permanent siege, until those state

---

[14] The list of seven books during that short period includes *L'Egypte Nasseriene* (1964) which Amin wrote under the pseudonym Hassan Riad. Inexplicably, this book has never been translated into English—at least to my knowledge— even though Amin himself kept referring to it in his later writings. For my generation of the left outside the Arab world this book, alongside Anouar Abdel-Malek's *Egypt: Military Society: the Regime, the Left, and Social Change under Nasser* (French original 1962; expanded English version 1968, New York: Random House), and (to a considerably lesser extent) the shoddily translated and edited book of Mahmoud Hussein *Class Conflict in Egypt, 1945–1970* (French edition 1971; English translation 1973, New York: Monthly Review Press) were the most significant book-length analyses of Nasserism. Interestingly, 'Mahmoud Hussein' was also a pseudonym—for the two Egyptian co-authors, Bahgat El-Nadi and Adel Rifaat.

systems too disintegrated at the end of what Eric Hobsbawm was to call the Short Twentieth Century (1914–1991). Liberalism thus succeeded where fascism had failed; by the 1980s, when the term 'neoliberalism' had not yet become common currency, some scholars were describing the U.S. variety of the liberal system itself as a 'friendly fascism'.[15]

The American project of a global empire that got going immediately after the Second World War had four major components. First, it was deemed supremely important that U.S. take economic and military command of the former centres of world capital in Western Europe and Japan: the Marshall Plan (1947), NATO (1949), the Treaty of San Francisco (1951). This also meant, quite centrally, that all the dominant political forces of Europe and Japan—from the Social Democrats to the Fascists—become part of a worldwide anti-communist crusade led by the U.S.[16] Second, there was a concerted effort to put in place an elaborate set of what in today's parlance might be called 'global governance'. Central to it were institutions such as the World Bank and the IMF for economic and financial management and the United Nations for political management. Literature on the World Bank, IMF, etc. and on the controlling power of the U.S. in such institutions in voluminous.[17] The bicameral institutional architecture of the United Nations was significant. All the nation-states, large and

---

[15] Bertram Gross, *Friendly Fascism: The New Face of Power in America*, Boston: South End Press, 1980.

[16] Among the founding members of NATO were the famous social democracies of Norway and Denmark as well as Salazar's fascist Portugal. It remained somewhat dormant for two years, then came into its own in 1951 for executing a war not in the North Atlantic, its supposed security zone and area of operation, but in Korea.

[17] Amin started his systematic analyses of U.S. imperialism per se well after giving final shape to his general theory of accumulation on the global scale which he published in 1970. One of the best books to appear at that point, though neglected at the time, was Michael Hudson's *Super Imperialism: The Economic Strategy of American Empire* (New York, 1972), which gives a detailed account of the institutional structure erected for that strategy.

small, that were considered sovereign in their own territories were given membership of the General Assembly which nevertheless had rather restricted decision-making powers. Real decision-making powers were basically reserved for the Security Council in which only the U.S. and its allies had permanent membership, plus the lone Soviet Union; Taiwan held the Chinese seat until 1971. Third, the whole of the Tricontinent was to be locked into a system of overlapping alliances headed by the United States, exemplified by the founding of the Organization of American States (OAS) in April 1948, the Southeast Asia Treaty Organization (SEATO) in September 1954 and the Middle East Treaty Organization (later to be renamed Central Treaty Organization—CENTO) in 1955. When a large number of countries declined to join such organizations they were declared 'immoral'.[18] Finally, a permanent worldwide war (hot as well as cold) was to be waged against communism as well as Third World economic nationalism. Any government anywhere in the Tricontinent that tried to pursue what Amin was to later call a 'sovereign project' was to be overthrown by whatever means necessary, from Lumumba and Nkrumah in Africa to Goulart to Allende in Latin America.

Samir Amin's work on imperialism can be divided roughly into two phases. There is the short early phase, 1957–1970, when he is preoccupied with the general theory of capitalist accumulation through both the long colonial period and the emerging neocolonial one, and with the effect of those processes in individual African countries. That kind of theoretical work continued in subsequent years as well, culminating in the short book of 2010 on the law of

---

[18] The historic Bandung Conference was held in April 1955 and became the foundational moment for the emergence of the Non-Aligned Movement (NAM). Two months later, in June, John Foster Dulles, Eisenhower's Secretary of State, declared that 'neutrality has increasingly become obsolete and, except under very special circumstances, it is an immoral and shortsighted conception'.

worldwide value, cited above.[19] After the early 1970s, though, he begins to write much more extensively on the political history of imperialism, communism and national liberation movements in his own time, and on the structural changes that the contemporary capitalist system has undergone at various points since the onset of what he came to conceptualize as an unending long-term crisis of capitalism that began around 1971 and has since been leading the system in more recent years to the brink of an 'implosion.' A robust stream of books and articles followed, some of which covering roughly the same territory but with the difference that the latter would always drop some of the earlier conceptual apparatus and analytic positions that were replaced by other concepts or insights that had been re-thought, refined, made new, either because he had changed his mind or, more often, because the object of thought had got transformed in some fundamental way. He also pursued other, related but somewhat distinct, trajectories of research and conceptualization, and two of his books may be mentioned here in this regard.

In *Class and Nation*,[20] Amin presented within the broadly Marxist methodological matrix novel propositions regarding both the transition from feudalism to capitalism as well as the formation of nations. Contrary to a general consensus, Amin proposed that the precapitalist world of the Eurasian landmass was comprised of a variety of tributary modes of production in which feudalism

---

[19] Two other books of the 1970s that extend the arguments first presented in his original dissertation can be cited here. His *Unequal Development: An Essay on the Social Formations of Peripheral Capitalism* (French original 1973; English translation 1976) shifts the focus of analysis from how values produced all over the world are utilized for accumulation in the imperial centres to the consequences of those processes for social formations of the peripheralized tricontinent. This was followed by *Imperialism and Unequal Development* (French edition 1976; English translation 1977), comprised of essays on related topics which address the debates that ensued around *Unequal Development*.

[20] Samir Amin, *Class and Nation, Historically and in the Current Crisis*, French original 1979; English translation 1980.

with its fragmented sovereignties was one, existing primarily at the peripheries of the entire system, at its West European and Japanese extremities, while the central formations such as those of China and India were far more prosperous and comparatively more advanced in various technologies, with complex systems of commercialization and centralization of the surplus and stabilization of sovereignties. He rejected the conception common among Marxists that the nation arose only after the rise and consolidation of capitalism. And he rejected even more vigorously the rather metaphysical conception, first given great currency by the European opponents of the Enlightenment and the French Revolution, that each nation is a primordial collectivity rooted in unique histories of ethnic origin, linguistic formation and religio-cultural disposition.[21] For Amin, centralization of the surplus and stable sovereign rule over extensive territory, which necessarily led to linguistic and cultural consolidations, were the preconditions for the emergence of national entities which, he argued, arose in a variety of premodern tributary systems—e.g., China, India, Persia, the Arab world—well before the national consolidations of the capitalist era.[22]

Almost a decade after the publication of *Class and Nation*, Amin returned in *Eurocentrism*[23] to this very conception of the multiplicity of tributary modes of production in the precapitalist

---

[21] Fichte was by no means a right-wing romantic of that kind. Even so, his *Addresses to the German Nation* (1808) is the classic statement of that position on the idea of the nation. No wonder Fichte is often cited on the more ideologically oriented websites of the self-styled American alt-right of today.

[22] For the Arab world in particular, Amin analysed the transition from precapitalist tributary mode to the modern bourgeois nationhood (with all its failures) that emerged in the course of the 20th century in his short book, *The Arab Nation: Nationalism and Class Struggle* (French original 1976; English translation 1978, Zed Books). Here, as in so much of his other writing, Amin explores the relationship, possibly an overlap, between the national (anti-imperialist) revolution and the struggle for socialism.

[23] Samir Amin, *Eurocentrism*, French original 1988; English translation 1989.

world, in which the central and advanced positions were held by formations outside Europe, to address a very different kind of question: what accounts for the emergence and very effective worldwide dissemination of the idea of an intrinsic European superiority which was supposed to have twin origins: the rise of Reason in Hellenic and Roman classical cultures, and the rise of Rome as the fountain of a trans-European Christian civilization?

In an argument converging with that of Martin Bernal, Amin proposed that throughout the history of precapitalist civilizations Europe and Asia were both divided and linked by a distinct cultural unit encompassing regions bordering the Mediterranean on all sides, which included Hellenic and Egyptian classicisms as well as the primary homes of the Abrahamic religions (even Islam which was born in the Arabian peninsula comes into its own only after it arrives in Egypt, the Levant and Turkey on the one side, Persia on the other).[24] In that world, there could neither be an ideology of Europe's intrinsic superiority nor the idea of the Hellenic world being a part of Europe whose unity and distinct identity, with Greece and Rome assimilated to it, was fabricated largely during the Renaissance. This ideology of an intrinsic European superiority—intellectual, religious, cultural, technological, even racial superiority—first emerged only when the capitalist system arising on the westernmost periphery of that time's world system acquired a technology that was able to bypass the central zones of the Mediterranean altogether by embarking on a project of world conquest across oceans and continents. In short, as Amin puts it in the Introduction to his book, Eurocentrism 'constitutes one dimension of the culture and ideology of the capitalist mode of production'. Asserting a certain correspondence between the

---

[24] Martin Bernal, *Black Athena: The Afroasiatic Roots of Classical Civilization* (three volumes: 1987, 1991, 2006), New Jersey: Rutgers University Press. The basic argument in favour of a distinct civilizational unity of the Mediterranean world was laid out in great detail in Volume 1, published the year before *Eurocentrism*.

ideological and the material, this concise and narrowly focused text thus locates what he calls 'the construction of Eurocentric culture' squarely in histories of commerce, colony and capital, in sharp contrast, for instance, to Edward Said's more capacious and elegantly composed *Orientalism*, a largely literary-critical and culturalist construction of a history in which what he describes as 'inferiorization' of the Orient appears to have been something constitutive and immanent in the very making of a European consciousness already present in Greek tragic drama.

III

Amin worked across a dozen fields of inquiry; his *ouvre* is by any measure magisterial, even though somewhat repetitious in the closing years. A bare skeletal sketch of this work is now in place, even though we have taken no note of some of his most important work, such as the thoughtful and provocative book on Russia, original in its conception, that he published toward the very end of his life.[25] What remains to be done now is to focus on some of the thematics that are the indispensable conceptual ground for the essays collected in this book.

For Amin, the foundational moment for the postwar world order was the making of what he called 'imperialism of the triad' (the United States, Western Europe and Japan). As he wrote punctually of U.S. hegemony and often exhorted Europe to define a 'sovereign project for itself', he clearly implied that relations among the three components of this triad were unequal. In relation to the rest of the world, though, what mattered was not the mutual inequality of the protagonists but their unity. Even in mutual relations, however, it was not always clear from Amin's formulations just what the extant or possible future consequences

---

[25] Samir Amin, *Russia and the Long Transition from Capitalism to Socialism*, 2016.

of this inequality might be. Were these relations unequal enough to possibly become truly antagonistic at some future point, leading to an 'inter-imperialist rivalry' of the kind that Lenin formulated on the eve of the First World War, leading not necessarily to military conflagration but to economic warfare so intractable as to possibly lead to worldwide systemic crack-up? This becomes a significant issue in light of the fact that he rejected the quite popular idea of an integrated worldwide capitalist class that was the ruling class of global capitalism as a whole.[26] He further argued that individual transnational corporations may obtain their capital from any number of countries but each is always rooted in particular nations, i.e., we have TNCs that are in the last instance American, German, Japanese, etc. If that indeed is the case, might there not develop an eventuality when deep fissures and competing tendencies appear inside the architecture of the triad's collective imperialism? Amin's analyses are not entirely clear on this. We are living in a historical moment when the Chinese, for instance, are beginning to work toward a financial architecture increasingly independent of the U.S. dollar domination while Germans are evidently not doing anything practical in that direction but are now beginning to at least talk of the need for precisely that kind of independent financial institutional structure for the European Union; many other countries may respond positively to such projects. Might such trends not become stronger and irreversible in case of a secular decline in the hegemonic global power of the U.S.? There is much talk of 'multipolarity' as the desirable goal for global order in the emerging epoch, and Amin undoubtedly approved of that. Might this multipolarity not become the harbinger of diminution in the 'collective' nature of contemporary imperialism and, on

---

[26] Significantly, Amin wrote a critical but enthusiastic review of William K. Carroll's *The Making of an International Capitalist Class: Corporate Power in the 21st Century*, London and New York: Zed Books, 2010. See his 'Transnational Capitalism or Collective Imperialism', Pambazuka News, May 23, 2011.

the contrary, emergence of some variant of an inter-imperialist rivalry?

Lacking adequate space for exposition, we shall leave aside Amin's analysis of the communist state systems in the 20th century. If anything, he has written even more extensively on the national liberation movements, the compradorization of Tricontinental bourgeoisies, and on the possible avenues and strategies for struggle against imperialism and eventual transition to communism. Much of that writing assumes a fundamental contradiction besetting the imperialist system: whereas the U.S. was extraordinarily successful in imposing a structural unity among all the states and populations in the imperial centre, no such stable system of governance or social integration could be devised for the Tricontinent (what he continues to designate as 'the periphery'). 'Up to this day,' he writes, 'imperialism has never found the terms of social and political compromise that could allow a system of rule to stabilize in its favour in the countries of the capitalist periphery. I interpret this failure as proof . . . [of] an objective situation in the periphery that is potentially revolutionary and always explosive and unstable.'[27]

Who, then, will make the revolution? And what will be the nature of that revolution?[28] In response to these dilemmas, Amin offered many an element of a theory that does not amount to a straight line of march any more than Marx and Engels were ever inclined to offer a blueprint for executing a communist revolution. At the broadest conceptual level, Amin offered two propositions: that the revolution would be both national and socialist, or it shall not be, the bourgeoisie having become altogether compradorized and reactionary; and that the onset of the process would need an initial phase preceding what in classical Marxism is understood

---

[27] *A Life*, p. 48.
[28] *The World We Wish to See: Revolutionary Objectives in the Twenty-First Century* (2008) is a good place to start for following Amin's thinking on these issues. My own exegesis in the following paragraphs is culled, however, from a broader range of his writings.

as the pre-communist phase of 'socialism'. The idea of a necessary pre-socialist phase would seem to have had three origins. First, the idea seems to be inspired by Mao's original conception of the New Democracy that was expected to be ushered in by a broad front of classes minus the comprador sections of the bourgeoisie. It can be plausibly argued that Mao abandoned that conception and speeded up the transition to socialism as a result of the lessons he learned from the experience of the Korean War in which U.S. imperialism was undoubtedly bent on destroying the People's Republic as such; Gen. MacArthur, at the helm of the U.S. forces in Korea, did propose the use of atomic bombs to defeat China, on the model of the Japanese surrender. Even so, Mao never risked breaking the worker-peasant alliance as it had been effectively broken during the collectivization drive in the Soviet Union. But, more problematically, for Amin's invocation of that model, Mao always thought of the compradors as a *fraction* that could be isolated while the bulk of the class, the *national* bourgeoisie, would be part of the multi-class alliance.[29]

The idea of a pre-socialist phase seems to have been premised, moreover, on the perception that the forces of production in the periphery were too undeveloped to be fruitfully socialized as a prelude to building the advanced communist society. That backwardness of the available productive forces was after all a significant element in the distortions that inevitably ensued in all the socialist experiments in the course of the 20th century. Thirdly, however, what seems also to have propelled this idea of a pre-socialist transitional phase in Amin's repertoire of conceptions is the ongoing process in China itself. In his view, China was the only country in the Tricontinent—indeed, in the world—that

---

[29] Mao's conception of a multi-class revolutionary alliance for the transitional period, which includes the national bourgeoisie, is sometimes invoked by the Chinese authorities these days not only in defining the specifically Chinese form of socialism but also to justify admitting a wide range of capitalists into the communist party, some of them reaching into the party's highest organs.

had defined for itself a sovereign project against U.S. hegemony which it was pursuing in an entirely novel historical form. He also believed that China could not be viewed as a country where capitalism had been fully restored, so long as land was not legally privatized. Fully committed to a sovereign project opposed to U.S. hegemony, still undecided between capitalism and socialism in its mode of production, rapidly advancing in its development of the productive forces, China, he thought, still had a chance to return from the precipice to take a renewed socialist direction. It could thus serve as a model for other countries in the peripheries. At his most optimistic, Amin saw possibilities of such sovereign projects also emerging in some of the other larger economies of the periphery, i.e., Russia, Brazil and, surprisingly enough, even India. Conceptually, this possibility seemed to be immanent in the very process of the development of the productive forces; the more powerful a peripheral economy grew the more it would want to be free of externally imposed hegemonies. This optimism was of course contradicted by some other convictions that were more central in Amin's thinking. He was convinced that the bourgeoisies of the periphery were so thoroughly compradorized that they no longer had a place in the bloc of forces likely to confront imperialism. If that is so, would it then not follow that regardless of how powerful a peripheral economy became the emergence of a sovereign project would require a prior transformation of state power away from comprador-imperialist domination? Short of that revolutionary change, it seems unlikely that, say, India would follow in China's footsteps and pursue a sovereign project opposed to U.S. imperialism. For one thing, other states cannot really follow the Chinese example precisely because the contemporary Chinese state is not a normal bourgeois state but one formed by a historic compromise between its original Maoist formation and its ultra-Dengist present. Whatever the potentialities of China's 'sovereign project' may be, the fortunes of Latin America's recent 'pink tide' should serve to remind us of the risks any genuinely socialist-oriented project would face that leaves the compradorized bourgeoisie, its political parties and media empires intact.

But then there is the even more vexed and exacting question of revolutionary agency: *who* makes the revolution in this age of 'generalized capitalist monopolies' (Amin's term), when the slum is the most widespread and expanding form of urban habitation, while a host of technologies such as cybernetic automation are intent, at the other end, on minimizing even the presence of any direct human labour in large-scale capitalist production.[30] Amin's thought on this score proceeds along two different lines that tend to converge only at particular nodal points. On the one hand, there is continued commitment to think of novel strategies for our time that in essence observe some degree of fidelity to the general Leninist scheme of the proletarian party, workers' mass organizations, worker-peasant alliance, the broad united front of popular masses. Thus, for instance, contrary to Hobsbawm who posited 'death of the peasantry' as an accomplished fact,[31] Amin insisted that peasants comprised roughly half of the world's population and would be the indispensable social base for revolution in a variety of countries in Asia and Africa—even pockets of Latin America. In keeping with this line of thought, and partly reacting to the collapse of other enthusiasms such as the World Social Forum, he insisted in the last years of his life on the feasibility of a revolutionary agency in the form of what he

---

[30] Foxconn isn't satisfied with employing the ill-paid, super-exploited Chinese workers. It wants to replace them with thousands of robots.

[31] 'The most dramatic and far-reaching social change of the second half this century, and the one that cuts us off for ever from the world of the past, is the death of the peasantry', says Eric Hobsbawm in *The Age of Extremes: A History of the World, 1914–1991*, New York: Pantheon Books, 1994. This is an inexplicably exaggerated claim. Even so, it is not clear just what proportion of the agrarian population can still be counted as 'peasants'; nor is it clear from the rapid rate of outward migration into urban slums just how long the countryside in the various Asian zones will remain so very densely populated.

described as a worldwide alliance of proletariats and peoples of the world under the leadership of their own (presumably national) parties.

Alongside this particular logic was a different line of thought that began to be crystallized in his writing with an essay, 'The Social Movements in the Periphery: An End to National Liberation?', that he contributed to a book he co-authored with his cohort in Dependency and World System theories.[32] The essay appeared in 1990, as the communist state system was unravelling across the Soviet Union and Southeastern Europe; the illusion that the national bourgeoisies of the newly independent countries in Asia and Africa would mount a challenge to imperialism had collapsed already, even though Amin remained attached to some variant of the Bandung project. It was quite possibly this conjunctural moment that accounts for Amin's shift of emphasis from class politics to 'peoples of the periphery' as the collective agent for revolution in our time and for his surprising and somewhat uncritical acceptance of the term 'social movement' as the imperative mobilizing form. For, the ideology of 'social movement' had arisen precisely in opposition to 'political party'; the focus on 'the social' as a turning away from 'the political'; with the attendant premise that the molecular, multiple, mostly local movements for social and cultural change ('a network of networks', as the highest organizational form) needed to replace a politics, essentially Marxist politics, that fought for state power so as to undo the political economy of capitalism *per se*. Amin was to spend many years, together with many others, in seeking to build global networks of such movements but, given his lasting Marxist and even Maoist predilections, he also strove to pull the social movements deeper into the orbit of more familiar kinds of

---

[32] See *Transforming the Revolution: Social Movements and the World-System*, Monthly Review Press, 1990, a collection of separate essays by Samir Amin, Giovanni Arrighi, Andre Gunder Frank and Immanuel Wallerstein.

left politics. Much of his thinking as well as practical activity in the closing decades of his life went into trying to formulate a proper mode of articulation between class and mass, social movement and class politics, the national and the transcontinental as two equally key sights for political mobilization. Yet, through all those experimentations in thought and practice, he never got quite unmoored from his communist origins. As late as the time of the Tahrir Square Uprising of 2011 in Egypt he was again found in the ranks of yet another communist organization.

Antonio Gramsci wrote that even though the basic ingredients of a socialist revolutionary practice had been discovered in the Paris Commune it was only after a long interregnum of almost half a century that a fully adequate revolutionary form came fully into view in all the minutiae of very elaborate and complex Bolshevik practice. It has seemed to me for some years now that we in our time are also going through precisely that kind of interregnum and the aftermath, after the Russian and Chinese Revolutions reached their limits and were unable to move further forward. A rich revolutionary tradition of thought and practice is there to draw upon but we are yet unable to perceive new forms of revolutionary practice that are adequate enough for the entirely changed historical conditions of the present to take the spirit of October forward to its next logical stage, as the Bolshevik Revolution itself was the determinate form for carrying forward as well as transcending the logics of the French Revolution. Samir Amin was a key intellectual of this interregnum, solving many riddles, speculating in various directions and always asking the right and difficult questions where he did not have the answers.

IV

Spending any time at all in Samir Amin's company was very much like sharing a patch of sunshine in the midst of the grey and the dark. His physical frame was rather small and began giving away whiffs of frailty in the last years, and yet his movements remained agile, exuding enthusiasm, as if the body was forever electrified by reservoirs of political and intellectual energy. He was unfailingly warm, polite, courteous, extraordinarily receptive in his connection with others, with a demeanour brimming with old-world charm that seemed to belie the granite hardness of his convictions. The combined qualities of his personal culture were rather unique and he had a very distinctive personality, unlike anyone else's that I have known, but he was by life-long habit basically a man in a group that served as both his social habitat and his political home. He was active and comfortable in many, many corners of the world, and political homes were thus variable, but there was always and everywhere a group for him to act and communicate with. Political belonging and a life of solidarities was something of an internalized second nature, though by no means free of conflicts large and small, as life neither of politics nor of the intellect can ever be free of dissentions or alignments. His mind was sharp and combative, and he had come to believe, with almost a child-like confidence, that he had managed to solve some of the great riddles of our time. Yet, in his dealings with others, he was genuinely and punctually humble.

Samir Amin was, in short, one of the rare diamond cutters of the age.

*   *   *

Footnotes by the editors of *Monthly Review* have been marked as such (—*Ed.*). The rest of the notes are Samir Amin's own.

THE POLITICAL ECONOMY
OF THE TWENTIETH CENTURY

THE BELLE ÉPOQUE

The twentieth century came to a close in an atmosphere astonishingly reminiscent of that which had presided over its birth—the 'belle époque' (and it *was* beautiful, at least for capital). The bourgeois choir of the European powers, the United States, and Japan (which I will call here 'the triad' and which, by 1910, constituted a distinct group) were singing hymns to the glory of their definitive triumph. The working classes of the centre were no longer the 'dangerous classes' they had been during the nineteenth century and the other peoples of the world were called upon to accept the 'civilizing mission' of the West.

The belle époque crowned a century of radical global trans-formations, marked by the emergence of the first industrial revolution and the formation of the modern bourgeois nation-state. The process spread from the northwestern quarter of Europe and conquered the rest of the continent, the United States, and Japan. The old peripheries of the mercantilist age (Latin America and the British and Dutch East Indies) were excluded from the dual revolution, while the old states of Asia (China, the Ottoman sultanate, and Persia) were being integrated as peripheries within the new globalization. The triumph of the centres of globalized capital asserted itself in a demographic explosion, which swelled the European population from 23 per cent of the world's total in 1800 to 36 per cent in 1900. At the same time, the concentration of industrial wealth in the triad created a polarization of wealth on a scale humanity had not witnessed during the entirety of its history. On the eve of the industrial revolution, the disproportion in the social productivity of work between the most productive fifth of humanity and the remainder had never exceeded a ratio of two to one. By 1900, this ratio was twenty to one.

The globalization celebrated in 1900, even then called 'the end of history', was nevertheless a recent fact, emerging during the second half of the nineteenth century. The opening of China and of the Ottoman Empire in 1840, the repression of the Sepoys in India in 1857, and the division of Africa that started in 1885 marked successive steps in the process. Globalization, far from accelerating the process of capital accumulation (a distinct process to which it cannot be reduced), in fact brought on a structural crisis between 1873 and 1896; almost exactly a century later, it did so again. The first crisis, however, was accompanied by a new industrial revolution (electricity, petroleum, automobiles, the airplane), which was expected to transform the human species; much the same is said today about electronics. In parallel, the first industrial and financial oligopolies were created—the transnational corporations (TNCs) of the time. Financial globalization seemed to be establishing itself in a stable fashion (and being thought of as eternal, a familiar contemporary belief) in the form of the gold-sterling standard. There was even talk of the internationalization of the transactions made possible by the new stock exchanges, with as much enthusiasm as accompanies talk of financial globalization today. Jules Verne was sending his hero (English, of course) around the world in eighty days—for him, the 'global village' was already a reality.

The political economy of the nineteenth century was dominated by the figures of the great classics—Adam Smith, Ricardo, then Marx and his devastating critique. The triumph of *fin-de-siécle* globalization brought to the foreground a new 'liberal' generation, driven by the desire to prove that capitalism was 'unsurpassable' because it expressed the demands of an eternal, transhistorical rationality. Walras, a central figure in this new generation (whose discovery by contemporary economists is no coincidence), did everything he could to prove that markets were self-regulating. He had as little success proving it then as neoclassical economists have today.

The ideology of triumphant liberalism reduced society to a mere multiplication of individuals. Then, following this reduction, it was asserted that the equilibrium produced by the market both constitutes the social optimum and guarantees stability and democracy. Everything was in place to substitute a theory of imaginary capitalism for an analysis of the contradictions in real capitalism. The vulgar version of this economistic social thought would find its expression in the manuals of the Briton Alfred Marshall, the bibles of economics at the time.

The promises of globalized liberalism, as they were then vaunted, seemed to be coming true for a while during the belle époque. After 1896, growth started again on the new bases of the second industrial revolution, oligopolies, and financial globalization. This 'emergence from the crisis' sufficed not only to convince organic ideologues of capitalism—the new economists— but also to shake the bewildered workers' movement. Socialist parties began to slide from their reformist positions to more modest ambitions: to be simple associates in managing the system. The shift was very similar to that found today in the discourse of Tony Blair and Gerhard Schröder. The modernist elites of the periphery also believed that nothing could be imagined outside the dominant logic of capitalism.

The triumph of the belle époque lasted less than two decades. A few dinosaurs, still young at the time (Lenin, for instance!), predicted its downfall but no one heard them. Liberalism, or the attempt to put into practice the individualist 'free market' utopia— what is, in fact, the unilateral domination of capital—could not reduce the intensity of the contradictions of every sort that the system carried within itself. On the contrary, it sharpened them. Behind the cheerful hymns sung by the workers' parties and trade unions as they mobilized for the cause of capitalist-utopian nonsense, one could hear the muted rumble of a fragmented social movement, confused, always on the verge of exploding, and crystallizing around the invention of new alternatives. A few Bolshevik intellectuals used their gift for sarcasm with regard to the narcotized discourse of the 'rentier political economy', as they described the 'pensée unique' of the time—the hegemonic rules of 'free market' thought. Liberal globalization could only engender the system's militarization in relations among the imperialist powers of the era, could only bring about a war which, on its cold and warm forms, lasted for just over thirty years—from 1914 to 1945. Behind the apparent calm of the belle époque it was possible to discern the rise of social struggles and violent domestic and international conflicts. In China, the first generation of critics of the bourgeois modernization project were clearing a path; their critique—still in its babbling stage in India, the Ottoman and Arab world, and Latin America—would finally conquer the three continents and dominate three-quarters of the twentieth century.

Between 1914 and 1945, the stage was held simultaneously by the thirty years' war between the United States and Germany, over who would inherit Britain's defunct hegemony, and by the attempts to contest, contain, and control—by any available means—the alternative hegemony described as the construction of socialism in the Soviet Union.

In the capitalist centres, both victors and vanquished in the war of 1914–1918 attempted persistently—against all the odds—to restore the utopia of globalized liberalism. We therefore witness a return to the gold standard; a colonial order maintained through violence; and economic management, regulated during the war years, once again liberalized. The results seemed positive for a brief time, and the 1920s saw renewed growth, pulled by the dynamism of the new mass automotive economy in the United States and the establishment of new forms of assembly line labour (parodied so brilliantly by Charlie Chaplin in *Modern Times*). But these developments would find ready ground for generalization, even within the core capitalist countries, only after the Second World War. The 1920s restoration was fragile and, as early as 1929, the financial underpinnings—the most globalized segment of the system—collapsed. The following decade, leading up to the war, was a nightmare. The great powers reacted to recession as they would again in the 1980s and 1990s, with systematically deflationist policies that served only to aggravate the crisis, creating a downward spiral characterized by massive unemployment—all the more tragic for its victims because the safety nets invented by the welfare state did not yet exist. Liberal globalization could not withstand the crisis; the monetary system based on gold was abandoned. The imperialist powers regrouped in the framework of colonial empires and protected zones of influence—the sources of the conflict that would lead to the Second World War.

Western societies reacted differently to the catastrophe. Some sank into fascism, choosing war as a means of reshuffling the deck on a global scale (Germany, Italy, Japan). The United States and France were the exceptions and, through Roosevelt's New Deal and the Front Populaire in France, launched another option: that of market management ('regulation') through active state intervention, backed by the working classes. These formulas remained timid and tentative in practice, however, and were expressed fully only after 1945.

In the peripheries, the collapse of the belle époque myths triggered an anti-imperialist radicalization. Some countries in Latin America, taking advantage of their independence, invented populist nationalism in a variety of forms: in Mexico, during the peasant revolution of the 1910s and 1920s; in Argentina, during Perónism in the 1940s. In the East, Turkish Kemalism was their counterpart. Following the 1911 revolution, China was torn by a long civil war between bourgeois modernists—the Kuo Min

37

Tang—and communists. Elsewhere, the yoke of colonial rule imposed a delay several decades long on the crystallization of similar national-populist projects.

Isolated, the Soviet Union sought to invent a new trajectory. During the 1920s, it had hoped in vain that the revolution would become global. Forced to fall back on its own forces, it followed Stalin into a series of Five-Year Plans meant to allow it to make up for lost time. Lenin had already defined this course as 'Soviet power plus electrification'. The reference here is to the new industrial revolution—electricity, not coal and steel. But 'electrification' (in fact, mainly coal and steel) would gain the upper hand over the power of the Soviets, emptied of meaning.

This centrally planned accumulation was, of course, managed by a despotic state, regardless of the social populism that characterized its policies. But then, neither German unity nor Japanese modernization had been the work of democrats. The Soviet system was efficient as long as the goals remained simple: to accelerate extensive accumulation (the country's industrialization) and to build up a military force that would be the first one capable of facing the challenge of the capitalist adversary, by beating Nazi Germany and then ending the American monopoly on atomic weapons and ballistic missiles during the 1960s.

THE CRISIS (1970–PRESENT)

The Second World War inaugurated a new phase in the world system. The takeoff of the postwar period (1945–1975) was based on the three social projects of the age, projects that stabilized and complemented each other. These three social projects were: (i) in the West, the welfare state project of national social democracy, based on the efficiency of productive interdependent national systems; (ii) the 'Bandung project' of bourgeois national construction on the system's periphery (development ideology);

and (iii) the Soviet-style project of 'capitalism without capitalists', existing in relative autonomy from the dominant world system. The double defeat of fascism and old colonialism had indeed created a conjuncture that allowed the popular classes, victims of capitalist accumulation, to impose variously limited or contested but stable forms of capital regulation and formation, to which capital itself was forced to adjust, and which were at the roots of this period of high growth and accelerated accumulation.

The crisis that followed (which started between 1968 and 1975) is one of the erosion, then the collapse, of the systems on which the previous takeoff had rested. This period, which has not yet come to a close, is therefore not that of the establishment of a new world order, as is too often claimed. Rather, this period is characterized by chaos that has not been overcome—far from it. The policies implemented under these conditions do not constitute a positive strategy of capital expansion but simply seek to manage the crisis of capital. They have not succeeded because the 'spontaneous' project produced by the unmediated, active domination of capital, in the absence of any framework imposed by social forces through coherent and efficient reaction, is still a utopia: that of world management through what is referred to as 'the market'—that is, the short-term interests of capital's dominant forces.

In modern history, phases of reproduction based on stable accumulation systems are succeeded by periods of chaos. In the first of these phases, as in the postwar takeoff, the succession of events gives the impression of a certain monotony, because the social and international relations that make up its architecture are stabilized. These relations are therefore reproduced through the functioning of the dynamics of the system. In these phases— and to the complete confusion of all 'methodological individualists'—active, defined, and precise sociohistorical subjects are clearly visible (active social classes, states, political parties, and dominant social organizations). Their practices appear to form a clear pattern and their reactions are predictable in most circumstances; the ideologies that motivate them benefit from a seemingly uncontested legitimacy. At these moments, conjunctures may change, but the structures remain stable. Prediction is then possible, even easy. The danger arises when we extrapolate too much from these predictions, as if the structures in question were eternal and marked 'the end of history'. Analysis of the contradictions that riddle these structures is then replaced by what the postmodernists rightly call 'grand narratives', 'the laws of history'. The subjects of history disappear, making room for supposedly objective structural logics.

But the contradictions of which we are speaking do their work quietly, and one day the 'stable' structures collapse. History then enters a phase that may be described later as transitional, but which is lived as a transition toward the unknown, during which new historical subjects crystallize slowly. These subjects inaugurate new practices, proceeding by trial and error, and legitimize them through new ideological discourses, often confused at the outset. Only when the processes of qualitative change have matured sufficiently do new social relations appear, defining post-transitional systems that are capable of sustained self-reproduction.

The postwar takeoff allowed for massive economic, political, and social transformations in all regions of the world. These transformations were the product of social regulations imposed on capital by the working and popular classes. They were not the product (and here liberal ideology is demonstrably false) of a logic of market expansion. But these transformations were so great that, despite the disintegrating process to which we are currently subject, they have defined a new framework for the challenges that confront the world's peoples now, on the threshold of the twenty-first century. For a long time—from the industrial revolution at the beginning of the nineteenth century to the 1930s (in the Soviet Union) or the 1950s (in the third world)—the contrast between the centre and the peripheries of the modern world system was almost identical to the opposition between industrialized and non-industrialized countries. The rebellions in the peripheries—and in this respect the socialist revolutions in Russia and China and national liberation movements were alike—revised this schema by engaging their societies in the modernization process. Industrialized peripheries appeared; the old polarization was revised. But then a new form of polarization came into clear view. Gradually, the axis around which the world capitalist system was reorganizing itself, and which would define the future forms of polarization, constituted itself on the basis of the 'five new monopolies' that benefited the countries of the dominant triad: the control of technology; global financial flows (through the banks, insurance cartels, and pension funds of the centre); access to the planet's natural resources; media and communications; and weapons of mass destruction.

Taken together, these five monopolies define the framework within which the law of globalized value expresses itself. The law of value is hardly the expression of a 'pure' economic rationality that can be detached from its social and political frame; rather, it is the condensed expression of the totality of these circumstances. It is these circumstances—rather than a calculus of 'rational', mythical individual choices made by the market—that cancel out the extent of industrialization of the peripheries, devalue the productive work incorporated in these products, and overvalue the supposed added value attached to the activities through which the new monopolies operate, to the benefit of the centres. They therefore produce a new hierarchy in the distribution of income on a world scale, more unequal than ever, while making subalterns of the peripheries' industries. Polarization finds its new basis here, a basis which will dictate its future form.

The industrialization that social forces, energized by the victories of national liberation, imposed on dominant capital produced unequal results. Today, we can differentiate the frontline peripheries, which have been capable of building productive national systems with potentially competitive industries within the framework of globalized capitalism, and the marginalized peripheries, which have not been as successful. The criteria that separates the active peripheries from the marginalized is not only seen in the presence of potentially competitive industries: it is also political.

The political authorities in the active peripheries—and, behind them, all of society (including the contradictions within society itself)—have a project and a strategy for its implementation. This is clearly the case for China, Korea, and to a lesser degree, for certain countries in Southeast Asia, India, and some countries in Latin America. These national projects are confronted with globally dominant imperialism; the outcome of this confrontation will contribute to the shape of tomorrow's world.

On the other hand, the marginalized peripheries have neither a project (even when rhetoric like that of political Islam claims the opposite) nor their own strategy. In this case, imperialist circles 'think for them' and take the initiative alone in elaborating 'projects' concerning these regions (like the European Community's African associations, the 'Middle Eastern' project of the United States and Israel, or Europe's vague Mediterranean schemes). No local forces offer any opposition; these countries are therefore the passive subjects of globalization.

This brief overview of the political economy of the transformation of the global capitalist system in the twentieth century must include a reminder about the stunning demographic revolution that has taken place on the periphery. The proportion of the global population formed by the populations of Asia (excluding Japan and the U.S.S.R.), Africa, Latin America, and the Caribbean was 68 per cent in 1900; it is 81 per cent today.

The third partner in the postwar world system, comprised of the countries where 'actually existing socialism' prevailed, has left the historical scene. The very existence of the Soviet system, with its successes in extensive industrialization and military accomplishments, was one of the principal motors of all the grand transformations of the twentieth century. Without the 'danger' that the communist model represented, Western social democracy would never have been able to impose the welfare state. The existence of the Soviet system, and the coexistence it imposed on the United States, reinforced the margin of autonomy available to the bourgeoisie of the South.

The Soviet system, however, did not manage to pass to a new stage of intensive accumulation; it therefore missed out on the new (computer-driven) industrial revolution with which the twentieth century ended. The reasons for this failure are complex; still, this failure forces us to place at the centre of our analysis the antidemocratic drift of Soviet power, which was ultimately unable to internalize the fundamental urgency of progress toward socialism demanded by the conditions that confronted it. I refer here to progress toward socialism as represented by the intensification of exactly that democratization of economy and society that would be capable of transcending the conditions defined and limited by the framework of historical capitalism. Socialism will be democratic or it cannot exist: this is the lesson of this first experience of the break with capitalism.

Social thought and the dominant economic, sociological, and political theories that legitimized the practices of autocentric, national-welfare-state development in the West, of the Soviet system in the East, and of populism in the South were largely inspired by Marx and Keynes. The new social relations of the postwar period, more favourable to labour, would inspire the practices of the welfare state, relegating the liberals to a position of insignificance. Marx's figure, of course, dominated the discourse of 'actually existing socialism'. But the two preponderant figures of the twentieth century gradually lost their quality as originators of fundamental critiques, becoming the mentors of the legitimation of the practices of state power. In both cases, there was a shift toward simplification and dogmatism.

Critical social thought moved, then, during the 1960s and 1970s, toward the periphery of the system. Here the practices of national populism—a poor version of Sovietism—triggered a brilliant explosion in the critique of 'actually existing socialism'. At the centre of this critique was a new awareness of the polarization created by capital's global expansion, which had been underestimated, if not purely and simply ignored, for over a century and a half. This critique—of actually existing capitalism, of the social thought that legitimated its expansion, and of the theoretical and practical socialist critique of both—was at the origin of the periphery's dazzling entry into modern thought. Here was a rich and variegated critique—which it would be a mistake to reduce to 'dependency theory', since this social thought reopened fundamental debates on socialism and the transition toward it. Furthermore, this critique revived the debate on Marxism and historical materialism, understanding from the start the necessity of transcending the limits of the Eurocentrism that dominated modern thought. Undeniably inspired for a moment by the Maoist eruption, it also initiated the critique of both Sovietism and the new globalism glimmering on the horizon.

FIN-DE-SIÉCLE CRISIS

Starting between 1968 and 1971, the collapse of the three postwar models of regulated accumulation opened up a structural crisis of the system reminiscent of that of the end of the nineteenth century. Growth and investment rates fell precipitously (to half of their previous levels); unemployment soared; pauperization intensified. The percentages used to measure inequality in the capitalist world increased sharply; the wealthiest 20 per cent of humanity increased their share of the global product from 60 to 80 per cent in the last two decades of this century. Globalization has been fortunate for some. For the vast majority, however—especially for the peoples of the South subjected to unilateral structural adjustment policies, and those of the East locked into a dramatic social demolition—it has been a disaster.

But this structural crisis, like its predecessor, is accompanied by a third technological revolution, which profoundly alters modes of labour organization, and (in the face of a fierce attack by global capital) divests the old forms of worker and popular organization and struggle of their efficiency and therefore of their legitimacy. The fragmented social movement has not yet found a formula strong enough to meet the challenges posed. But it has made remarkable breakthroughs in directions that enrich its impact: principally, women's powerful entry into social life, as well as a new awareness of environmental destruction on a scale which, for the first time in history, threatens all highly organized forms of life on this planet. Thus as the capitalist centre's 'five new monopolies' came gradually into view, an emerging multipolar global social movement (that is its potential counterweight, alternative, and successor) had elements already visible in outline.

The management of the crisis, based on a brutal reversal of relations of power in capital's favour, has made it possible for liberal 'free market' recipes to impose themselves anew. Marx and Keynes have been erased from social thought and the 'theoreticians' of 'pure economics' have replaced analysis of the real world with that of an imaginary capitalism. But the temporary success of this highly reactionary utopian thought is simply the symptom of a decline—witchcraft taking the place of rationality—that testifies to the fact that capitalism is objectively ready to be transcended.

Crisis management has already entered the phase of collapse. The crises in Southeast Asia and Korea were predictable. During the 1980s, these countries (and China as well), managed to benefit from the world crisis through greater involvement in world exchanges (based on their 'comparative advantage' of cheap labour), attracting foreign investment but remaining on the sidelines of financial globalization, and (in the cases of China and Korea) inscribing their development projects in a nationally controlled strategy. In the 1990s, Korea and Southeast Asia opened up to financial globalization, while China and India began to shift in the same direction.

Attracted by the region's high growth levels, the surplus of floating foreign capital flowed in, producing not accelerated growth but asset inflation in stocks and real estate. As had been predicted, the financial bubble burst only a few years later. Political reaction to this massive crisis has been new in several respects—different from that provoked by the Mexican crisis, for instance. The United States, with Japan following closely, attempted to take advantage of the Korean crisis to dismantle the country's productive system (under the fallacious pretext that it was controlled oligopolistically!) and to subordinate it to the strategies of U.S. and Japanese oligopolies. Regional powers attempted to resist by challenging the question of their insertion into financial globalization through reestablishing exchange controls in Malaysia or by removing immediate participation from their list of priorities in China and India.

This collapse of the financial dimension of globalization forced the G7 countries (the group of seven most advanced capitalist countries) to envisage a new strategy, provoking a crisis in liberal thought. It is in light of this crisis that we must examine the outline of the counterattack launched by the G7. Overnight, they changed their tune: the term 'regulation', forbidden until then, reappeared in the group's resolutions. It became necessary to 'regulate international financial flows'. Joseph Stiglitz, chief economist of the World Bank at the time, suggested a debate on defining a new 'post-Washington consensus'. But this was too much for the current mouthpiece of U.S. hegemony, Treasury

Secretary Lawrence Summers, who saw to Stiglitz's removal.

WILL NOT BE AMERICAN

In this chaotic conjuncture, the United States took the offensive once more, in order to reestablish its global hegemony and accordingly to organize the world system in its economic, political, and military dimensions. Has U.S. hegemony entered its decline? Or has it begun a renewal that will make the twenty-first century America's?

If we examine the economic dimension in the narrow sense of the term, measured roughly in terms of per capita Gross Domestic Product (GDP), and the structural tendencies of the balance of trade, we might conclude that American hegemony, so crushing in 1945, receded as early as the 1960s and 1970s, with the brilliant resurgence of Europe and Japan. The Europeans bring it up continuously, in familiar terms: the European Union is the first economic and commercial force on a world scale. The statement is hasty, however. For, if it is true that a single European market does exist, and even that a single currency is perhaps emerging, the same cannot be said of a European economy (at least not yet). There is no such thing as a 'European productive system'; such a productive system, on the contrary, can be spoken of in the United States. The economies set up in Europe through the constitution of the historical bourgeoisie in the relevant states, and the shaping within this framework of autocentric national productive systems (even if these are open, even aggressively so), have stayed more or less the same. There are still no European TNCs: only British, German, or French TNCs. Capital interpenetration is no denser in inter-European relations than in the bilateral relations between each European nation and the United States or Japan. If Europe's productive systems have indeed been eroded, and if 'globalized interdependence' has weakened them to such an extent that national policies lose a good deal of their efficiency, this is precisely to the advantage of globalization and the (U.S.) forces that dominate it, not to that of 'European integration', which does not yet exist.

The hegemony of the United States rests on a second pillar, however: that of military power. Built up systematically since 1945, it now covers the whole of the planet, which is parcelled out into regions—each under the requisite U.S. military command. This hegemony had been forced to accept the peaceful coexistence imposed by Soviet military might. Now that page has turned and the United States has gone on the offensive to reinforce its global domination. Henry Kissinger summed it up in a memorably arrogant phrase: 'Globalization is only another word for U.S. domination.' This American global strategy has five aims: to neutralize and subjugate the other partners in the triad (Europe and Japan), while minimizing their ability to act outside the orbit of the United States; to establish military control over NATO while 'Latin-Americanizing' the fragments of the former Soviet world; to exert uncontested influence in the Middle East and Central Asia, especially over their petroleum resources; to dismantle China, ensure the subordination of the other great nations (India and Brazil), and prevent the constitution of regional blocs potentially capable of negotiating the terms of globalization; and to marginalize the regions of the South that represent no strategic interest.

The favoured instrument of this hegemony is therefore military, as the highest-ranking representatives of the United States never tire of repeating. This hegemony, which guarantees the superiority of the triad over the world system, therefore demands that America's allies agree to follow in its wake. Great Britain, Germany, and Japan make no bones (not even cultural ones) about this imperative. But this means that the speeches about Europe's economic power (with which European politicians shower their audiences) have no real significance. By positioning itself exclusively on the terrain of mercantile squabbles, Europe (which has no political or social project of its own) has lost before the race has even started. Washington knows this well.

The principal body that implements Washington's chosen strategy is NATO, which explains why it has survived the collapse of the adversary that constituted the organization's *raison d'être*. NATO still speaks today in the name of the 'international community', expressing its contempt for the democratic principle that governs this community through the UN. Yet NATO acts only to serve Washington's aims—no more and no less—as the history of the past decade, from the Gulf War to Kosovo, illustrates.

The strategy employed by the triad, under U.S. direction, takes as its aim the construction of a unipolar world organized along two complementary principles: the unilateral dictatorship of dominant TNC capital and the unfurling of a U.S. military empire, to which all nations must be compelled to submit. No other project may be tolerated within this perspective, not even the European project of subaltern NATO allies, and especially not a project entailing some degree of autonomy, like China's, which must be broken by force if necessary.

This vision of a unipolar world is being increasingly opposed by that of a multipolar globalization, the only strategy that would allow the different regions of the world to achieve acceptable social development, and would thereby foster social democratization and the reduction of the motives for conflict. The hegemonic strategy of the United States and its NATO allies is today the main enemy of social progress, democracy, and peace.

The twenty-first century will not be America's century. It will be one of vast conflicts, and the rise of social struggles that question the ambitions of Washington and of capital. The crisis is exacerbating contradictions within the dominant classes. These conflicts must take on increasingly acute international dimensions, and therefore pit states and groups of states against each other.

One can already discern the first hints of a conflict between the United States, Japan, and their faithful Australian ally on the one hand, and China and other Asian countries on the other. Nor is it difficult to envisage the rebirth of a conflict between the United States and Russia, if the latter manages to extricate itself from the nightmarish spiral of death and disintegration into which Boris Yeltsin and his U.S. 'advisors' have plunged it. And if the European Left could free itself from submission to the double dictates of capital and Washington, it would be possible to imagine that the new European strategy could be intertwined with those of Russia, China, India, and the third world in general, in a necessary, multipolar construction effort. If this does not come about, the European project itself will fade away.

The central question, therefore, is how conflicts and social struggles (it is important to differentiate between the two) will be articulated. Which will triumph? Will social struggles be subordinated, framed by conflicts, and therefore mastered by the dominant powers, even made instruments to the benefit of those powers? Or will social struggles surmount their autonomy and force the major powers to respond to their urgent demands?

Of course, I do not imagine that the conflicts and struggles of the twenty-first century will produce a remake of the previous century. History does not repeat itself according to a cyclical model. Today's societies are confronted by new challenges at all levels. But precisely because the immanent contradictions of capitalism are sharper at the end of the century than they were at its beginning, and because the means of destruction are also far greater than they were, the alternatives for the twenty-first century are (more than ever before) 'socialism or barbarism'.

June 01, 2000

WORLD POVERTY, PAUPERIZATION AND CAPITAL ACCUMULATION

A discourse on poverty and the necessity of reducing its magnitude, if not eradicating it, has become fashionable today. It is a discourse of charity, in the nineteenth-century style, which does not seek to understand the economic and social mechanisms that generate poverty, although the scientific and technological means to eradicate it are now available.

CAPITALISM AND THE NEW AGRARIAN QUESTION

All societies before modern (capitalist) times were peasant societies. Their production was ruled by various specific systems and logics—but not those which rule capitalism in a market society such as the maximization of the return on capital.

Modern capitalist agriculture—encompassing both rich, large-scale family farming and agribusiness corporations—is now engaged in a massive attack on third world peasant production. The green light for this was given at the November 2001 session of the World Trade Organization (WTO) in Doha, Qatar. There are many victims of this attack—and most are third world peasants, who still make up half of humankind.

Capitalist agriculture governed by the principle of return on capital, which is localized almost exclusively in North America, Europe, Australia, and in the Southern Cone of Latin America employs only a few tens of millions of farmers who are no longer peasants. Because of the degree of mechanization and the extensive size of the farms managed by one farmer, their productivity generally ranges between 1 to 2 million kilograms (2 and 4.5 million pounds) of cereals per farmer.

In sharp contrast, three billion farmers are engaged in peasant farming. Their farms can be grouped into two distinct sectors, with greatly different scales of production, economic and social characteristics, and levels of efficiency. One sector, able to benefit from the green revolution, obtained fertilizers, pesticides, and improved seeds and has some degree of mechanization. The productivity of these peasants ranges between 10,000 and 50,000 kilograms (20,000 and 110,000 pounds) of cereals per year. However, the annual productivity of peasants excluded from new technologies is estimated to be around 1,000 kilograms (2,000 pounds) of cereals per farmer.

The ratio of the productivity of the most advanced capitalist segment of the world's agriculture to the poorest, which was around 10 to 1 before 1940, is now approaching 2000 to 1! That means that productivity has progressed much more unequally in the area of agriculture and food production than in any other area. Simultaneously this evolution has led to the reduction of the relative prices of food products (in relation to other industrial and service products) to one fifth of what they were fifty years ago. The new agrarian question is the result of that unequal development.

Modernization has always combined constructive dimensions, namely the accumulation of capital and increasing productivity, with destructive aspects—reducing labour to the state of a commodity sold on the market, often destroying the natural ecological basis needed for the reproduction of life and production, and polarizing the distribution of wealth on a global level. Modernization has always simultaneously *integrated* some, as expanding markets created employment, and *excluded* others, who were not integrated in the new labour force after having lost their positions in the previous systems. In its ascending phase, capitalist global expansion integrated many along with its excluding processes. But now, in the third world peasant societies, it is excluding massive numbers of people while including relatively few.

The question raised here is precisely whether this trend will continue to operate with respect to the three billion human beings still producing and living in peasant societies in Asia, Africa, and Latin America.

Indeed, what would happen if agriculture and food production were treated as any other form of production submitted to the rules of competition in an open and deregulated market, as decided in principle at the November 2001 WTO meeting in Doha. Would such principles foster the acceleration of production?

One can imagine that the food brought to market by today's three billion peasants, after they ensure their own subsistences, would instead be produced by twenty million new modern farmers. The conditions for the success of such an alternative would include: (1) the transfer of important pieces of good land to the new capitalist farmers (and these lands would have to be taken out of the hands of present peasant populations); (2) capital (to buy supplies and equipment); and (3) access to the consumer markets. Such farmers would indeed compete successfully with the billions of present peasants. But what would happen to those billions of people?

Under the circumstances, agreeing to the general principle of competition for agricultural products and foodstuffs, as imposed by WTO, means accepting the elimination of billions of non-competitive producers within the short historic time of a few decades. What will become of these billions of humans beings, the majority of whom are already poor among the poor, who feed themselves with great difficulty? In fifty years' time, industrial development, even in the fanciful hypothesis of a continued growth rate of 7 per cent annually, could not absorb even one-third of this reserve.

The major argument presented to legitimate the WTO's competition doctrine is that such development did happen in nineteenth- and twentieth-century Europe and the United States where it produced a modern, wealthy, urban-industrial and post-industrial society with modern agriculture able to feed the nation and even export food. Why should not this pattern be repeated in the contemporary third world countries?

The argument fails to consider two major factors that make the reproduction of the pattern in third world countries almost impossible. The first is that the European model developed throughout a century and a half along with labour-intensive industrial technologies. Modern technologies use far less labour and the newcomers of the third world have to adopt them if their industrial exports are to be competitive in global markets. The second is that, during that long transition, Europe benefited from the massive migration of its surplus population to the Americas.

The contention that capitalism has indeed solved the agrarian question in its developed centres has always been accepted by large sections of the left, an example being Karl Kautsky's famous book, *The Agrarian Question*, written before the First World War. Soviet ideology inherited that view and on its basis undertook modernization through the Stalinist collectivization, with poor results. What was always overlooked was that capitalism, while it solved the question in its centres, did it through generating a gigantic agrarian question in the peripheries, which it can only solve through the genocide of half of humankind. Within the Marxist tradition only Maoism understood the magnitude of the challenge. Therefore, those who accused Maoism of a 'peasant deviation' show by this very criticism that they lack the analytical capacity to understand imperialist capitalism, which they reduce to an abstract discourse on capitalism in general.

Modernization through capitalist market liberalization, as suggested by WTO and its supporters, finally aligns side by side, without even necessarily combining, the two components: the production of food on a global scale by modern competitive farmers mostly based in the North but also possibly in the future in some pockets of the South; and, the marginalization, exclusion, and further impoverishment of the majority of the three billion peasants of the present third world and finally their seclusion in some kinds of reserves. It therefore combines a pro-modernization and efficiency-dominant discourse with an ecological-cultural-reserve set of policies allowing the victims to survive in a state of material (including ecological) impoverishment. These two components might therefore complement, rather than conflict with, one another.

Can we imagine other alternatives and have them widely debated? Ones in which peasant agriculture would be maintained throughout the visible future of the twenty-first century, but, which simultaneously engage in a process of continuous technological and social progress? In this way, changes could happen at a rate that would allow a progressive transfer of the peasants into non-rural and non-agricultural employment.

Such a strategic set of targets involves complex policy mixes at national, regional, and global levels.

At the national level it implies macro policies protecting peasant food production from the unequal competition of modernized farmers and agribusiness corporations—local and international. This will help guarantee acceptable internal food prices—disconnected from international market prices, which are additionally biased by the agricultural subsidies of the wealthy North.

Such policy targets also question the patterns of industrial and urban development, which should be based less on export-oriented priorities (e.g., keeping wages low which implies low prices for food) and more attentive to a socially-balanced expansion of the internal market.

Simultaneously, this involves an overall pattern of policies to ensure national food security—an indispensable condition for a country to be an active member of the global community, enjoying the indispensable margin of autonomy and negotiating capacity.

At regional and global levels it implies international agreements and policies that move away from the doctrinaire liberal principles ruling the WTO—replacing them with imaginative and specific solutions for different areas, taking into consideration the specific issues and concrete historical and social conditions.

THE NEW LABOUR QUESTION

The planet's urban population now represents about half of humanity, at least three billion individuals, with peasants making up all but a statistically insignificant percentage of the other half. The data on this population allow us to distinguish between what we can call the middle classes and the popular classes.

In the contemporary stage of capitalist evolution, the dominant classes—formal owners of the principal means of production and senior managers associated with bringing them into play—represent only a very minor fraction of the global population even though the share they draw from their societies' available income is significant. To this we add the middle classes in the old sense of the term—non-wage-earners, owners of small enterprises, and middle managers, who are not necessarily in decline.

The large mass of workers in the modern segments of production consists of wage-earners who now make up more than four-fifths of the urban population of the developed centres. This mass is divided into at least two categories, the border between which is both visible to the outside observer and truly lived in the consciousness of affected individuals.

There are those who we can label *stabilized* popular classes in the sense that they are relatively secure in their employment, thanks among other things to professional qualifications which give them negotiating power with employers and, therefore, they are often organized, at least in some countries, into powerful unions. In all cases this mass carries a political weight that reinforces its negotiating capacity.

Others make up the *precarious* popular classes that include workers weakened by their low capacity for negotiation (as a result of their low skill levels, their status as non-citizens, or their race or gender) as well as non-wage-earners (the formally unemployed and the poor with jobs in the informal sector). We can label this second category of the popular classes 'precarious', rather than 'non-integrated' or 'marginalized', because these workers are perfectly integrated into the systemic logic that commands the accumulation of capital.

From the available information for developed countries and certain Southern countries (from which we extrapolate data) we obtain the relative proportions that each of the above-defined categories represent in the planet's urban population.

Although the centres account for only 18 per cent of the planet's population, since their population is 90 per cent urban, they are home to a third of the world's urban population (see Table 1).

Table 1. *Percentages of Total World Urban Population*

	Centres	Peripheries	World
Wealthy and middle classes	11	13	25
Popular classes	24	54	75
Stabilized	(13)	(11)	(25)
Precarious	9	(43)	(50)
Total	33	67	100
Population concerned (millions)	(1,000)	(2,000)	(3,000)

Note: Percentages may not add up exactly due to statistical approximations.

The popular classes account for three-quarters of the world's urban population, while the precarious subcategory represents two-thirds of the popular classes on a world scale. (About 40 per cent of the popular classes in the centres and 80 per cent in the peripheries are in the precarious subcategory.) In other words, the precarious popular classes represent half (at least) of the world's urban population and far more than that in the peripheries.

A look at the composition of the urban popular classes a half century ago, following the Second World War, shows that the proportions that characterize the structure of the popular classes were very different from what they have become.

At the time, the third world's share did not exceed half of the global urban population (then on the order of a billion individuals) versus two-thirds today. Megacities, like those that we know today in practically all countries of the South, did not yet exist. There were only a few large cities, notably in China, India, and Latin America.

In the centres, the popular classes benefited, during the postwar period, from an exceptional situation based on the historic compromise imposed on capital by the working classes. This compromise permitted the stabilization of the majority of workers in forms of a work organization known as the 'Fordist' factory system. In the peripheries, the proportion of the precarious—which was, as always, larger than in the centres—did not exceed half of the urban popular classes (versus more than 70 per cent today). The other half still consisted, in part, of stabilized wage-earners in the forms of the new colonial economy and of the modernized society and, in part, in old forms of craft industries.

The main social transformation that characterizes the second half of the twentieth century can be summarized in a single statistic: the proportion of the precarious popular classes rose from less than one-quarter to more than one-half of the global urban population, and this phenomenon of pauperization has reappeared on a significant scale in the developed centres themselves. This destabilized urban population has increased in a half-century from less than a quarter of a billion to more than a billion-and-a-half individuals, registering a growth rate which surpasses those that characterize economic expansion, population growth, or the process of urbanization itself.

Pauperization—there is no better term to name the evolutionary trend during the second half of the twentieth century.

Overall, the fact in itself is recognized and reaffirmed in the new dominant language: 'reducing poverty' has become a recurring theme of the objectives which government policies claim to achieve. But the poverty in question is only presented as an empirically measured fact, either very crudely by income distribution (poverty lines) or a little less crudely by composite indices (such as the human development indices proposed by the United Nations Development Program), without ever raising the question of the logics and mechanisms which generate this poverty.

Our presentation of these same facts goes further because it allows us precisely to begin explaining the phenomenon and its evolution. Middle strata, stabilized popular strata, and precarious popular strata are all integrated into the same system of social production, but they fulfil distinct functions within it. Some are indeed excluded from the benefits of prosperity. The excluded are very much a part of the system and are not marginalized in the sense of not being integrated—functionally—into the system.

Pauperization is a modern phenomenon which is not at all reducible to a lack of sufficient income for survival. It is really the modernization of poverty and has devastating effects in all dimensions of social life. Emigrants from the countryside were relatively well integrated into the stabilized popular classes during the golden age (1945-1975)—they tended to become factory workers. Now those who have recently arrived and their children are situated on the margins of the main productive systems, creating favourable conditions for the substitution of community solidarities for class consciousness. Meanwhile, women are even more victimized by economic precariousness than are men, resulting in deterioration of their material and social conditions. And if feminist movements have without doubt achieved important advances in the realm of ideas and behaviour, the beneficiaries of these gains are almost exclusively middle-class women, certainly not those of the pauperized popular classes. As for democracy, its credibility—and therefore its legitimacy—is sapped by its inability to curb the degradation of conditions of a growing fraction of the popular classes.

Pauperization is a phenomenon inseparable from polarization on a world scale—an inherent product of the expansion of really-existing capitalism, which for this reason we must call imperialist by nature.

Pauperization in the urban popular classes is closely linked to the developments which victimize third world peasant societies. The submission of these societies to the demands of capitalist market expansion supports new forms of social polarization which exclude a growing proportion of farmers from access to use of the land. These peasants who have been impoverished or become landless feed—even more than population growth—the migration to the shantytowns. Yet all these phenomena are destined to get worse as long as liberal dogmas are not challenged, and no corrective policy within this liberal framework can check their spread.

Pauperization calls into question both economic theory and the strategies of social struggles.

Conventional vulgar economic theory avoids the real questions that are posed by the expansion of capitalism. This is because it substitutes for an analysis of really-existing capitalism a theory of an imaginary capitalism, conceived as a simple and continuous extension of exchange relations (the market), whereas the system functions and reproduces itself on the basis of capitalist production and exchange relations (not simple market relations). This substitution is easily coupled with the *a priori* notion, which neither history nor rational argument confirm, that the market is self-regulating and produces a social optimum. Poverty can then only be explained by causes decreed to be outside of economic logic, such as population growth or policy errors. The relation of poverty to the very process of accumulation is dismissed by conventional economic theory. The resulting liberal virus, which pollutes contemporary social thought and annihilates the capacity to understand the world, let alone transform it, has deeply penetrated the various lefts constituted since the Second World War. The movements currently engaged in social struggles for 'another world' and an alternative globalization will only be able to produce significant social advances if they get rid of this virus in order to construct an authentic theoretical debate. As long as they have not gotten rid of this virus, social movements, even the best intentioned, will remain locked in the shackles of conventional thought and therefore prisoners of ineffective corrective propositions—those which are fed by the rhetoric concerning poverty reduction.

The analysis sketched above should contribute to opening this debate. This is because it reestablishes the pertinence of the link between capital accumulation on the one hand and the phenomenon of social pauperization on the other. One hundred and fifty years ago, Marx initiated an analysis of the mechanisms behind this link, which has hardly been pursued since then—and scarcely at all on a global scale.

October 01, 2003

POLITICAL ISLAM IN THE SERVICE OF IMPERIALISM

All the currents that claim adherence to political Islam proclaim the 'specificity of Islam'. According to them, Islam knows nothing of the separation between politics and religion, something supposedly distinctive of Christianity. It would accomplish nothing to remind them, as I have done, that their remarks reproduce, almost word for word, what European reactionaries at the beginning of the nineteenth century (such as Bonald and de Maistre) said to condemn the rupture that the Enlightenment and the French Revolution had produced in the history of the Christian West!

On the basis of this position, every current of political Islam chooses to conduct its struggle on the terrain of culture—but 'culture' reduced in actual fact to the conventional affirmation of belonging to a particular religion. In reality, the militants of political Islam are not truly interested in discussing the dogmas that form religion. The ritual assertion of membership in the community is their exclusive preoccupation. Such a vision of the reality of the modern world is not only distressing because of the immense emptiness of thought that it conceals, but it also justifies imperialism's strategy of substituting a so-called conflict of cultures for the one between imperialist centres and dominated peripheries. The exclusive emphasis on culture allows political Islam to eliminate from every sphere of life the real social confrontations between the popular classes and the globalized capitalist system that oppresses and exploits them. The militants of political Islam have no real presence in the areas where actual social conflicts take place and their leaders repeat incessantly that such conflicts are unimportant. Islamists are only present in these areas to open schools and health clinics. But these are nothing but works of charity and means for indoctrination. They are not means of support for the struggles of the popular classes against the system responsible for their poverty.

On the terrain of the real social issues, political Islam aligns itself with the camp of dependent capitalism and dominant imperialism. It defends the principle of the sacred character of property and legitimizes inequality and all the requirements of capitalist reproduction. The support by the Muslim Brotherhood in the Egyptian parliament for the recent reactionary laws that reinforce the rights of property owners to the detriment of the rights of tenant farmers (the majority of the small peasantry) is but one example among hundreds of others. There is no example of even one reactionary law promoted in any Muslim state to which the Islamist movements are opposed. Moreover, such laws are promulgated with the agreement of the leaders of the imperialist system. Political Islam is not anti-imperialist, even if its militants think otherwise! It is an invaluable ally for imperialism and the latter knows it. It is easy to understand, then, that political Islam has always counted in its ranks the ruling classes of Saudi Arabia and Pakistan. Moreover, these classes were among its most active promoters from the very beginning. The local comprador bourgeoisies, the nouveaux riches, beneficiaries of current imperialist globalization, generously support political Islam. The latter has renounced an anti-imperialist perspective and substituted for it an 'anti-Western' (almost 'anti-Christian') position, which obviously only leads the societies concerned into an impasse and hence does not form an obstacle to the deployment of imperialist control over the world system.

Political Islam is not only reactionary on certain questions (notably concerning the status of women) and perhaps even responsible for fanatic excesses directed against non-Muslim citizens (such as the Copts in Egypt)—it is fundamentally reactionary and therefore obviously cannot participate in the progress of people's liberation.

Three major arguments are nevertheless advanced to encourage social movements as a whole to enter into dialogue with the movements of political Islam. The first is that political Islam mobilizes numerous popular masses, which cannot be ignored or scorned. Numerous images certainly reinforce this claim. Still, one should keep a cool head and properly assess the mobilizations in question. The electoral 'successes' that have been organized are put into perspective as soon as they are subjected to more rigorous analyses. I mention here, for example, the huge proportion of abstentions—more than 75 per cent!—in the Egyptian elections. The power of the Islamist street is, in large part, simply the reverse side of the weaknesses of the organized left, which is absent from the spheres in which current social conflicts are occurring.

Even if it were agreed that political Islam actually mobilizes significant numbers, does that justify concluding that the left must seek to include political Islamic organizations in alliances for political or social action? If political Islam successfully mobilizes large numbers of people, that is simply a fact, and any effective political strategy must include this fact in its considerations, proposals, and options. But seeking alliances is not necessarily the best means to deal with this challenge. It should be pointed out that the organizations of political Islam—the Muslim Brotherhood in particular—are not seeking such an alliance, indeed even reject it. If, by chance, some unfortunate leftist organizations come to believe that political Islamic organizations have accepted them, the first decision the latter would make, after having succeeded in coming to power, would be to liquidate their burdensome ally with extreme violence, as was the case in Iran with the Mujahideen and the Fidayeen Khalq.

The second reason put forward by the partisans of 'dialogue' is that political Islam, even if it is reactionary in terms of social proposals, is 'anti-imperialist'. I have heard it said that the criterion for this that I propose (unreserved support for struggles carried out for social progress) is 'economistic' and neglects the political dimensions of the challenge that confronts the peoples of the South. I do not believe that this critique is valid given what I have said about the democratic and national dimensions of the desirable responses for handling this challenge. I also agree that in their response to the challenge that confronts the peoples of the South, the forces in action are not necessarily consistent in their manner of dealing with its social and political dimensions. It is, thus, possible to imagine a political Islam that is anti-imperialist, though regressive on the social plane. Iran, Hamas in Palestine, Hezbollah in Lebanon, and certain resistance movements in Iraq immediately come to mind. I will discuss these particular situations later. What I contend is that political Islam as a whole is quite simply not anti-imperialist but is altogether lined up behind the dominant powers on the world scale.

The third argument calls the attention of the left to the necessity of combating Islamophobia. Any left worthy of the name cannot ignore the *question des banlieues*, that is, the treatment of the popular classes of immigrant origin in the metropolises of contemporary developed capitalism. Analysis of this challenge and the responses provided by various groups (the interested parties themselves, the European electoral left, the radical left) lies outside the focus of this text. I will content myself with expressing my viewpoint in principle: the progressive response cannot be based on the institutionalization of communitarianism,[1] which is essentially and necessarily always associated with inequality, and ultimately originates in a racist culture. A specific ideological product of the reactionary political culture of the United States, communitarianism (already triumphant in Great Britain) is beginning to pollute political life on the European continent. Islamophobia, systematically promoted by important sections of

---

[1] A political theory based on 'collective cultural identities' as central to understanding dynamic social reality.—*Ed.*

the political elite and the media, is part of a strategy for managing community diversity for capital's benefit, because this supposed respect for diversity is, in fact, only the means to deepen divisions within the popular classes.

The question of the so-called problem neighbourhoods (*banlieues*) is specific and confusing it with the question of imperialism (i.e., the imperialist management of the relations between the dominant imperialist centres and the dominated peripheries), as is sometimes done, will contribute nothing to making progress on each of these completely distinct terrains. This confusion is part of the reactionary toolbox and reinforces Islamophobia, which, in turn, makes it possible to legitimize both the offensive against the popular classes in the imperialist centres and the offensive against the peoples of the peripheries concerned. This confusion and Islamophobia, in turn, provide a valuable service to reactionary political Islam, giving credibility to its anti-Western discourse. I say, then, that the two reactionary ideological campaigns promoted, respectively, by the racist right in the West and by political Islam mutually support each other, just as they support communitarian practices.

MODERNITY, DEMOCRACY, SECULARISM, AND ISLAM

The image that the Arab and Islamic regions give of themselves today is that of societies in which religion (Islam) is at the forefront in all areas of social and political life, to the point that it appears strange to imagine that it could be different. The majority of foreign observers (political leaders and the media) conclude that modernity, perhaps even democracy, will have to adapt to the strong presence of Islam, *de facto* precluding secularism. Either this reconciliation is possible and it will be necessary to support it, or it is not and it will be necessary to deal with this region of the world as it is. I do not at all share this so-called realist vision.

The future—in the long view of a globalized socialism—is, for the peoples of this region as for others, democracy and secularism. This future is possible in these regions as elsewhere, but nothing is guaranteed and certain, anywhere.

Modernity is a rupture in world history, initiated in Europe during the sixteenth century. Modernity proclaims that human beings are responsible for their own history, individually and collectively, and consequently breaks with the dominant pre-modern ideologies. Modernity, then, makes democracy possible, just as it demands secularism, in the sense of separation of the religious and the political. Formulated by the eighteenth-century Enlightenment, implemented by the French Revolution, the complex association of modernity, democracy, and secularism, its advances and retreats, has been shaping the contemporary world ever since. But modernity by itself is not only a cultural revolution. It derives its meaning only through the close relation that it has with the birth and subsequent growth of capitalism. This relation has conditioned the historic limits of 'really existing' modernity. The concrete forms of modernity, democracy, and secularism found today must, then, be considered as products of the concrete history of the growth of capitalism. They are shaped by the specific conditions in which the domination of capital is expressed—the historical compromises that define the social contents of hegemonic blocs (what I call the historical course of political cultures).

This condensed presentation of my understanding of the historical materialist method is evoked here simply to situate the diverse ways of combining capitalist modernity, democracy, and secularism in their theoretical context.

The Enlightenment and the French Revolution put forward a model of radical secularism. Atheist or agnostic, deist or believer (in this case Christian), the individual is free to choose, the state knows nothing about it. On the European continent—and in France beginning with the Restoration—the retreats and compromises which combined the power of the bourgeoisie with that of the dominant classes of the pre-modern systems were the basis for attenuated forms of secularism, understood as tolerance, without excluding the social role of the churches from the political system. As for the United States, its particular historical path resulted in the forming of a fundamentally reactionary political culture, in which genuine secularism is practically unknown. Religion here is a recognized social actor and secularism is confused with the multiplicity of official religions (any religion—or even sect—is official).

There is an obvious link between the degree of radical secularism upheld and the degree of support for shaping society in accord with the central theme of modernity. The left, be it radical or even moderate, which believes in the effectiveness of politics to orient social evolution in chosen directions, defends strong concepts of secularism. The conservative right claims that things should be allowed to evolve on their own whether the question is economic, political, or social. As to economy the choice in favour of the 'market' is obviously favourable to capital. In politics low-intensity democracy becomes the rule, alternation is substituted for alternative. And in society, in this context, politics has no need for active secularism—'communities' compensate for the deficiencies of the state. The market and representative democracy make history and they should be allowed to do so. In the current moment of the left's retreat, this conservative version of social thought is widely dominant, in formulations that run the gamut from those of Touraine to those of Negri. The reactionary political culture of the United States goes even further in negating the responsibility of political action. The repeated assertion that God inspires the 'American' nation, and the massive adherence to this 'belief', reduce the very concept of secularism to nothing. To say that God makes history is, in fact, to allow the market alone to do it.

From this point of view, where are the peoples of the Middle East region situated? The image of bearded men bowed low and groups of veiled women give rise to hasty conclusions about the intensity of religious adherence among individuals. Western 'culturalist' friends who call for respect for the diversity of beliefs rarely find out about the procedures implemented by the authorities to present an image that is convenient for them. There are certainly those who are 'crazy for God' (*fous de Dieu*). Are they proportionally more numerous than the Spanish Catholics who march on Easter? Or the vast crowds who listen to televangelists in the United States?

In any case, the region has not always projected this image of itself. Beyond the differences from country to country, a large region can be identified that runs from Morocco to Afghanistan, including all the Arab peoples (with the exception of those in the Arabian peninsula), the Turks, Iranians, Afghans, and peoples of the former Soviet Central Asian republics, in which the possibilities for the development of secularism are far from negligible. The situation is different among other neighbouring peoples, the Arabs of the peninsula or the Pakistanis.

In this larger region, political traditions have been strongly marked by the radical currents of modernity: the ideas of the Enlightenment, the French Revolution, the Russian Revolution, and the communism of the Third International were present in the minds of everyone and were much more important than the parliamentarianism of Westminster, for example. These dominant currents inspired the major models for political transformation implemented by the ruling classes, which could be described, in some of their aspects, as forms of enlightened despotism.

This was certainly the case in the Egypt of Mohammed Ali or Khedive Ismail. Kemalism in Turkey and modernization in Iran were similar. The national populism of more recent stages of history belongs to the same family of modernist political projects.

The variants of the model were numerous (the Algerian National Liberation Front, Tunisian Bourguibism, Egyptian Nasserism, the Baathism of Syria and Iraq), but the direction of movement was analogous. Apparently extreme experiences—the so-called communist regimes in Afghanistan and South Yemen—were really not very different. All these regimes accomplished much and, for this reason, had very wide popular support. This is why, even though they were not truly democratic, they opened the way to a possible development in this direction. In certain circumstances, such as those in Egypt from 1920 to 1950, an experiment in electoral democracy was attempted, supported by the moderate anti-imperialist centre (the Wafd party), opposed by the dominant imperialist power (Great Britain) and its local allies (the monarchy). Secularism, implemented in moderate versions, to be sure, was not 'refused' by the people. On the contrary, it was religious people who were regarded as obscurantists by general public opinion, and most of them were.

The modernist experiments, from enlightened despotism to radical national populism, were not products of chance. Powerful movements that were dominant in the middle classes created them. In this way, these classes expressed their will to be viewed as fully-fledged partners in modern globalization. These projects, which can be described as national bourgeois, were modernist, secularizing and potential carriers of democratic developments. But precisely because these projects conflicted with the interests of dominant imperialism, the latter fought them relentlessly and systematically mobilized declining obscurantist forces for this purpose.

The history of the Muslim Brotherhood is well known. It was literally created in the 1920s by the British and the monarchy to block the path of the democratic and secular Wafd. Their mass return from their Saudi refuge after Nasser's death, organized by the CIA and Sadat, is also well known. We are all acquainted with the history of the Taliban, formed by the CIA in Pakistan to fight the 'communists' who had opened the schools to everyone, boys and girls. It is even well known that the Israelis supported Hamas at the beginning in order to weaken the secular and democratic currents of the Palestinian resistance.

Political Islam would have had much more difficulty in moving out from the borders of Saudi Arabia and Pakistan without the continual, powerful, and resolute support of the United States. Saudi Arabian society had not even begun its move out of tradition when petroleum was discovered under its soil. The alliance between imperialism and the traditional ruling class, sealed immediately, was concluded between the two partners and gave a new lease on life to Wahabi political Islam. On their side, the British succeeded in breaking Indian unity by persuading the Muslim leaders to create their own state, trapped in political Islam at its very birth. It should be noted that the theory by which this curiosity was legitimated—attributed to Maududi—had been completely drawn up beforehand by the English Orientalists in His Majesty's service.[2]

It is, thus, easy to understand the initiative taken by the United States to break the united front of Asian and African states set up at Bandung (1955) by creating an 'Islamic Conference', immediately promoted (from 1957) by Saudi Arabia and Pakistan. Political Islam penetrated into the region by this means.

The least of the conclusions that should be drawn from the observations made here is that political Islam is not the spontaneous result of the assertion of authentic religious convictions by the peoples concerned. Political Islam was constructed by the systematic action of imperialism, supported, of course, by obscurantist reactionary forces and subservient comprador

---

[2] The origin of the force of today's political Islam in Iran does not show the same historical connection with imperialist manipulation, for reasons discussed in the next section.—*Ed.*

classes. That this state of affairs is also the responsibility of left forces that neither saw nor knew how to deal with the challenge remains indisputable.

QUESTIONS RELATIVE TO THE FRONT LINE COUNTRIES (AFGHANISTAN, IRAQ, PALESTINE, AND IRAN)

The project of the United States, supported to varying degrees by their subaltern allies in Europe and Japan, is to establish military control over the entire planet. With this prospect in mind, the Middle East was chosen as the 'first strike' region for four reasons: (1) it holds the most abundant petroleum resources in the world and its direct control by the armed forces of the United States would give Washington a privileged position, placing its allies—Europe and Japan—and possible rivals (China) in an uncomfortable position of dependence for their energy supplies; (2) it is located at the crossroads of the Old World and makes it easier to put in place a permanent military threat against China, India, and Russia; (3) the region is experiencing a moment of weakness and confusion that allows the aggressor to be assured of an easy victory, at least for the moment; and (4) Israel's presence in the region, Washington's unconditional ally.

This aggression has placed the countries and nations located on the front line (Afghanistan, Iraq, Palestine, and Iran) in the particular situation of being destroyed (the first three) or threatened with destruction (Iran).

Afghanistan

Afghanistan experienced the best period in its modern history during the so-called communist republic. This was a regime of modernist enlightened despotism that opened up the educational system to children of both sexes. It was an enemy of obscurantism and, for this reason, had decisive support within the society. The agrarian reform that it had undertaken was, for the most part, a group of measures intended to reduce the tyrannical powers of tribal leaders. The support—at least tacitly—of the majority of the peasantry guaranteed the probable success of this well-begun change. The propaganda conveyed by the Western media as well as by political Islam presented this experiment as communist and atheist totalitarianism rejected by the Afghan people. In reality, the regime was far from being unpopular, much like Ataturk in his time.

The fact that the leaders of this experiment, in both of the major factions (Khalq and Parcham), were self-described as communists is not surprising. The model of the progress accomplished by the neighbouring peoples of Soviet Central Asia (despite everything that has been said on the subject and despite the autocratic practices of the system) in comparison with the ongoing social disasters of British imperialist management in other neighbouring countries (India and Pakistan included) had the effect, here as in many other countries of the region, of encouraging patriots to assess the full extent of the obstacle formed by imperialism to any attempt at modernization. The invitation extended by one faction to the Soviets to intervene in order to rid themselves of the others certainly had a negative effect and mortgaged the possibilities of the modernist national populist project.

The United States in particular and its allies of the Triad in general have always been tenacious opponents of the Afghan modernizers, communists or not. It is they who mobilized the obscurantist forces of Pakistan-style political Islam (the Taliban) and the warlords (the tribal leaders successfully neutralized by the so-called communist regime), and they who trained and armed them. Even after the Soviet retreat, the Najibullah government demonstrated the capability for resistance. It probably would have gained the upper hand but for the Pakistani military offensive that came to the support of the Taliban, and then the offensive of the reconstituted forces of the warlords, which increased the chaos.

Afghanistan was devastated by the intervention of the United States and its allies and agents, the Islamists in particular. Afghanistan cannot be reconstructed under their authority, barely disguised behind a clown without roots in the country, who was parachuted there by the Texas transnational by whom he was employed. The supposed 'democracy', in the name of which Washington, NATO, and the UN, called to the rescue, claim to justify the continuation of their presence (in fact, occupation), was a lie from the very beginning and has become a huge farce.

There is only one solution to the Afghan problem: all foreign forces should leave the country and all powers should be forced to refrain from financing and arming their allies. To those who are well-intended and express their fear that the Afghan people will then tolerate the dictatorship of the Taliban (or the warlords), I would respond that the foreign presence has been up until now and remains the best support for this dictatorship! The Afghan people had been moving in another direction—potentially the best possible—at a time when the West was forced to take less interest in its affairs. To the enlightened despotism of 'communists', the civilized West has always preferred obscurantist despotism, infinitely less dangerous for its interests!

Iraq

The armed diplomacy of the United States had the objective of literally destroying Iraq well before pretexts were actually given to it to do so on two different occasions: the invasion of Kuwait in 1990 and then after September 11, 2001—exploited for this purpose by Bush with Goebbels-style cynicism and lies ('If you tell a lie big enough and keep repeating it, people will eventually come to believe it'). The reason for this objective is simple and has nothing to do with the discourse calling for the liberation of the Iraqi people from the bloody dictatorship (real enough) of Saddam

Hussein. Iraq possesses a large part of the best petroleum resources of the planet. But, what is more, Iraq had succeeded in training scientific and technical cadres that were capable, through their critical mass, of supporting a coherent and substantial national project. This danger had to be eliminated by a preventive war that the United States gave itself the right to carry out when and where it decided, without the least respect for international law.

Beyond this obvious observation, several serious questions should be examined: (1) How could Washington's plan appear— even for a brief historical moment—to be such a dazzling success so easily? (2) What new situation has been created and confronts the Iraqi nation today? (3) What responses are the various elements of the Iraqi population giving to this challenge? And (4) what solutions can the democratic and progressive Iraqi, Arab, and international forces promote?

Saddam Hussein's defeat was predictable. Faced with an enemy whose main advantage lies in its capability to effect genocide with impunity by aerial bombardment (the use of nuclear weapons is to come), the people have only one possible effective response: carry out resistance on their invaded territory. Saddam's regime was devoted to eliminating every means of defence within reach of its people through the systematic destruction of any organization and every political party (beginning with the Communist Party) that had made the history of modern Iraq, including the Baath itself, which had been one of the major actors in this history. It is not surprising in these conditions that the Iraqi people allowed their country to be invaded without a struggle, nor even that some behaviours (such as apparent participation in elections organized by the invader or the outburst of fratricidal fighting among Kurds, Sunni Arabs, and Shia Arabs) seemed to be signs of a possible acceptance of defeat (on which Washington had based its calculations). But what is worthy of note is that the resistance on the ground grows stronger every day (despite all of the serious weaknesses displayed by the various resistance forces), that it has already made it impossible to establish a regime of lackeys capable of maintaining the appearance of order; in a way, that it has already demonstrated the failure of Washington's project.

A new situation has, nevertheless, been created by the foreign military occupation. The Iraqi nation is truly threatened. Washington is incapable of maintaining its control over the country (so as to pillage its petroleum resources, which is its number one objective) through the intermediary of a seeming national government. The only way it can continue its project, then, is to break the country apart. The division of the country into at least three states (Kurd, Sunni Arab, and Shia Arab) was, perhaps from the very beginning, Washington's objective, in alignment with Israel (the archives will reveal the truth of that in the future). Today, the 'civil war' is the card that Washington plays to legitimize the continuation of its occupation. Clearly, permanent occupation was—and remains—the objective: it is the only means by which Washington can guarantee its control of the petroleum resources. Certainly, no credence can be given to Washington's declarations of intent, such as 'we will leave the country as soon as order has been restored'. It should be remembered that the British never said of their occupation of Egypt, beginning in 1882, that it was anything other than provisional (it lasted until 1956!). Meanwhile, of course, the United States destroys the country, its schools, factories, and scientific capacities, a little more each day, using all means, including the most criminal.

The responses given by the Iraqi people to the challenge—so far, at least—do not appear to be up to facing the seriousness of the situation. That is the least that can be said. What are the reasons for this? The dominant Western media repeat *ad nauseam* that Iraq is an artificial country and that the oppressive domination of Saddam's 'Sunni' regime over the Shia and Kurds is the origin of the inevitable civil war (which can only be suppressed, perhaps, by continuing the foreign occupation).The resistance, then, is limited to a few pro-Saddam hard-core Islamists from the Sunni triangle. It is surely difficult to string together so many falsehoods.

Following the First World War, the British had great difficulty in defeating the resistance of the Iraqi people. In complete harmony with their imperial tradition, the British imported a monarchy and created a class of large landowners to support their power, thereby giving a privileged position to the Sunnis. But, despite their systematic efforts, the British failed. The Communist Party and the Baath Party were the main organized political forces that defeated the power of the 'Sunni' monarchy detested by everyone, Sunni, Shia, and Kurd. The violent competition between these two forces, which occupied centre stage between 1958 and 1963, ended with the victory of the Baath Party, welcomed at the time by the Western powers as a relief. The Communist project carried in itself the possibility for a democratic evolution; this was not true of the Baath. The latter was nationalist and pan-Arab in principle, admired the Prussian model for constructing German unity, and recruited its members from the secular, modernist petite bourgeoisie, hostile to obscurantist expressions of religion. In power, the Baath evolved, in predictable fashion, into a dictatorship that was only half anti-imperialist, in the sense that, depending on conjunctures and circumstances, a compromise could be accepted by the two partners (Baathist power in Iraq and U.S. imperialism, dominant in the region).

This deal encouraged the megalomaniacal excesses of the leader, who imagined that Washington would accept making him its main ally in the region. Washington's support for Baghdad (the delivery of chemical weapons is proof of this) in the absurd and criminal war against Iran from 1980 to 1989 appeared to lend credence to this calculation. Saddam never imagined Washington's deceit, that modernization of Iraq was unacceptable to imperialism and that the decision to destroy the country had already been made.

Saddam fell into the open trap when the green light was given to annex Kuwait (in fact attached in Ottoman times to the provinces that constitute Iraq, and detached by the British imperialists in order to make it one of their petroleum colonies). Iraq was then subjected to ten years of sanctions intended to bleed the country dry so as to facilitate the glorious conquest of the resulting vacuum by the armed forces of the United States.

The successive Baathist regimes, including the last one in its declining phase under Saddam's leadership, can be accused of everything, except for having stirred up the conflict between the Sunni and Shia. Who then is responsible for the bloody clashes between the two communities? One day, we will certainly learn how the CIA (and undoubtedly Mossad) organized many of these massacres. But, beyond that, it is true that the political desert created by the Saddam regime and the example that it provided of unprincipled opportunist methods encouraged succeeding aspirants to power of all kinds to follow this path, often protected by the occupier. Sometimes, perhaps, they were even naive to the point of believing that they could be of service to the occupying power. The aspirants in question, be they religious leaders (Shia or Sunni), supposed (para-tribal) 'notables', or notoriously corrupt businessmen exported by the United States, never had any real political standing in the country. Even those religious leaders whom the believers respected had no political influence that was acceptable to the Iraqi people. Without the void created by Saddam, no one would know how to pronounce their names. Faced with the new political world created by the imperialism of liberal globalization, will other authentically popular and national, possibly even democratic, political forces have the means to reconstruct themselves?

There was a time when the Iraqi Communist Party was the focus for organizing the best of what Iraqi society could produce. The Communist Party was established in every region of the country and dominated the world of intellectuals, often of Shia origin. (I note in passing that the Shia produced revolutionaries or religious leaders above all, rarely bureaucrats or compradors!) The Communist Party was authentically popular and anti-imperialist, little inclined to demagoguery and potentially democratic. After the massacre of thousands of its best militants by the Baathist dictatorships, the collapse of the Soviet Union (for which the Iraqi Communist Party was not prepared), and the behaviour of those intellectuals who believed it acceptable to return from exile as camp followers of the armed forces of the United States, is the Iraqi Communist Party henceforth fated to disappear permanently from history? Unfortunately, this is all too possible, but not inevitable—far from it.

The Kurdish question is real, in Iraq as in Iran and Turkey. But on this subject also, it should be remembered that the Western powers have always practised, with great cynicism, double standards. The repression of Kurdish demands has never attained in Iraq and Iran the level of police, military, political, and moral violence carried out by Ankara. Neither Iran nor Iraq has ever gone so far as to deny the very existence of the Kurds. However, Turkey must be pardoned for everything as a member of NATO, an organization of democratic nations, as the media remind us. Among the eminent democrats proclaimed by the West was Portugal's Salazar, one of NATO's founding members, and the no less ardent admirers of democracy, the Greek colonels and Turkish generals!

Each time that the Iraqi popular fronts, formed around the Communist Party and the Baath in the best moments of its turbulent history, exercised political power, they always found an area of agreement with the principal Kurdish parties. The latter, moreover, have always been their allies. The anti-Shia and anti-Kurd excesses of the Saddam regime were certainly real: for example, the bombing of the Basra region by Saddam's army after its defeat in Kuwait in 1990 and the use of gas against the Kurds. These excesses came in response to the manoeuvres of Washington's armed diplomacy, which had mobilized sorcerer's apprentices among Shia and Kurds. They remain no less criminal excesses, and stupid, moreover, since the success of Washington's appeals was quite limited. But can anything else be expected from dictators like Saddam?

The force of the resistance to foreign occupation, unexpected under these conditions, might seem to be miraculous. This is not the case, since the basic reality is that the Iraqi people as a whole (Arab and Kurd, Sunni and Shia) detest the occupiers and are familiar with its crimes on a daily basis (assassinations, bombings, massacres, torture). Given this a united front of national resistance (call it what you want) might even be imagined, proclaiming itself as such, posting the names, lists of organizations, and parties composing it and their common programme. This, however, is not actually the case up to the present for all of the reasons described above, including the destruction of the social and political fabric caused by the Saddam dictatorship and the occupation. Regardless of the reasons, this weakness is a serious handicap, which makes it easier to divide the population, encourage opportunists, even so far as making them collaborators, and throw confusion over the objectives of the liberation.

Who will succeed in overcoming these handicaps? The communists should be well placed to do so. Already, militants who are present on the ground are separating themselves from the leaders of the Communist Party (the only ones known by the dominant media) who, confused and embarrassed, are attempting to give a semblance of legitimacy to their rallying to the collaborationist government, even pretending that they are adding to the effectiveness of armed resistance by such action! But, under the circumstances, many other political forces could make decisive initiatives in the direction of forming this front.

It remains the case that, despite its weaknesses, the Iraqi people's resistance has already defeated (politically if not yet militarily) Washington's project. It is precisely this that worries the Atlanticists in the European Union, faithful allies of the United States. Today, they fear a U.S. defeat, because this would strengthen the capacity of the peoples of the South to force globalized transnational capital of the imperialist triad to respect the interests of the nations and peoples of Asia, Africa, and Latin America.

The Iraqi resistance has offered proposals that would make it possible to get out of the impasse and aid the United States to withdraw from the trap. It proposes: (1) formation of a transitional administrative authority set up with the support of the UN Security Council; (2) the immediate cessation of resistance actions and military and police interventions by occupying forces; (3) the departure of all foreign military and civilian authorities within six months. The details of these proposals have been published in the prestigious Arab review *Al Moustaqbal al Arabi* (January 2006), published in Beirut.

The absolute silence with which the European media oppose the dissemination of this message is a testament to the solidarity of the imperialist partners. Democratic and progressive European forces have the duty to dissociate themselves from this policy of the imperialist triad and support the proposals of the Iraqi resistance. To leave the Iraqi people to confront its opponent alone is not an acceptable option: it reinforces the dangerous idea that nothing can be expected from the West and its peoples, and consequently encourages the unacceptable—even criminal—excesses in the activities of some of the resistance movements.

The sooner the foreign occupation troops leave the country and the stronger the support by democratic forces in the world and in Europe for the Iraqi people, the greater will be the possibilities for a better future for this martyred people. The longer the occupation lasts, the more dismal will be the aftermath of its inevitable end.

Palestine

The Palestinian people have, since the Balfour Declaration during the First World War, been the victim of a colonization project by a foreign population, who reserve for them the fate of the 'redskins', whether one acknowledges it or pretends to be ignorant of it. This project has always had the unconditional support of the dominant imperialist power in the region (yesterday Great Britain, today the United States), because the foreign state in the region formed by that project can only be the unconditional ally, in turn, of the interventions required to force the Arab Middle East to submit to the domination of imperialist capitalism.

This is an obvious fact for all the peoples of Africa and Asia. Consequently, on both continents, they are spontaneously united on the assertion and defence of the rights of the Palestinian people. In Europe, however, the 'Palestinian question' causes division, produced by the confusions kept alive by Zionist ideology, which is frequently echoed favourably.

Today more than ever, in conjunction with the implementation of the U.S. 'Greater Middle East project', the rights of the Palestinian people have been abolished. All the same, the PLO accepted the Oslo and Madrid plans and the roadmap drafted by Washington. It is Israel that has openly gone back on its agreement, and implemented an even more ambitious expansion plan. The PLO has been undermined as a result: public opinion can justly reproach it with having naively believed in the sincerity of its adversaries. The support provided by the occupation authorities to its Islamist adversary (Hamas), in the beginning, at least, and the spread of corrupt practices in the Palestinian administration (on which the fund donors—the World Bank, Europe, and the NGOs—are silent, if they are not party to it) had to lead to the Hamas electoral victory (it was predictable). This then became an additional pretext immediately put forward to justify unconditional alignment with Israeli policies no matter what they may be.

The Zionist colonial project has always been a threat, beyond Palestine, for neighbouring Arab peoples. Its ambitions to annex the Egyptian Sinai and its effective annexation of the Syrian Golan are testimony to that. In the Greater Middle East project, a particular place is granted to Israel, to its regional monopoly of nuclear military equipment and its role as 'indispensable partner' (under the fallacious pretext that Israel has technological expertise of which the Arab people are incapable. What an indispensable racism!).

It is not the intention here to offer analyses concerning the complex interactions between the resistance struggles against Zionist colonial expansion and the political conflicts and choices in Lebanon and Syria. The Baathist regimes in Syria have resisted, in their own way, the demands of the imperialist powers and Israel. That this resistance has also served to legitimize more questionable ambitions (control of Lebanon) is certainly not debatable. Moreover, Syria has carefully chosen the least dangerous allies in Lebanon. It is well known that the Lebanese Communist Party had organized resistance to the Israeli incursions in South Lebanon (diversion of water included). The Syrian, Lebanese, and Iranian authorities closely cooperated to destroy this dangerous base and replace it with Hezbollah. The assassination of Rafiq al-Hariri (a still unresolved case) obviously gave the imperialist powers (the United States in front, France behind) the opportunity to intervene with two objectives in mind: (1) force Damascus to align itself permanently with the vassal Arab states (Egypt and Saudi Arabia)—or, failing that, eliminate the vestiges of a deteriorated Baathist power; and (2) demolish what remains of the capability to resist Israeli incursions (by demanding the disarmament of Hezbollah). Rhetoric about democracy can be invoked within this context, if useful.

Today to accept the implementation of the Israeli project in progress is to ratify the abolition of the primary right of peoples:

the right to exist. This is the supreme crime against humanity. The accusation of 'anti-Semitism' addressed to those who reject this crime is only a means for appalling blackmail.

Iran

It is not our intention here to develop the analyses called for by the Islamic Revolution. Was it, as it has been proclaimed to be among supporters of political Islam as well as among foreign observers, the declaration of and point of departure for a change that ultimately must seize the entire region, perhaps even the whole Muslim world, renamed for the occasion the *umma* (the 'nation', which has never been)? Or was it a singular event, particularly because it was a unique combination of the interpretations of Shia Islam and the expression of Iranian nationalism?

From the perspective of what interests us here, I will only make two observations. The first is that the regime of political Islam in Iran is not by nature incompatible with integration of the country into the globalized capitalist system such as it is, since the regime is based on liberal principles for managing the economy. The second is that the Iranian nation as such is a 'strong nation', one whose major components, if not all, of both popular classes and ruling classes, do not accept the integration of their country into the globalized system in a dominated position. There is, of course, a contradiction between these two dimensions of the Iranian reality. The second one accounts for Teheran's foreign policy tendencies, which bear witness to the will to resist foreign diktats.

It is Iranian nationalism—powerful and, in my opinion, altogether historically positive—that explains the success of the modernization of scientific, industrial, technological, and military capabilities undertaken by the Shah's regime and the Khomeinist regime that followed. Iran is one of the few states of the South (with China, India, Korea, Brazil, and maybe a few others, but not many!) to have a national bourgeois project. Whether it be possible in the long term to achieve this project or not (my opinion is that it is not) is not the focus of our discussion here. Today this project exists and is in place.

It is precisely because Iran forms a critical mass capable of attempting to assert itself as a respected partner that the United States has decided to destroy the country by a new preventive war. As is well known, the conflict is taking place around the nuclear capabilities that Iran is developing. Why should not this country, just like others, have the right to pursue these capabilities, up to and including becoming a nuclear military power? By what right can the imperialist powers and their Israeli accomplice boast about granting themselves a monopoly over weapons of mass destruction? Can one give any credit to the discourse that argues that 'democratic' nations will never make use of such weapons like 'rogue states' could, when it is common knowledge that the democratic nations in question are responsible for the greatest genocides of modern times, including the one against the Jews, and that the United States has already used atomic weapons and still today rejects an absolute and general ban on their use?

CONCLUSION

Today, political conflicts in the region find three groups of forces opposed to one another: those that proclaim their nationalist past (but are, in reality, nothing more than the degenerate and corrupt inheritors of the bureaucracies of the national-populist era); those that proclaim political Islam; and those that are attempting to organize around 'democratic' demands that are compatible with economic liberalism. The consolidation of power by any of these forces is not acceptable to a left that is attentive to the interests of the popular classes. In fact, the interests of the comprador classes affiliated with the current imperialist system are expressed through these three tendencies. U.S. diplomacy keeps all three irons in the fire, since it is focused on using the conflicts among them for its exclusive benefit. For the left to attempt to become involved in these conflicts solely through alliances with one or another of the tendencies[3] (preferring the regimes in place to avoid the worst, i.e., political Islam, or else seeking to be allied with the latter in order to get rid of the regimes) is doomed to fail. The left must assert itself by undertaking struggles in areas where it finds its natural place: defence of the economic and social interests of the popular classes, democracy, and assertion of national sovereignty, all conceptualized together as inseparable.

The region of the Greater Middle East is today central in the conflict between the imperialist leader and the peoples of the entire world. To defeat the Washington establishment's project is the condition for providing the possibility of success for advances in any region of the world. Failing that, all these advances will remain vulnerable in the extreme. That does not mean that the importance of struggles carried out in other regions of the world, in Europe or Latin America or elsewhere, should be underestimated. It means only that they should be part of a comprehensive perspective that contributes to defeating Washington in the region that it has chosen for its first criminal strike of this century.

December 01, 2007

---

[3] Tactical alliances arising from the concrete situation are another matter, e.g., the joint action of the Lebanese Communist Party with Hezbollah in resisting the Israeli invasion of Lebanon in the summer of 2006.—*Ed.*

THE TRAJECTORY OF HISTORICAL CAPITALISM AND MARXISM'S TRICONTINENTAL VOCATION

THE LONG RISE OF CAPITALISM

The long history of capitalism is composed of three distinct, successive phases: (1) a lengthy preparation—the transition from the tributary mode, the usual form of organization of pre-modern societies—which lasted eight centuries, from 1000 to 1800; (2) a short period of maturity (the nineteenth century), during which the 'West' affirmed its domination; (3) the long 'decline' caused by the 'Awakening of the South' (to use the title of my book, published in 2007) in which the peoples and their states regained the major initiative in transforming the world—the first wave having taken place in the twentieth century. This struggle against an imperialist order that is inseparable from the global expansion of capitalism is itself the potential agent in the long road of transition, beyond capitalism, toward socialism. In the twenty-first century, there are now the beginnings of a second wave of independent initiatives by the peoples and states of the South.

The internal contradictions that were characteristic of all the advanced societies in the pre-modern world—and not only those specific to 'feudal' Europe—account for the successive waves of the social-technological innovation that were to constitute capitalist modernity.

The oldest wave came from China, where changes began in the Sung era (eleventh century) and developing further in the Ming and Qing epochs gave China a head start in terms of technological inventiveness and the social productivity of collective work—not to be surpassed by Europe until the nineteenth century. The 'Chinese' wave was to be followed by a 'Middle Eastern' wave, which took place in the Arabo-Persian Caliphate and then via the Crusades and their aftermath, in the towns of Italy.

The last wave concerns the long transition of the ancient tributary world to the modern capitalist world. This began in earnest in the Atlantic part of Europe following the conquest/encounter with the Americas, and for three centuries (1500-1800) took the form of mercantilism. Capitalism, which gradually came to dominate the world, is the product of this last wave of social-technological innovation. The European ('Western') form of historical capitalism that emerged in Atlantic and Central Europe, in its offspring in the United States, and later, in Japan, developed its own characteristics—notably a mode of accumulation based on the dispossession, first, of the peasants and then of the peoples in the peripheries, who were integrated as dependencies into its global system. This historical form is therefore inseparable from the centres/peripheries contradiction that it endlessly constructs, reproduces, and deepens.

Historical capitalism took on its final form at the end of the eighteenth century with the English Industrial Revolution that invented the new 'machine factory' (together with the creation of the new industrial proletariat) and the French Revolution that gave rise to modern politics.

Mature capitalism developed over the short period that marked the apogee of this system in the nineteenth century. Capital accumulation then took on its definitive form and became the basic law that governed society. From the beginning, this form of accumulation was constructive (it enabled a prodigious and continuous acceleration in the productivity of social labour). But it was, at the same time, destructive. Marx observed that accumulation destroys the two bases of wealth: the human being (victim of commodity alienation) and nature.

In my analyses of historical capitalism I particularly stressed a third dimension of accumulation's destructiveness: the material and cultural dispossession of the dominated peoples of the periphery—whom Marx had somewhat overlooked. This was no doubt because, in the short period when Marx was producing his works, Europe seemed almost exclusively dedicated to the requirements of internal accumulation. Marx thus relegated this dispossession to a temporary phase of 'primitive accumulation' that I, on the contrary, have described as permanent.

The fact remains that during its short mature period, capitalism fulfilled undeniable progressive functions. It created the conditions that made it possible and necessary for it to be overtaken by socialism/communism, both on the material level and on that of the new political and cultural consciousness that accompanied it. Socialism (and even more so, communism) is not, as some have thought, to be conceived as a superior 'mode of production' because it is capable of accelerating the development of the forces of production and of associating them with an 'equitable' distribution of income. Socialism is something else again: a higher stage in the development of human civilization. It is not, therefore, by chance that the working-class movement took root in the exploited population and became committed to the fight for socialism, as evident in nineteenth century Europe, and expressed in *The Communist Manifesto* in 1848. Nor is it by chance that this challenge took the form of the first socialist revolution in history: the Paris Commune in 1871.

MONOPOLY CAPITALISM: THE BEGINNING OF THE LONG DECLINE

At the end of the nineteenth century, capitalism entered into its long period of decline. I mean by this that the destructive dimensions of accumulation now won out, at a growing rate, over its progressive, constructive dimension. This qualitative transformation of capitalism took shape with the setting up of new production monopolies (no longer only in the areas of trade and colonial conquest, as in the mercantilist period) at the end of the nineteenth century. This was in response to the first long structural crisis of capitalism that started in the 1870s, shortly after the defeat of the Paris Commune. The emergence of monopoly capitalism (as famously highlighted by Hilferding and Hobson) showed that classic, freely competitive capitalism, and indeed capitalism itself, had by now 'had its day', and become 'obsolete'. The bell sounded for the necessary and possible expropriation of the expropriators. This decline found its expression in the first wave of wars and revolutions that marked the history of the twentieth century. Lenin was therefore right in describing monopoly capitalism as the 'highest stage of capitalism'.

But, optimistically, Lenin thought that this first long crisis would be the last, with the socialist revolution on the agenda. History later proved that capitalism was able to overcome this crisis, at the cost of two world wars, and was even able to adapt to the setbacks imposed on it by the Russian and Chinese Revolutions and national liberation in Asia and Africa. But after the short period of monopoly capitalist revival (1945–1975), there followed a second, long structural crisis of the system, starting in the 1970s. Capital reacted to this renewed challenge by a qualitatively new transformation that took the form of what I have described as 'generalized-monopoly capitalism'.

A host of major questions arise from this interpretation of the 'long decline' of capitalism, which concern the nature of the 'revolution' that was the order of the day. Could the 'long decline' of historical monopoly capitalism be synonymous with the 'long transition' to socialism/communism? Under what conditions?

From 1500 (the beginning of the Atlantic mercantilist form of the transition to mature capitalism) to 1900 (the beginning of the challenge to the unilateral logic of accumulation), the Westerners (Europeans, then North Americans and, later, the Japanese) remained the masters of the game. They alone shaped the structures of the new world of historical capitalism. The peoples and nations of the periphery who had been conquered and dominated did, of course, resist as well as they could, but they were always defeated in the end and forced to adapt themselves to their subordinate status.

The domination of the Euro-Atlantic world was accompanied by its demographic explosion: the Europeans, who had constituted 18 per cent of the planet's population in 1500, represented 36 per cent by 1900—increased by their descendants emigrating to the Americas and Australia. Without this massive emigration, the accumulation model of historical capitalism, based on the accelerated disappearance of the peasant world, would have simply been impossible. This is why the model cannot be reproduced in the peripheries of the system, which have no 'Americas' to conquer. 'Catching up' in the system being impossible, people of the peripheries have no alternative than to opt for a different development path.

THE INITIATIVE PASSES TO THE PEOPLES
AND NATIONS OF THE PERIPHERY

In 1871 the Paris Commune which, as mentioned, was the first socialist revolution, was also the last one to take place in a country that was part of the capitalist centre. The twentieth century inaugurated—with the 'awakening of the peoples of the peripheries'—a new chapter in history. Its first manifestations were the revolutions in Iran (1907), in Mexico (1910–1920), China (1911), and 'semi-peripheral' Russia in 1905. This awakening of the peoples and nations of the periphery was carried forward in the Revolution of 1917, the Arabo-Muslim Nahda, the constitution of the Young Turk movement (1908), the Egyptian Revolution of 1919, and the formation of the Indian Congress (1885).

In reaction to the first long crisis of historical capitalism (1875–1950), the peoples of the periphery began to liberate themselves around 1914–1917, mobilizing themselves under the flags of socialism (Russia, China, Vietnam, Cuba) or of national liberation (India, Algeria) associated to different degrees with progressive social reforms. They took the path to industrialization, hitherto forbidden by the domination of the (old) 'classic' imperialism, forcing the latter to 'adjust' to this first wave of independent initiatives of the peoples, nations, and states of the peripheries. From 1917 to the time when the 'Bandung project' (1955–1980) ran out of steam and Sovietism collapsed in 1990, these were the initiatives that dominated the scene.

I do not see the two long crises of aging monopoly capitalism in terms of long Kondratieff cycles, but as two stages in both the decline of historical globalized capitalism and the possible transition to socialism. Nor do I see the 1914–1945 period exclusively as 'the 30 years' war for the succession to 'British hegemony'. I see this period also as the long war conducted by the imperialist centres against the first awakening of the peripheries (East and South).

This first wave of the awakening of the peoples of the periphery wore out for many reasons, including its own internal limitations and contradictions, and imperialism's success in finding new ways of dominating the world system (through the control of technological invention, access to resources, the globalized financial system, communication and information technology, weapons of mass destruction).

Nevertheless, capitalism underwent a second long crisis that began in the 1970s, exactly one hundred years after the first one. The reactions of capital to this crisis were the same as it had had to the previous one: reinforced concentration, which gave rise to generalized-monopoly capitalism, globalization ('liberal'), and financialization. But the moment of triumph—the second 'belle époque', from 1990 to 2008, echoing the first 'belle époque', from 1890 to 1914—of the new collective imperialism of the Triad (the United States, Europe, and Japan) was indeed brief. A new epoch of chaos, wars, and revolutions emerged. In this situation, the second wave of the awakening of the nations of the periphery (which had already started), now refused to allow the collective imperialism of the Triad to maintain its dominant positions, other than through the military control of the planet. The Washington establishment, by giving priority to this strategic objective, proves that it is perfectly aware of the real issues at stake in the struggles and decisive conflicts of our epoch, as opposed to the naive vision of the majority currents in Western 'alterworldism'.

IS GENERALIZED-MONOPOLY CAPITALISM THE LAST PHASE OF CAPITALISM?

Lenin described the imperialism of the monopolies as the 'highest stage of capitalism'. I have described imperialism as a 'permanent phase of capitalism' in the sense that globalized historical capitalism has built up, and never ceases from reproducing and deepening, the centre/periphery polarization. The first wave of constituting monopolies at the end of the nineteenth century certainly involved a qualitative transformation in the fundamental structures of the capitalist mode of production. Lenin deduced from this that the socialist revolution was on the agenda, and Rosa Luxemburg believed that the alternatives were now 'socialism or barbarism'. Lenin was certainly too optimistic, having underestimated the devastating effects of the imperialist rent—and the transfer associated with it—on the revolution from the West (the centres) to the East (the peripheries).

The second wave of the centralization of capital, which took place in the last third of the twentieth century, constituted a second qualitative transformation of the system, which I have described as 'generalized monopolies'. From now on, they not only commanded the heights of the modern economy; they also succeeded in imposing their direct control over the whole production system. The small and medium enterprises (and even the large ones outside the monopolies), such as the farmers, were literally dispossessed, reduced to the status of sub-contractors, with their upstream and downstream operations, and subjected to rigid control by the monopolies.

At this highest phase of the centralization of capital, its ties with a living organic body—the bourgeoisie—have broken. This is an immensely important change: the historical bourgeoisie, constituted of families rooted locally, has given way to an anonymous oligarchy/plutocracy that controls the monopolies, in spite of the dispersion of the title deeds of their capital. The range of financial operations invented over the last decades bears witness to this supreme form of alienation: the speculator can now sell what he does not even possess, so that the principle of property is reduced to a status that is little less than derisory.

The function of socially productive labour has disappeared. The high degree of alienation had already attributed a productive virtue to money ('money makes little ones'). Now alienation has reached new heights: it is time ('time is money') that by its virtue alone 'produces profit'. The new bourgeois class that responds to the requirements of the reproduction of the system has been reduced to the status of 'waged servants' (precarious, to boot), even when they are, as members of the upper sectors of the middle classes, privileged people who are very well paid for their 'work'.

This being so, should one not conclude that capitalism has had its day? There is no other possible answer to the challenge: the monopolies must be nationalized. This is a first, unavoidable step toward a possible socialization of their management by workers and citizens. Only this will make it possible to progress along the long road to socialism. At the same time, it will be the only way of developing a new macro economy that restores a genuine space for the operations of small and medium enterprises. If that is not done, the logic of domination by abstract capital can produce nothing but the decline of democracy and civilization, to a 'generalized apartheid' at the world level.

MARXISM'S TRICONTINENTAL VOCATION

My interpretation of historical capitalism stresses the polarization of the world (the contrast of centre/periphery) produced by the historical form of the accumulation of capital. This perspective questions the visions of the 'socialist revolution', and, more broadly, the transition to socialism, that the historical Marxisms have developed. The 'revolution'—or the transition—before us is not necessarily the one on which these historical visions were based. Nor are the strategies for surmounting capitalism the same.

It has to be recognized that what the most important social and political struggles of the twentieth century tried to challenge was not so much capitalism in itself as the permanent imperialist dimension of actually existing capitalism. The issue is therefore whether this transfer of the centre of gravity of the struggles necessarily calls capitalism into question, at least potentially.

Marx's thinking associates 'scientific' clarity in the analysis of reality with social and political action (the class struggle in its broadest sense) aimed at 'changing the world'. Confronting the basics—i.e., the discovery of the real source of surplus value produced by the exploitation of social labour by capital—is indispensable to this struggle. If this fundamental and lucid contribution of Marx is abandoned, a double failure is inevitably the result. Any such abandonment of the theory of exploitation (law of value) reduces the analysis of reality to that of appearances only, a way of thinking that is limited by its abject submission to the requirements of commodification, itself engendered by the system. Similarly, such abandonment of the labour value-based critique of the system annihilates the effectiveness of strategies and struggles to change the world, which are thereby conceived within this alienating framework, the 'scientific' claims of which have no real basis.

Nevertheless, it is not enough just to cling to the lucid analysis formulated by Marx. This is not only because 'reality' itself changes, and there are always 'new' things to be taken into account in the development of the critique of the real world that started with Marx. But more fundamentally, it is because, as we know, the analysis that Marx put forward in *Capital* was left incomplete. In the planned sixth volume of this work (which was never written), Marx proposed treating the globalization of capitalism. This now has to be done by others, which is why I have dared to advocate the formulation of the 'law of globalized value', restoring the place of the unequal development (through the centre/periphery polarization) that is inseparable from the global expansion of historical capitalism. In this formulation, 'imperialist rent' is integrated into the whole process of the production and circulation of capital and the distribution of the surplus value. This rent is at the origin of the challenge: it accounts for why the struggles for socialism in the imperialist centres have faded, and it highlights the anti-imperialist dimensions of the struggles in the peripheries against the system of capitalist/imperialist globalization.

I shall not return here to discuss what an exegesis of Marx's texts on this question would suggest. Marx, who is nothing less than a giant, with his critical acumen and the incredible subtlety of his thought, must have had at least an intuition that he was coming up against a serious question here. This is suggested by his observations on the disastrous effects of the alignment of the English working class with the chauvinism associated with the colonial exploitation of Ireland. Marx was therefore not surprised that it was in France—less developed than England economically, but more advanced in political consciousness—that the first socialist revolution took place. He, like Engels, also hoped that the 'backwardness' of Germany would enable an original form of advance to develop, fusing together both the bourgeois and the socialist revolutions.

Lenin went still further. He emphasized the qualitative transformation that was involved in the passage to monopoly capitalism, and he drew the necessary conclusions: that capitalism had ceased to be a necessary progressive stage in history and that it was now 'putrefied' (Lenin's own term). In other words, it had become 'obsolete' and 'senile' (my terms), so that the passing to socialism was on the agenda, which was both necessary and possible. He conceived and implemented, in this framework, a revolution that began in the periphery (Russia, the 'weak link'). Then, seeing the failure of his hopes in a European revolution, he conceived of the transfer of the revolution to the East, where he saw that the fusion of the objectives of the anti-imperialist struggle with those of the struggle against capitalism had become possible.

But it was Mao who rigorously formulated the complex and contradictory nature of the objectives in the transition to the socialism that were to be pursued in these conditions. 'Marxism' (or, more exactly, the historical Marxisms) was confronted by a new challenge—one which did not exist in the most lucid political consciousness of the nineteenth century, but which arose because of the transfer of the initiative to transform the world to the peoples, nations, and states of the periphery.

Imperialist rent not 'only' benefited the monopolies of the dominant centre (in the form of super profits), it was also the basis of the reproduction of society as a whole, in spite of its evident class structure and the exploitation of its workers. This is what Perry Anderson analysed so clearly as 'Western Marxism', which he described as 'the product of defeat' (the abandonment of the socialist perspective)—and which is relevant here. This Marxism was then condemned, having renounced 'changing the world' and committing itself to 'academic' studies, without political impact.

The liberal drift of social democracy—and its rallying both to the U.S. ideology of 'consensus' and to Atlanticism at the service of the imperialist domination of the world—were the consequences.

'Another world' (a very vague phrase to indicate a world committed to the long road toward socialism) is obviously impossible unless it provides a solution to the problems of the peoples in the periphery—only 80 per cent of the world population! 'Changing the world' therefore means changing the living conditions of this majority. Marxism, which analyses the reality of the world in order to make the forces acting for change as effective as possible, necessarily acquires a decisive tricontinental (Africa, Asia, Latin America) vocation.

How is this related to the terrain of struggle that confronts us? What I propose, in answer to this question, is an analysis of the transformation of imperialist monopoly capitalism ('senile') into generalized-monopoly capitalism (still more senile for this reason). This is a qualitative transformation in response to the second long crisis of the system that began in the 1970s, and that has still not been resolved. From this analysis, I draw two main conclusions: (1) The imperialist system is transformed into the collective imperialism of the Triad, in reaction to the industrialization of the peripheries, imposed by the victories of the first wave of their 'awakening'. (2) This occurs together with the implementation by the new imperialism of new means of control of the world system, based on the military control of the planet and its resources, the super-protection of the exclusive appropriation of technology by the oligopolies and their control over the world financial system. There is an accompanying transformation of the class structures of contemporary capitalism with the emergence of an exclusive dominant oligarchy.

'Western Marxism' has ignored the decisive transformation represented by the emergence of generalized-monopoly capitalism. The intellectuals of the new Western radical left refuse to measure the decisive effects of the concentration of the oligopolies that now dominate the production system as a whole, in the same way that they dominate all political, social, cultural, and ideological life. Having eliminated the term 'socialism' (and, *a fortiori,* 'communism') from their language, they no longer envisage the necessary expropriation of the expropriators, but only an impossible 'other capitalism' with what they call a 'human face'. The drift of the 'post' discourses (post-modernist, post-Marxist, etc.) is the inevitable result. Negri, for example, says not a word concerning this decisive transformation that, for me, is at the heart of the issues of our time.

The newspeak of these crazy ravings should be seen in the literal sense of the term, as an illusory imaginary detached from all reality. In French, *le peuple* (and better still, *les classes populaires*), as in Spanish *el pueblo* (*los clases populares*), is not a synonym for 'everyone'. It refers to the dominated and exploited classes and therefore also emphasizes their diversity (of the kinds of relationship they have with capital), which makes it possible to build effective concrete strategies and to make them into active change agents. This is in contrast to the English equivalent: 'people' does not have this meaning, being synonymous with *les gens* (everyone) and, in Spanish, *la gente*. Newspeak ignores these concepts (marked by Marxism and formulated in French or Spanish) and substitutes for them some vague word like Negri's 'multitude'. It is a philosophical delirium to attribute to this word (which adds nothing but subtracts a lot) a so-called analytical power, by invoking its use by Spinoza, who lived at a time and in conditions which have nothing to do with our own.

The fashionable political thought of new Western radical leftists also ignores the imperialist character of the domination of the generalized monopolies, replacing it with the empty term of 'Empire' (Negri). This Western-centrism, taken to the extreme, omits any reflection on the imperialist rent without which neither the mechanisms of social reproduction nor the challenges that they thus constitute can be understood.

In contrast, Mao presented a view that was both profoundly revolutionary and 'realistic' (scientific, lucid) about the terms in which the challenge should be analysed, making it possible to deduce effective strategies for successive advances along the long road of transition to socialism. For this reason, he distinguishes and connects the three dimensions of reality: peoples, nations, states.

The people (popular classes) 'want the revolution'. This means that it is possible to construct a hegemonic bloc that brings together the different dominated and exploited classes, as opposed to the one that enables the reproduction of the system of the domination of imperialist capitalism, exercised through the comprador hegemonic bloc and the state at its service.

Mention of nations refers to the fact that imperialist domination denies the dignity of the 'nations' (call them what you will), forged by the history of the societies of the peripheries. Such domination has systematically destroyed all that give the nations their originality—in the name of 'Westernization' and the proliferation of cheap junk. The liberation of the people is therefore inseparable from that of the nations to which they belong. And this is the reason why Maoism replaced the short slogan, 'Workers of all countries, unite!' by a more embracing one: 'Workers of all countries, oppressed peoples, unite!' Nations want their 'liberation', seen as being complementary to the struggle of the people and not conflictual with it. The liberation in question is not, therefore, the restoration of the past—the illusion fostered by a culturalist attachment to the past—but the invention of the future. This is based on the radical transformation of the nation's historical heritage, rather than the artificial importation of a false 'modernity'. The culture that is inherited and subjected to the test of transformation is understood here as political culture—

care being taken not to use the undifferentiated term of 'culture' (encompassing 'religious' and innumerable other forms), which neither means anything, because genuine culture is not abstract, nor is a historical invariant.

The reference to the state is based on the necessary recognition of the relative autonomy of its power in its relations with the hegemonic bloc that is the base of its legitimacy, even if this is popular and national. This relative autonomy cannot be ignored as long as the state exists, that is, at least for the whole duration of the transition to communism. It is only after this that we can think of a 'stateless society'—not before. This is not only because the popular and national advances must be protected from the permanent aggression of imperialism, which still dominates the world, but also, and perhaps above all, because 'to advance on the long transition' also requires 'developing productive forces'. In other words, the goal is to achieve that which imperialism has been preventing in the countries of the periphery, and to obliterate the heritage of world polarization, which is inseparable from the world expansion of historical capitalism. The programme is not the same as 'catching up' through the imitation of central capitalism—a catching up which is, incidentally, impossible and above all, undesirable. It imposes a different conception of 'modernization/industrialization', based on the genuine participation of the popular classes in the process of implementation, with immediate benefits for them at each stage as it advances. We must therefore reject the dominant reasoning that demands that people wait indefinitely until the development of the productive forces have finally created the conditions of a 'necessary' passage to socialism. These forces must be developed right from the beginning with the prospect of constructing socialism. The power of the state is evidently at the heart of the conflicts between these contradictory requirements of 'development' and 'socialism'.

'The states want independence.' This must be seen as a twofold objective: independence (extreme form of autonomy) vis-à-vis the popular classes; independence from the pressures of the capitalist world system. The 'bourgeoisie' (broadly speaking, the governing class in commanding positions of the state, whose ambitions always tend toward a bourgeois evolution) is both national and comprador. If circumstances enable them to increase their autonomy vis-à-vis dominant imperialism, they choose to 'defend the national interest'. But if circumstances do not so permit, they will opt for 'comprador' submission to the requirements of imperialism. The 'new governing class' (or 'governing group') is still in an ambiguous position, even when it is based on a popular bloc, by the fact that it is animated by a 'bourgeois' tendency, at least partially.

The correct articulation of reality at these three levels—peoples, nations, and states—conditions the success of the progress on the long road of the transition. It is a question of reinforcing the complementarity of the advances of the people, of the liberation of the nation, and of the achievements by the power of the state. But if contradictions between the popular agent and the state agent are allowed to develop, any advances are finally doomed.

There will be an impasse if one of these levels is not concerned about its articulation with the others. The abstract notion of the 'people' as being the only entity that counts, and the thesis of the abstract 'movement', capable of transforming the world without worrying about taking over power, are simply naive. The idea of national liberation, 'at all costs'—viewed as independent of the social content of the hegemonic bloc—leads to the cultural illusion of irretrievable attachment to the past (political Islam, Hinduism, and Buddhism are examples) and is, in fact, powerless. This generates a notion of power, conceived as being capable of 'attaining achievements' for the people, but which is, in fact, to be exercised without them. It thus leads to the drift to authoritarianism and the crystallization of a new bourgeoisie. The deviation of Sovietism, which evolved from a 'capitalism without capitalists' (state capitalism) to a 'capitalism with capitalists', is the most tragic example of this.

Since peoples, nations, and states of the periphery do not accept the imperialist system, the 'South' is the 'storm zone', one of permanent uprisings and revolts. Beginning in 1917, history has consisted mainly of these revolts and independent initiatives (in the sense of independence of the tendencies that dominate the existing imperialist capitalist system) of the peoples, nations, and states of the peripheries. It is these initiatives, despite their limits and contradictions, that have shaped the most decisive transformations of the contemporary world, far more than the progress of the productive forces and the relatively easy social adjustments that accompanied them in the heartlands of the system.

The second wave of independent initiatives of the countries of the South has begun. The 'emerging' countries and others, like their peoples, are fighting the ways in which the collective imperialism of the Triad tries to perpetuate its domination. The military interventions of Washington and their subaltern NATO allies have also proved a failure. The world financial system is collapsing and, in its place, autonomous regional systems are in the process of being set up. The technological monopoly of the oligopolies has been thwarted.

Recovering control over natural resources is now the order of the day. The Andean nations, victims of the internal colonialism that succeeded foreign colonization, are making themselves felt on the political level.

The popular organizations and the parties of the radical left in struggle have already defeated some liberal programmes (in Latin America) or are on the way to doing so. These initiatives, which are, first of all, fundamentally anti-imperialist, are potentially able to commit themselves along the long road to the socialist transition.

How do these two possible futures relate to each other? The 'other world' that is being built is always ambiguous: it carries the worst and the best within it, both of them 'possible' (there are no laws in history previous to history itself to give us an indication). A first wave of initiatives by the peoples, nations, and states of the periphery took place in the twentieth century, until 1980. Any analysis of its components makes no sense unless thought is given to the complementarities and conflicts on how the three levels relate to each other. A second wave of initiatives in the periphery has already started. Will it be more effective? Can it go further than the preceding one?

ENDING THE CRISIS OF CAPITALISM?

The oligarchies in power of the contemporary capitalist system are trying to restore the system as it was before the financial crisis of 2008. For this, they need to convince people through a 'consensus' that does not challenge their supreme power. To succeed in this, they are prepared to make some rhetorical concessions about the ecological challenges (in particular about the question of the climate), green-washing their domination, and even hinting that they will carry out social reforms (the 'war on poverty') and political reforms ('good governance').

To take part in this game of convincing people of the need to forge a new consensus—even defined in terms that are clearly better—will end up in failure. Worse, still, it will prolong fatal illusions. This is because the response to the challenge raised by the crisis of the global system first requires the transformation of power relationships to the benefit of the workers, as well as of international relationships to the benefit of the peoples of the peripheries. The United Nations has organized a whole series of global conferences, which have yielded nothing—as one might have expected.

History has proved that this is a necessary requirement. The response to the first long crisis of ageing capitalism took place between 1914 and 1950, mainly through the conflicts that opposed the peoples of the peripheries to the domination of the imperial powers and, to different degrees, through the internal social relationships benefiting the popular classes. In this way, they prepared the path for the three systems of the post-Second World War period: the really existing socialisms of that time, the national and popular regimes of Bandung, and the social-democrat compromise in the countries of the North, which had been made particularly necessary by the independent initiatives of the peoples of the peripheries.

In 2008 the second long crisis of capitalism moved into a new phase. Violent international conflicts have already begun and are visible: will they challenge the domination of the generalized monopolies, based on anti-imperialist positions? How do they relate to the social struggles of the victims of the austerity policies pursued by the dominant classes in response to the crisis? In other words, will the peoples employ a strategy of extricating themselves from a capitalism in crisis, instead of the strategy to extricate the system from its crisis, as pursued by the powers that be?

The ideologues serving power are running out of steam, making futile remarks about the 'world after the crisis'. The CIA can only envisage a restoration of the system—attributing the greater participation of 'emerging markets' in liberal globalization as to the detriment of Europe, rather than the United States. It is incapable of recognizing that the deepening crisis will not be 'overcome', except through violent international and social conflict. No one knows how it will turn out: it could be for the better (progress in the direction of socialism) or for the worse (world apartheid).

The political radicalization of the social struggles is the condition for overcoming their internal fragmentation and their exclusively defensive strategy ('safeguarding social benefits'). Only this will make it possible to identify the objectives needed for undertaking the long road to socialism. Only this will enable the 'movements' to generate real empowerment.

The empowerment of the movements requires a framework of macro political and economic conditions that make their concrete projects viable. How to create these conditions? Here we come to the central question of the power of the state. Would a renewed state, genuinely popular and democratic, be capable of carrying out effective policies in the globalized conditions of the contemporary world? An immediate, negative response on the left has led to calls for initiatives to achieve a minimal global consensus, as a basis for universal political change, circumventing the state. This response and its corollary are proving fruitless. There is no other solution than to generate advances at the national level, perhaps reinforced by appropriate action at the regional level. They must aim at dismantling the world system ('delinking') prior to eventual reconstruction, on a different social basis, with the prospect of going beyond capitalism. The principle is as valid for the countries of the South which, incidentally, have started to move in this direction in Asia and Latin America, as it is for the countries of the North where, alas, the need for dismantling the European institutions (and that of the Euro) is not yet envisaged, even by the radical left.

THE INDISPENSABLE INTERNATIONALISM OF THE WORKERS AND THE PEOPLES

The limits of the advances made by the awakening of the South in the twentieth century and the exacerbation of the contradictions that resulted were the cause of the first liberation wave losing its impetus. This was greatly reinforced by the permanent hostility of the states in the imperialist centre, which went to the extent of waging open warfare that—it has to be said—was supported, or at least accepted, by the peoples of the North. The benefits of the imperialist rent were certainly an important factor in this rejection of internationalism by the popular forces of the North. The communist minorities, who adopted another attitude, sometimes strongly so, nevertheless failed to build effective alternative blocs around themselves. And the passing of the socialist parties en masse into the 'anticommunist' camp largely contributed to the success of the capitalist powers in the imperialist camp. These parties have not, however, been 'rewarded', as the very day after the collapse of the first wave of struggles of the twentieth century, monopoly capitalism shook off their alliance. They have not learned the lesson of their defeat by radicalizing themselves: on the contrary, they have chosen to capitulate by sliding into the 'social-liberal' positions with which we are familiar. This is the proof, if such was needed, of the decisive role of the imperialist rent in the reproduction of the societies in the North. Thus, the second capitulation was not so much a tragedy as a farce.

The defeat of internationalism shares part of the responsibility for the authoritarian drifts toward autocracy in the socialist experiences of the past century. The explosion of inventive expressions of democracy during the course of the Russian and Chinese Revolutions gives the lie to the too easy judgement that these countries were not 'ripe' for democracy. The hostility of the imperialist countries, facilitated by the support of their peoples, largely contributed to making the pursuit of democratic socialism even harder in conditions that were already difficult, a consequence of the inheritance of peripheral capitalism.

Thus, the second wave of the awakening of the peoples, nations, and states of the peripheries of the twenty-first century starts out in conditions that are hardly better, in fact, are even more difficult. The so-called characteristic of U.S. ideology of the 'consensus' (meaning submission to the requirements of the power of the generalized-monopoly capitalism); the adoption of 'presidential' political regimes that destroy the effectiveness of the anti-establishment potential of democracy; the indiscriminate eulogy of a false, manipulated individualism, together with inequality (seen as a virtue); the rallying of the subaltern NATO countries to the strategies implemented by the Washington establishment—all these are making rapid headway in the European Union which cannot be, in these conditions, anything other than what it is, a constitutive bloc of imperialist globalization.

In this situation, the collapse of this military project becomes the first priority and the preliminary condition for the success of the second wave of the liberation being undertaken through the struggles of the peoples, nations, and states of the three continents. Until this happens, their present and future advances will remain vulnerable. A possible remake of the twentieth century is not, therefore, to be excluded even if, obviously, the conditions of our epoch are quite different from those of the last century.

This tragic scenario is not, however, the only possible one. The offensive of capital against the workers is already under way in the very heartlands of the system. This is proof, if it were necessary, that capital, when it is reinforced by its victories against the peoples of the periphery, is then able to attack frontally the positions of the working classes in the centres of the system. In this situation, it is no longer impossible to visualize the radicalization of the struggles. The heritage of European political cultures is not yet lost, and it should facilitate the rebirth of an international consciousness that meets the requirements of its globalization. An evolution in this direction, however, comes up against the obstacle of the imperialist rent.

This is not only a major source of exceptional profits for the monopolies; it also conditions the reproduction of the society as a whole. And, with the indirect support of those popular elements seeking to preserve at all costs the existing electoral model of 'democracy' (however undemocratic in reality), the weight of the middle classes can in all likelihood destroy the potential strength arising from the radicalization of the popular classes. Because of this, it is probable that the progress in the tricontinental South will continue to be at the forefront of the scene, as in the last century. However, as soon as the advances have had their effects and seriously restricted the extent of the imperialist rent, the peoples of the North should be in a better position to understand the failure of strategies that submit to the requirements of the generalized imperialist monopolies. The ideological and political forces of the radical left should then take their place in this great movement of liberation, built on the solidarity of peoples and workers.

The ideological and cultural battle is decisive for this renaissance—which I have summed up as the strategic objective of building a Fifth International of workers and peoples.

February 01, 2011

CHINA 2013

The debates concerning the present and future of China—an 'emerging' power—always leave me unconvinced. Some argue that China has chosen, once and for all, the 'capitalist road' and intends even to accelerate its integration into contemporary capitalist globalization. They are quite pleased with this and hope only that this 'return to normality' (capitalism being the 'end of history') is accompanied by development towards Western-style democracy (multiple parties, elections, human rights). They believe—or need to believe—in the possibility that China shall by this means 'catch up' in terms of per capita income to the opulent societies of the West, even if gradually, which I do not believe is possible. The Chinese right shares this point of view. Others deplore this in the name of the values of a 'betrayed socialism'. Some associate themselves with the dominant expressions of the practice of China bashing[1] in the West. Still others—those in power in Beijing—describe the chosen path as 'Chinese-style socialism', without being more precise. However, one can discern its characteristics

[1] *China bashing* refers to the favoured sport of Western media of all tendencies—including the left, unfortunately—that consists of systematically denigrating, even criminalizing, everything done in China. China exports cheap junk to the poor markets of the third world (this is true), a horrible crime. However, it also produces high-speed trains, airplanes, satellites, whose marvellous technological quality is praised in the West, but to which China should have no right! They seem to think that the mass construction of housing for the working class is nothing but the abandonment of workers to slums and liken 'inequality' in China (working-class houses are not opulent villas) to that in India (opulent villas side-by-side with slums), etc. China bashing panders to the infantile opinion found in some currents of the powerless Western 'left': if it is not the communism of the twenty-third century, it is a betrayal! China bashing participates in the systematic campaign of maintaining hostility towards China, in view of a possible military attack. This is nothing less than a question of destroying the opportunities for an authentic emergence of a great people from the South.

by reading official texts closely, particularly the Five-Year Plans, which are precise and taken quite seriously.

In fact the question, 'Is China capitalist or socialist?' is badly posed, too general and abstract for any response to make sense in terms of this absolute alternative. In fact, China has actually been following an original path since 1950, and perhaps even since the Taiping Revolution in the nineteenth century. I shall attempt here to clarify the nature of this original path at each of the stages of its development from 1950 to today—2013.

THE AGRARIAN QUESTION

Mao described the nature of the revolution carried out in China by its Communist Party as an anti-imperialist/anti-feudal revolution looking toward socialism. Mao never assumed that, after having dealt with imperialism and feudalism, the Chinese people had 'constructed' a socialist society. He always characterized this construction as the first phase of the long path to socialism.

I must emphasize the quite specific nature of the response given to the agrarian question by the Chinese Revolution. The distributed (agricultural) land was not privatized; it remained the property of the nation represented by village communes and only the use was given to rural families. That had not been the case in Russia where Lenin, faced with the *fait accompli* of the peasant insurrection in 1917, recognized the private property of the beneficiaries of land distribution.

Why was the implementation of the principle that agricultural land is not a commodity possible in China (and Vietnam)? It is constantly repeated that peasants around the world long for property and that alone. If such had been the case in China, the decision to nationalize the land would have led to an endless peasant war, as was the case when Stalin began forced collectivization in the Soviet Union.

The attitude of the peasants of China and Vietnam (and nowhere else) cannot be explained by a supposed 'tradition' in which they are unaware of property. It is the product of an intelligent and exceptional political line implemented by the Communist Parties of these two countries.

The Second International took for granted the inevitable aspiration of peasants for property, real enough in nineteenth-century Europe. Over the long European transition from feudalism to capitalism (1500–1800), the earlier institutionalized feudal forms of access to the land through rights shared among king, lords, and peasant serfs had gradually been dissolved and replaced by modern bourgeois private property, which treats land as a commodity—a good that the owner can freely dispose of (buy and sell). The socialists of the Second International accepted this *fait accompli* of the 'bourgeois revolution', even if they deplored it.

They also thought that small peasant property had no future, which belonged to large mechanized agricultural enterprise modelled on industry. They thought that capitalist development by itself would lead to such a concentration of property and to the most effective forms of its exploitation (see Kautsky's writings on this subject). History proved them wrong. Peasant agriculture gave way to capitalist family agriculture in a double sense; one that produces for the market (farm consumption having become insignificant) and one that makes use of modern equipment, industrial inputs, and bank credit. What is more, this capitalist family agriculture has turned out to be quite efficient in comparison with large farms, in terms of volume of production per hectare per worker/year. This observation does not exclude the fact that the modern capitalist farmer is exploited by generalized-monopoly capital, which controls the upstream supply of inputs and credit and the downstream marketing of the products. These farmers have been transformed into subcontractors for dominant capital.

Thus (wrongly) persuaded that large enterprise is always

more efficient than small in every area—industry, services, and agriculture—the radical socialists of the Second International assumed that the abolition of landed property (nationalization of the land) would allow the creation of large socialist farms (analogous to the future Soviet *sovkhozes* and *kolkhozes*). However, they were unable to put such measures to the test since revolution was not on the agenda in their countries (the imperialist centres).

The Bolsheviks accepted these theses until 1917. They contemplated the nationalization of the large estates of the Russian aristocracy, while leaving property in communal lands to the peasants. However, they were subsequently caught unawares by the peasant insurrection, which seized the large estates.

Mao drew the lessons from this history and developed a completely different line of political action. Beginning in the 1930s in southern China, during the long civil war of liberation, Mao based the increasing presence of the Communist Party on a solid alliance with the poor and landless peasants (the majority), maintained friendly relations with the middle peasants, and isolated the rich peasants at all stages of the war, without necessarily antagonizing them. The success of this line prepared the large majority of rural inhabitants to consider and accept a solution to their problems that did not require private property in plots of land acquired through distribution. I think that Mao's ideas, and their successful implementation, have their historical roots in the nineteenth-century Taiping Revolution. Mao thus succeeded where the Bolshevik Party had failed: in establishing a solid alliance with the large rural majority. In Russia, the *fait accompli* of summer 1917 eliminated later opportunities for an alliance with the poor and middle peasants against the rich ones (the *kulaks*) because the former were anxious to defend their acquired private property and, consequently, preferred to follow the *kulaks* rather than the Bolsheviks.

This 'Chinese specificity'—whose consequences are of

major importance—absolutely prevents us from characterizing contemporary China (even in 2013) as 'capitalist' because the capitalist road is based on the transformation of land into a commodity.

PRESENT AND FUTURE OF PETTY PRODUCTION

However, once this principle is accepted, the forms of using this common good (the land of the village communities) can be quite diverse. In order to understand this, we must be able to distinguish petty production from small property.

Petty production—peasant and artisanal—dominated production in all past societies. It has retained an important place in modern capitalism, now linked with small property—in agriculture, services, and even certain segments of industry. Certainly in the dominant triad of the contemporary world (the United States, Europe, and Japan) it is receding. An example of that is the disappearance of small businesses and their replacement by large commercial operations. Yet this is not to say that this change is 'progress', even in terms of efficiency, and all the more so if the social, cultural, and civilizational dimensions are taken into account. In fact, this is an example of the distortion produced by the domination of rent-seeking generalized monopolies. Hence, perhaps in a future socialism the place of petty production will be called upon to resume its importance.

In contemporary China, in any case, petty production—which is not necessarily linked with small property—retains an important place in national production, not only in agriculture but also in large segments of urban life.

China has experienced quite diverse and even contrasting forms of the use of land as a common good. We need to discuss, on the one hand, efficiency (volume of production from a hectare per worker/year) and, on the other, the dynamics of the transformations set in motion. These forms can strengthen tendencies towards capitalist development, which would end up calling into question the non-commodity status of the land, or can be part of development in a socialist direction. These questions can be answered only through a concrete examination of the forms at issue, as they were implemented in successive moments of Chinese development from 1950 to the present.

At the beginning, in the 1950s, the form adopted was petty family production combined with simpler forms of cooperation for managing irrigation, work requiring coordination, and the use of certain kinds of equipment. This was associated with the insertion of such petty family production into a state economy that maintained a monopoly over purchases of produce destined for the market and the supply of credit and inputs, all on the basis of planned prices (decided by the centre).

The experience of the communes that followed the establishment of production cooperatives in the 1970s is full of lessons. It was not necessarily a question of passing from small production to large farms, even if the idea of the superiority of the latter inspired some of its supporters. The essentials of this initiative originated in the aspiration for decentralized socialist construction. The Communes not only had responsibility for managing the agricultural production of a large village or a collective of villages and hamlets (this organization itself was a mixture of forms of small family production and more ambitious specialized production), they also provided a larger framework: (1) attaching industrial activities that employed peasants available in certain seasons; (2) articulating productive economic activities together with the management of social services (education, health, housing); and (3) commencing the decentralization of the political administration of the society. Just as the Paris Commune had intended, the socialist state was to become, at least partially, a federation of socialist Communes.

Undoubtedly, in many respects, the Communes were in advance of their time and the dialectic between the decentralization of decision-making powers and the centralization assumed by the omnipresence of the Communist Party did not always operate smoothly. Yet the recorded results are far from having been disastrous, as the right would have us believe. A Commune in the Beijing region, which resisted the order to dissolve the system, continues to record excellent economic results linked with the persistence of high-quality political debates, which disappeared elsewhere. Current projects of 'rural reconstruction', implemented by rural communities in several regions of China, appear to be inspired by the experience of the Communes.

The decision to dissolve the Communes made by Deng Xiaoping in 1980 strengthened small family production, which remained the dominant form during the three decades following this decision. However, the range of users' rights (for village Communes and family units) has expanded considerably. It has become possible for the holders of these land use rights to 'rent' that land out (but never 'sell' it), either to other small producers—thus facilitating emigration to the cities, particularly of educated young people who do not want to remain rural residents—or to firms organizing a much larger, modernized farm (never a *latifundia*, which does not exist in China, but nevertheless considerably larger than family farms). This form is the means used to encourage specialized production (such as good wine, for which China has called on the assistance of experts from Burgundy) or test new scientific methods (GMOs and others).

To 'approve' or 'reject' the diversity of these systems *a priori* makes no sense, in my opinion. Once again, the concrete analysis of each of them, both in design and the reality of its implementation, is imperative. The fact remains that the inventive diversity of forms of using commonly held land has led to phenomenal results. First of all, in terms of economic efficiency, although urban population has grown from 20 to 50 per cent of total population, China has succeeded in increasing agricultural production to keep pace with the gigantic needs of urbanization. This is a remarkable and exceptional result, unparalleled in the countries of the 'capitalist' South. It has preserved and strengthened its food sovereignty, even though it suffers from a major handicap: its agriculture feeds 22 per cent of the world's population reasonably well while it has only 6 per cent of the world's arable land. In addition, in terms of the way (and level) of life of rural populations, Chinese villages no longer have anything in common with what is still dominant elsewhere in the capitalist third world. Comfortable and well-equipped permanent structures form a striking contrast, not only with the former China of hunger and extreme poverty, but also with the extreme forms of poverty that still dominate the countryside of India or Africa.

The principles and policies implemented (land held in common, support for petty production without small property) are responsible for these unequalled results. They have made possible a relatively controlled rural-to-urban migration. Compare that with the capitalist road, in Brazil, for example. Private property in agricultural land has emptied the countryside of Brazil—today only 11 per cent of the country's population. But at least 50 per cent of urban residents live in slums (the *favelas*) and survive only thanks to the 'informal economy' (including organized crime). There is nothing similar in China, where the urban population is, as a whole, adequately employed and housed, even in comparison with many 'developed countries', without even mentioning those where the GDP per capita is at the Chinese level!

The population transfer from the extremely densely populated Chinese countryside (only Vietnam, Bangladesh, and Egypt are similar) was essential. It improved conditions for rural petty production, making more land available. This transfer, although relatively controlled (once again, nothing is perfect in the history of humanity, neither in China nor elsewhere), is perhaps threatening to become too rapid. This is being discussed in China.

CHINESE STATE CAPITALISM

The first label that comes to mind to describe Chinese reality is state capitalism. Very well, but this label remains vague and superficial so long as the specific content is not analysed.

It is indeed capitalism in the sense that the relation to which the workers are subjected by the authorities who organize production is similar to the one that characterizes capitalism: submissive and alienated labour, extraction of surplus labour. Brutal forms of extreme exploitation of workers exist in China, e.g., in the coal mines or in the furious pace of the workshops that employ women. This is scandalous for a country that claims to want to move forward on the road to socialism. Nevertheless, the establishment of a state capitalist regime is unavoidable, and will remain so everywhere. The developed capitalist countries themselves will not be able to enter a socialist path (which is not on the visible agenda today) without passing through this first stage. It is the preliminary phase in the potential commitment of any society to liberating itself from historical capitalism on the long route to socialism/communism. Socialization and reorganization of the economic system at all levels, from the firm (the elementary unit) to the nation and the world, require a lengthy struggle during an historical time period that cannot be foreshortened.

Beyond this preliminary reflection, we must concretely describe the state capitalism in question by bringing out the nature and the project of the state concerned, because there is not just one type of state capitalism, but many different ones. The state capitalism of France of the Fifth Republic from 1958 to 1975 was designed to serve and strengthen private French monopolies, not to commit the country to a socialist path.

Chinese state capitalism was built to achieve three objectives: (i) construct an integrated and sovereign modern industrial system; (ii) manage the relation of this system with rural petty production; and (iii) control China's integration into the world system, dominated by the generalized monopolies of the imperialist triad (United States, Europe, Japan). The pursuit of these three priority objectives is unavoidable. As a result it permits a possible advance on the long route to socialism, but at the same time it strengthens tendencies to abandon that possibility in favour of pursuing capitalist development pure and simple. It must be accepted that this conflict is both inevitable and always present. The question then is this: Do China's concrete choices favour one of the two paths?

Chinese state capitalism required, in its first phase (1954–1980), the nationalization of all companies (combined with the nationalization of agricultural lands), both large and small alike. Then followed an opening to private enterprise, national and/or foreign, and liberalized rural and urban petty production (small companies, trade, services). However, large basic industries and the credit system established during the Maoist period were not denationalized, even if the organizational forms of their integration into a 'market' economy were modified. This choice went hand in hand with the establishment of means of control over private initiative and potential partnership with foreign capital. It remains to be seen to what extent these means fulfil their assigned functions or, on the contrary, if they have not become empty shells, collusion with private capital (through 'corruption' of management) having gained the upper hand.

Still, what Chinese state capitalism has achieved between 1950 and 2012 is quite simply amazing. It has, in fact, succeeded in building a sovereign and integrated modern productive system to the scale of this gigantic country, which can only be compared with that of the United States. It has succeeded in leaving behind the tight technological dependence of its origins (importation of Soviet, then Western models) through the development of its own capacity to produce technological inventions. However, it has not (yet?) begun the reorganization of labour from the perspective of socialization of economic management. The Plan—and not the 'opening'—has remained the central means for implementing this systematic construction.

In the Maoist phase of this development planning, the Plan remained imperative in all details: nature and location of new establishments, production objectives, and prices. At that stage, no reasonable alternative was possible. I will mention here, without pursuing it further, the interesting debate about the nature of the law of value that underpinned planning in this period. The very success—and not the failure—of this first phase required an alteration of the means for pursuing an accelerated development project. The 'opening' to private initiative—beginning in 1980, but above all from 1990—was necessary in order to avoid the stagnation that was fatal to the U.S.S.R. Despite the fact that this opening coincided with the globalized triumph of neo-liberalism— with all the negative effects of this coincidence, to which I shall return—the choice of a 'socialism *of* the market', or better yet, a 'socialism *with* the market', as fundamental for this second phase of accelerated development is largely justified, in my opinion.

The results of this choice are, once again, simply amazing. In a few decades, China has built a productive, industrial urbanization that brings together 600 million human beings, two-thirds of whom were urbanized over the last two decades (almost equal to Europe's population!). This is due to the Plan and not to the market. China now has a truly sovereign productive system. No other country in the South (except for Korea and Taiwan) has succeeded in doing this. In India and Brazil there are only a few disparate elements of a sovereign project of the same kind, nothing more.

The methods for designing and implementing the Plan have been transformed in these new conditions. The Plan remains imperative for the huge infrastructure investments required by the project: to house 400 million new urban inhabitants in adequate conditions, and to build an unparalleled network of highways, roads, railways, dams, and electric power plants; to open up all or almost all of the Chinese countryside; and to transfer the centre of gravity of development from the coastal regions to the continental west. The Plan also remains imperative—at least in part—for the objectives and financial resources of publicly owned enterprises (state, provinces, municipalities). As for the rest, it points to possible and probable objectives for the expansion of small urban commodity production as well as industrial and other private activities. These objectives are taken seriously and the political-economic resources required for their realization are specified. On the whole, the results are not too different from the 'planned' predictions.

Chinese state capitalism has integrated into its development project visible social (I am not saying 'socialist') dimensions. These objectives were already present in the Maoist era: eradication of illiteracy, basic health care for everyone, etc. In the first part of the post-Maoist phase (the 1990s), the tendency was undoubtedly to neglect the pursuit of these efforts. However, it should be noted that the social dimension of the project has since won back its place and, in response to active and powerful social movements, is expected to make more headway. The new urbanization has no parallel in any other country of the South. There are certainly 'chic' quarters and others that are not at all opulent; but there are no slums, which have continued to expand everywhere else in the cities of the third world.

THE INTEGRATION OF CHINA
INTO CAPITALIST GLOBALIZATION

We cannot pursue the analysis of Chinese state capitalism (called 'market socialism' by the government) without taking into consideration its integration into globalization.

The Soviet world had envisioned a delinking from the world capitalist system, complementing that delinking by building an integrated socialist system encompassing the U.S.S.R. and Eastern Europe. The U.S.S.R. achieved this delinking to a great extent, imposed moreover by the West's hostility; even blaming the blockade for its isolation. However, the project of integrating Eastern Europe never advanced very far, despite the initiatives of Comecon. The nations of Eastern Europe remained in uncertain and vulnerable positions, partially delinked—but on a strictly national basis—and partially open to Western Europe beginning in 1970. There was never a question of a U.S.S.R.-China integration, not only because Chinese nationalism would not have accepted it, but even more because China's priority tasks did not require it. Maoist China practised delinking in its own way. Should we say that, by reintegrating itself into globalization beginning in the 1990s, it has fully and permanently renounced delinking?

China entered globalization in the 1990s by the path of the accelerated development of manufactured exports possible for its productive system, giving first priority to exports whose rates of growth then surpassed those of the growth in GDP. The triumph of neoliberalism favoured the success of this choice for fifteen years (from 1990 to 2005). The pursuit of this choice is questionable not only because of its political and social effects, but also because it is threatened by the implosion of neoliberal globalized capitalism, which began in 2007. The Chinese government appears to be aware of this and very early began to attempt a correction by giving greater importance to the internal market and to development of western China.

To say, as one hears ad nauseam, that China's success should be attributed to the abandonment of Maoism (whose 'failure' was obvious), the opening to the outside, and the entry of foreign capital is quite simply idiotic. The Maoist construction put in place the foundations without which the opening would not have achieved its well-known success. A comparison with India, which has not made a comparable revolution, demonstrates this. To say that China's success is mainly (even 'completely') attributable to the initiatives of foreign capital is no less idiotic. It is not multinational capital that built the Chinese industrial system and achieved the objectives of urbanization and the construction of infrastructure. The success is 90 per cent attributable to the sovereign Chinese project. Certainly, the opening to foreign capital has fulfilled useful functions: it has increased the import of modern technologies. However, because of its partnership methods, China absorbed these technologies and has now mastered their development. There is nothing similar elsewhere, even in India or Brazil, *a fortiori* in Thailand, Malaysia, South Africa, and other places.

China's integration into globalization has remained, moreover, partial and controlled (or at least controllable, if one wants to put it that way). China has remained outside of financial globalization. Its banking system is completely national and focused on the country's internal credit market. Management of the yuan is still a matter for China's sovereign decision making. The yuan is not subject to the vagaries of the flexible exchanges that financial globalization imposes. Beijing can say to Washington, 'The yuan is our money and your problem,' just like Washington said to the Europeans in 1971, 'The dollar is our money and your problem.' Moreover, China retains a large reserve for deployment in its public credit system. The public debt is negligible compared with the rates of indebtedness (considered intolerable) in the United States, Europe, Japan, and many of the countries in the South. China can thus increase the expansion of its public expenditures without serious danger of inflation.

The attraction of foreign capital to China, from which it has benefited, is not behind the success of its project. On the contrary, it is the success of the project that has made investment in China attractive for Western transnationals. The countries of the South that opened their doors much wider than China and unconditionally accepted their submission to financial globalization have not become attractive to the same degree. Transnational capital is not attracted to China to pillage the natural resources of the country, nor, without any transfer of technology, to outsource and benefit from low wages for labour; nor to seize the benefits from training and integration of offshored units unrelated to nonexistent national productive systems, as in Morocco and Tunisia; nor even to carry out a financial raid and allow the imperialist banks to dispossess the national savings, as was the case in Mexico, Argentina, and Southeast Asia. In China, by contrast, foreign investments can certainly benefit from low wages and make good profits, on the condition that their plans fit into China's and allow technology transfer. In sum, these are 'normal' profits, but more can be made if collusion with Chinese authorities permits!

CHINA, EMERGING POWER

No one doubts that China is an emerging power. One current idea is that China is only attempting to recover the place it had occupied for centuries and lost only in the nineteenth century. However, this idea—certainly correct, and flattering, moreover—does not help us much in understanding the nature of this emergence and its real prospects in the contemporary world. Incidentally, those who propagate this general and vague idea have no interest in considering whether China will emerge by rallying to the general principles of capitalism (which they think is probably necessary) or whether it will take seriously its project of 'socialism with Chinese characteristics'. For my part, I argue that if China is indeed an emerging power, this is precisely because it has not chosen the capitalist path of development pure and simple; and that, as a consequence, if it decided to follow that capitalist path, the project of emergence itself would be in serious danger of failing.

The thesis that I support implies rejecting the idea that peoples cannot leap over the necessary sequence of stages and that China must go through a capitalist development before the question of its possible socialist future is considered. The debate on this question between the different currents of historical Marxism was never concluded. Marx remained hesitant on this question. We know that right after the first European attacks (the Opium Wars), he wrote: the next time that you send your armies to China they will be welcomed by a banner, 'Attention, you are at the frontiers of the bourgeois Republic of China.' This is a magnificent intuition and shows confidence in the capacity of the Chinese people to respond to the challenge, but at the same time an error because in fact the banner read: 'You are at the frontiers of the People's Republic of China.' Yet we know that, concerning Russia, Marx did not reject the idea of skipping the capitalist stage (see his correspondence with Vera Zasulich). Today, one might believe that the first Marx was right and that China is indeed on the route to capitalist development.

But Mao understood—better than Lenin—that the capitalist path would lead to nothing and that the resurrection of China could only be the work of communists. The Qing Emperors at the end of the nineteenth century, followed by Sun Yat Sen and the Guomindang, had already planned a Chinese resurrection in response to the challenge from the West. However, they imagined no other way than that of capitalism and did not have the intellectual wherewithal to understand what capitalism really is and why this path was closed to China, and to all the peripheries of the world capitalist system for that matter. Mao, an independent Marxist spirit, understood this. More than that, Mao understood that this battle was not won in advance—by the 1949 victory—and that the conflict between commitment to the long route to socialism, the condition for China's renaissance, and return to the capitalist fold would occupy the entire visible future.

Personally, I have always shared Mao's analysis and I shall return to this subject in some of my thoughts concerning the role of the Taiping Revolution (which I consider to be the distant origin of Maoism), the 1911 revolution in China, and other revolutions in the South at the beginning of the twentieth century, the debates at the beginning of the Bandung period and the analysis of the impasses in which the so-called emergent countries of the South committed to the capitalist path are stuck. All these considerations are corollaries of my central thesis concerning the polarization (i.e., construction of the centre/periphery contrast) immanent to the world development of historical capitalism. This polarization eliminates the possibility for a country from the periphery to 'catch up' within the context of capitalism. We must draw the conclusion: if 'catching up' with the opulent countries is impossible, something else must be done—it is called following the socialist path.

China has not followed a particular path just since 1980, but since 1950, although this path has passed through phases that are different in many respects. China has developed a coherent, sovereign project that is appropriate for its own needs. This is certainly not capitalism, whose logic requires that agricultural land be treated as a commodity. This project remains sovereign insofar as China remains outside of contemporary financial globalization.

The fact that the Chinese project is not capitalist does not mean that it 'is' socialist, only that it makes it possible to advance on the long road to socialism. Nevertheless, it is also still threatened with a drift that moves it off that road and ends up with a return, pure and simple, to capitalism.

China's successful emergence is completely the result of this sovereign project. In this sense, China is the only authentically emergent country (along with Korea and Taiwan, about which we will say more later). None of the many other countries to which the World Bank has awarded a certificate of emergence is really emergent because none of these countries is persistently pursuing a coherent sovereign project. All subscribe to the fundamental principles of capitalism pure and simple, even in potential sectors of their state capitalism. All have accepted submission to contemporary globalization in all its dimensions, including financial. Russia and India are partial exceptions to this last point, but not Brazil, South Africa, and others. Sometimes there are pieces of a 'national industry policy', but nothing comparable with the systematic Chinese project of constructing a complete, integrated, and sovereign industrial system (notably in the area of technological expertise).

For these reasons all these other countries, too quickly characterized as emergent, remain vulnerable in varying degrees, but always much more than China. For all these reasons, the appearances of emergence—respectable rates of growth, capacities to export manufactured products—are always linked with the processes of pauperization that impact the majority of their populations (particularly the peasantry), which is not the case with China. Certainly the growth of inequality is obvious everywhere, including China; but this observation remains superficial and deceptive. Inequality in the distribution of benefits from a model of growth that nevertheless excludes no one (and is even accompanied with a reduction in pockets of poverty—this is the case in China) is one thing; the inequality connected with a growth that benefits only a minority (from 5 per cent to 30 per cent of the population, depending on the case) while the fate of the others remains desperate is another thing. The practitioners of China bashing are unaware—or pretend to be unaware—of this decisive difference. The inequality that is apparent from the existence of quarters with luxurious villas, on the one hand, and quarters with comfortable housing for the middle and working classes, on the other, is not the same as the inequality apparent from the juxtaposition of wealthy quarters, middle-class housing, and slums for the majority. The Gini coefficients are valuable for measuring the changes from one year to another in a system with a fixed structure. However, in international comparisons between systems with different structures, they lose their meaning, like all other measures of macroeconomic magnitudes in national accounts. The emergent countries (other than China) are indeed 'emergent markets', open to penetration by the monopolies of the imperialist triad. These markets allow the latter to extract, to their benefit, a considerable part of the surplus value produced in the country in question. China is different: it is an emergent nation in which the system makes possible the retention of the majority of the surplus value produced there.

Korea and Taiwan are the only two successful examples of an authentic emergence in and through capitalism. These two countries owe this success to the geostrategic reasons that led the United States to allow them to achieve what Washington prohibited others from doing. The contrast between the support of the United States to the state capitalism of these two countries and the extremely violent opposition to state capitalism in Nasser's Egypt or Boumedienne's Algeria is, on this account, quite illuminating.

I will not discuss here potential projects of emergence, which appear quite possible in Vietnam and Cuba, or the conditions of a possible resumption of progress in this direction in Russia. Nor will I discuss the strategic objectives of the struggle by progressive forces elsewhere in the capitalist South, in India, Southeast Asia, Latin America, the Arab World, and Africa, which could facilitate moving beyond current impasses and encourage the emergence of sovereign projects that initiate a true rupture with the logic of dominant capitalism.

GREAT SUCCESSES, NEW CHALLENGES

China has not just arrived at the crossroads; it has been there every day since 1950. Social and political forces from the right and left, active in society and the party, have constantly clashed.

Where does the Chinese right come from? Certainly, the former comprador and bureaucratic bourgeoisies of the Guomindang were excluded from power. However, over the course of the war of liberation, entire segments of the middle classes, professionals, functionaries, and industrialists, disappointed by the ineffectiveness of the Guomindang in the face of Japanese aggression, drew closer to the Communist Party, even joining it. Many of them—but certainly not all—remained nationalists, and nothing more. Subsequently, beginning in 1990 with the opening to private initiative, a new, more powerful, right made its appearance. It should not be reduced simply to 'businessmen' who have succeeded and made (sometimes colossal) fortunes, strengthened by their clientele—including state and party officials, who mix control with collusion, and even corruption.

This success, as always, encourages support for rightist ideas in the expanding educated middle classes. It is in this sense that the growing inequality—even if it has nothing in common with inequality characteristic of other countries in the South—is a major political danger, the vehicle for the spread of rightist ideas, depoliticization, and naive illusions.

Here I shall make an additional observation that I believe is important: petty production, particularly peasant, is not motivated by rightist ideas, like Lenin thought (that was accurate in Russian conditions). China's situation contrasts here with that of the ex-

U.S.S.R. The Chinese peasantry, as a whole, is not reactionary because it is not defending the principle of private property, in contrast with the Soviet peasantry, whom the communists never succeeded in turning away from supporting the kulaks in defence of private property. On the contrary, the Chinese peasantry of petty producers (without being small property owners) is today a class that does not offer rightist solutions, but is part of the camp of forces agitating for the adoption of the most courageous social and ecological policies. The powerful movement of 'renovating rural society' testifies to this. The Chinese peasantry largely stands in the leftist camp, with the working class. The left has its organic intellectuals and it exercises some influence on the state and party apparatuses.

The perpetual conflict between the right and left in China has always been reflected in the successive political lines implemented by the state and party leadership. In the Maoist era, the leftist line did not prevail without a fight. Assessing the progress of rightist ideas within the party and its leadership, a bit like the Soviet model, Mao unleashed the Cultural Revolution to fight it. 'Bombard the Headquarters', that is, the Party leadership, where the 'new bourgeoisie' was forming. However, while the Cultural Revolution met Mao's expectations during the first two years of its existence, it subsequently deviated into anarchy, linked to the loss of control by Mao and the left in the party over the sequence of events. This deviation led to the state and party taking things in hand again, which gave the right its opportunity. Since then, the right has remained a strong part of all leadership bodies. Yet the left is present on the ground, restricting the supreme leadership to compromises of the 'centre'—but is that centre right or centre left?

To understand the nature of challenges facing China today, it is essential to understand that the conflict between China's sovereign project, such as it is, and North American imperialism and its subaltern European and Japanese allies will increase in intensity to the extent that China continues its success. There are several areas of conflict: China's command of modern technologies, access to the planet's resources, the strengthening of China's military capacities, and pursuit of the objective of reconstructing international politics on the basis of the sovereign rights of peoples to choose their own political and economic system. Each of these objectives enters into direct conflict with the objectives pursued by the imperialist triad.

The objective of U.S. political strategy is military control of the planet, the only way that Washington can retain the advantages that give it hegemony. This objective is being pursued by means of the preventive wars in the Middle East, and in this sense these wars are the preliminary to the preventive (nuclear) war against China, cold-bloodedly envisaged by the North American establishment as possibly necessary 'before it is too late'. Fomenting hostility to China is inseparable from this global strategy, which is manifest in the support shown for the slaveowners of Tibet and Sinkiang, the reinforcement of the U.S. naval presence in the China Sea, and the unstinting encouragement to Japan to build its military forces. The practitioners of *China bashing* contribute to keeping this hostility alive.

Simultaneously, Washington is devoted to manipulating the situation by appeasing the possible ambitions of China and the other so-called emergent countries through the creation of the G20, which is intended to give these countries the illusion that their adherence to liberal globalization would serve their interests. The G2 (United States/China) is—in this vein—a trap that, in making China the accomplice of the imperialist adventures of the United States, could cause Beijing's peaceful foreign policy to lose all its credibility.

The only possible effective response to this strategy must proceed on two levels: (i) strengthen China's military forces and equip them with the potential for a deterrent response, and (ii) tenaciously pursue the objective of reconstructing a polycentric international political system, respectful of all national sovereignties, and, to this effect, act to rehabilitate the United Nations, now marginalized by NATO. I emphasize the decisive importance of the latter objective, which entails the priority of reconstructing a 'front of the South' (Bandung 2?) capable of supporting the independent initiatives of the peoples and states of the South. It implies, in turn, that China becomes aware that it does not have the means for the absurd possibility of aligning with the predatory practices of imperialism (pillaging the natural resources of the planet), since it lacks a military power similar to that of the United States, which in the last resort is the guarantee of success for imperialist projects. China, in contrast, has much to gain by developing its offer of support for the industrialization of the countries of the South, which the club of imperialist 'donors' is trying to make impossible.

The language used by Chinese authorities concerning international questions, restrained in the extreme (which is understandable), makes it difficult to know to what extent the leaders of the country are aware of the challenges analysed above. More seriously, this choice of words reinforces naive illusions and depoliticization in public opinion.

The other part of the challenge concerns the question of democratizing the political and social management of the country.

Mao formulated and implemented a general principle for the political management of the new China that he summarized in these terms: rally the left, neutralize (I add: and not eliminate) the right, govern from the centre left. In my opinion, this is the best way to conceive of an effective manner for moving through successive advances, understood and supported by the great majority. In this way, Mao gave a positive content to the concept of democratization of society combined with social progress on the long road to socialism. He formulated the method for implementing this: 'the mass line' (go down into the masses, learn their struggles, go back to the summits of power). Lin Chun has analysed with precision the method and the results that it makes possible.

The question of democratization connected with social progress—in contrast with a 'democracy' disconnected from social progress (and even frequently connected with social regression)—does not concern China alone, but all the world's peoples. The methods that should be implemented for success cannot be summarized in a single formula, valid in all times and places. In any case, the formula offered by Western media propaganda—multiple parties and elections—should quite simply be rejected. Moreover, this sort of 'democracy' turns into farce, even in the West, more so elsewhere. The 'mass line' was the means for producing consensus on successive, constantly progressing, strategic objectives. This is in contrast with the 'consensus' obtained in Western countries through media manipulation and the electoral farce, which is nothing more than alignment with the requirements of capital.

Yet today, how should China begin to reconstruct the equivalent of a new mass line in new social conditions? It will not be easy because the power of the leadership, which has moved mostly to the right in the Communist Party, bases the stability of its management on depoliticization and the naive illusions that go along with that. The very success of the development policies strengthens the spontaneous tendency to move in this direction. It is widely believed in China, in the middle classes, that the royal road to catching up with the way of life in the opulent countries is now open, free of obstacles; it is believed that the states of the triad (United States, Europe, Japan) do not oppose that; U.S. methods are even uncritically admired; etc. This is particularly true for the urban middle classes, which are rapidly expanding and whose conditions of life are incredibly improved. The brainwashing to which Chinese students are subject in the United States, particularly in the social sciences, combined with a rejection of the official unimaginative and tedious teaching of Marxism, have contributed to narrowing the spaces for radical critical debates.

The government in China is not insensitive to the social question, not only because of the tradition of a discourse founded on Marxism, but also because the Chinese people, who learned how to fight and continue to do so, force the government's hand. If, in the 1990s, this social dimension had declined before the immediate priorities of speeding up growth, today the tendency is reversed. At the very moment when the social-democratic conquests of social security are being eroded in the opulent West, poor China is implementing the expansion of social security in three dimensions—health, housing, and pensions. China's popular housing policy, vilified by the China bashing of the European right and left, would be envied, not only in India or Brazil, but equally in the distressed areas of Paris, London, or Chicago!

Social security and the pension system already cover 50 per cent of the urban population (which has increased, recall, from 200 to 600 million inhabitants!) and the Plan (still carried out in China) anticipates increasing the covered population to 85 per cent in the coming years. Let the journalists of China bashing give us comparable examples in the 'countries embarked on the democratic path', which they continually praise. Nevertheless, the debate remains open on the methods for implementing the system. The left advocates the French system of distribution based on the principle of solidarity between these workers and different generations—which prepares for the socialism to come—while the right, obviously, prefers the odious U.S. system of pension funds, which divides workers and transfers the risk from capital to labour.

However, the acquisition of social benefits is insufficient if it is not combined with democratization of the political management of society, with its re-politicization by methods that strengthen the creative invention of forms for the socialist/communist future.

Following the principles of a multi-party electoral system as advocated ad nauseam by Western media and the practitioners of

China bashing, and defended by 'dissidents' presented as authentic 'democrats', does not meet the challenge. On the contrary, the implementation of these principles could only produce in China, as all the experiences of the contemporary world demonstrate (in Russia, Eastern Europe, the Arab world), the self-destruction of the project of emergence and social renaissance, which is in fact the actual objective of advocating these principles, masked by an empty rhetoric ('there is no other solution than multi-party elections'!). Yet it is not sufficient to counter this bad solution with a fallback to the rigid position of defending the privilege of the 'party', itself sclerotic and transformed into an institution devoted to recruitment of officials for state administration. Something new must be invented.

The objectives of re-politicization and creation of conditions favourable to the invention of new responses cannot be obtained through 'propaganda' campaigns. They can only be promoted through social, political, and ideological struggles. That implies the preliminary recognition of the legitimacy of these struggles and legislation based on the collective rights of organization, expression, and proposing legislative initiatives. That implies, in turn, that the party itself is involved in these struggles; in other words, reinvents the Maoist formula of the mass line. Re-politicization makes no sense if it is not combined with procedures that encourage the gradual conquest of responsibility by workers in the management of their society at all levels—company, local, and national. A programme of this sort does not exclude recognition of the rights of the individual person. On the contrary, it supposes their institutionalization. Its implementation would make it possible to reinvent new ways of using elections to choose leaders.

March 01, 2013

ACKNOWLEDGEMENTS

This paper owes much to the debates organized in China (November–December 2012) by Lau Kin Chi (Lingnan University, Hong Kong), in association with the South West University of Chongqing (Wen Tiejun), Renmin and Xinhua Universities of Beijing (Dai Jinhua, Wang Hui), the CASS (Huang Ping) and to meetings with groups of activists from the rural movement in the provinces of Shanxi, Shaanxi, Hubei, Hunan and Chongqing. I extend to all of them my thanks and hope that this paper will be useful for their ongoing discussions. It also owes much to my reading of the writings of Wen Tiejun and Wang Hui.

SOURCES

The Chinese Path and the Agrarian Question

Karl Kautsky, *On the Agrarian Question*, 2 vols. (London: Zwan Publications, 1988). Originally published 1899.

Samir Amin, 'Forerunners of the Contemporary World: The Paris Commune (1871) and the Taiping Revolution (1851–1864)', *International Critical Thought* 3, No. 2, 2013, pp. 159–164.

Samir Amin, 'The 1911 Revolution in a World Historical Perspective: A Comparison with the Meiji Restoration and the Revolutions in Mexico, Turkey and Egypt', published in Chinese in 1990.

Samir Amin, *Ending the Crisis of Capitalism or Ending Capitalism?* (Oxford: Pambazuka Press, 2011). (Chapter 5: The Agrarian Question)

Contemporary Globalization, the Imperialist Challenge

Samir Amin, *A Life Looking Forward: Memoirs of An Independent Marxist* (London: Zed Books, 2006). (Chapter 7: Deployment and Erosion of the Bandung Project)

Samir Amin, *The Law of Worldwide Value* (New York: Monthly Review Press, 2010). (Initiatives from the South, section 4, 121ff)

Samir Amin, *The Implosion of Contemporary Capitalism* (New York: Monthly Review Press, 2013). (Chapter 2: The South: Emergence and Lumpen Development)

Samir Amin, *Beyond US Hegemony* (London: Zed Books, 2006). (The Project of the American Ruling Class; China, Market Socialism?; Russia, Out of the Tunnel?; India, A Great Power?; and Multipolarity in the 20th Century)

Samir Amin, *Obsolescent Capitalism* (London: Zed Books, 2003). (Chapter 5: The Militarization of the New Collective Imperialism)

Andre Gunder Frank, *ReOrient: Global Economy in the Asian Age* (Berkeley: University of California Press, 1998)

Yash Tandon, *Ending Aid Dependence* (Oxford: Fahamu, 2008)

The Democratic Challenge

Samir Amin, 'The Democratic Fraud and the Universalist Alternative', *Monthly Review* 63, No. 5, October 2011, pp. 29–45.

Lin Chun, *The Transformation of Chinese Socialism* (Durham, N.C.: Duke University Press, 1996)

THE RETURN OF FASCISM
IN CONTEMPORARY CAPITALISM

It is not by chance that the very title of this contribution links the return of fascism on the political scene with the crisis of contemporary capitalism. Fascism is not synonymous with an authoritarian police regime that rejects the uncertainties of parliamentary electoral democracy. Fascism is a particular political response to the challenges with which the management of capitalist society may be confronted in specific circumstances.

UNITY AND DIVERSITY OF FASCISM

Political movements that can rightly be called fascist were in the forefront and exercised power in a number of European countries, particularly during the 1930s up to 1945. These included Italy's Benito Mussolini, Germany's Adolf Hitler, Spain's Francisco Franco, Portugal's António de Oliveira Salazar, France's Philippe Pétain, Hungary's Miklós Horthy, Romania's Ion Antonescu, and Croatia's Ante Pavelić. The diversity of societies that were the victims of fascism—both major developed capitalist societies and minor dominated capitalist societies, some connected with a victorious war, others the product of defeat—should prevent us from lumping them all together. I shall thus specify the different effects that this diversity of structures and conjunctures produced in these societies.

Yet, beyond this diversity, all these fascist regimes had two characteristics in common:

(1) In the circumstances, they were all willing to manage the government and society in such a way as not to call the fundamental principles of capitalism into question, specifically private capitalist

property, including that of modern monopoly capitalism. That is why I call these different forms of fascism particular ways of managing capitalism and not political forms that challenge the latter's legitimacy, even if 'capitalism' or 'plutocracies' were subject to long diatribes in the rhetoric of fascist speeches. The lie that hides the true nature of these speeches appears as soon as one examines the 'alternative' proposed by these various forms of fascism, which are always silent concerning the main point—private capitalist property. It remains the case that the fascist choice is not the only response to the challenges confronting the political management of a capitalist society. It is only in certain conjunctures of violent and deep crisis that the fascist solution appears to be the best one for dominant capital, or sometimes even the only possible one. The analysis must, then, focus on these crises.

(2) The fascist choice for managing a capitalist society in crisis is always based—by definition even—on the categorical rejection of 'democracy'. Fascism always replaces the general principles on which the theories and practices of modern democracies are based—recognition of a diversity of opinions, recourse to electoral procedures to determine a majority, guarantee of the rights of the minority, etc.—with the opposed values of submission to the requirements of collective discipline and the authority of the supreme leader and his main agents. This reversal of values is then always accompanied by a return of backward-looking ideas, which are able to provide an apparent legitimacy to the procedures of submission that are implemented. The proclamation of the supposed necessity of returning to the ('medieval') past, of submitting to the state religion or to some supposed characteristic of the 'race' or the (ethnic) 'nation' make up the panoply of ideological discourses deployed by the fascist powers.

The diverse forms of fascism found in modern European history share these two characteristics and fall into one of the following four categories:

(1) The fascism of the major 'developed' capitalist powers that aspired to become dominant hegemonic powers in the world, or at least in the regional, capitalist system.

Nazism is the model of this type of fascism. Germany became a major industrial power beginning in the 1870s and a competitor of the hegemonic powers of the era (Great Britain and, secondarily, France) and of the country that aspired to become hegemonic (the United States). After the 1918 defeat, it had to deal with the consequences of its failure to achieve its hegemonic aspirations. Hitler clearly formulated his plan: to establish over Europe, including Russia and maybe beyond, the hegemonic domination of 'Germany', i.e., the capitalism of the monopolies that had supported the rise of Nazism. He was disposed to accept a compromise with his major opponents: Europe and Russia would be given to him, China to Japan, the rest of Asia and Africa to Great Britain, and the Americas to the United States. His error was in thinking that such a compromise was possible: Great Britain and the United States did not accept it, while Japan, in contrast, supported it.

Japanese fascism belongs to the same category. Since 1895, modern capitalist Japan aspired to impose its domination over all of East Asia. Here the slide was made 'softly' from the 'imperial' form of managing a rising national capitalism—based on apparently 'liberal' institutions (an elected Diet), but in fact completely controlled by the Emperor and the aristocracy transformed by modernization—to a brutal form, managed directly by the military High Command. Nazi Germany made an alliance with imperial/ fascist Japan, while Great Britain and the United States (after Pearl Harbor, in 1941) clashed with Tokyo, as did the resistance in China—the deficiencies of the Guomindang being compensated for by the support of the Maoist Communists.

(2) The fascism of second rank capitalist powers.

Italy's Mussolini (the inventor of fascism, including its name) is the prime example. Mussolinism was the response of the Italian right (the old aristocracy, new bourgeoisie, middle classes) to the crisis of the 1920s and the growing communist threat. But neither Italian capitalism nor its political instrument, Mussolini's fascism, had the ambition to dominate Europe, let alone the world. Despite all the boasts of the Duce about reconstructing the Roman Empire (!), Mussolini understood that the stability of his system rested on his alliance—as a subaltern—either with Great Britain (master of the Mediterranean) or Nazi Germany. Hesitation between the two possible alliances continued right up to the eve of the Second World War.

The fascism of Salazar and Franco belong to this same type. They were both dictators installed by the right and the Catholic Church in response to the dangers of republican liberals or socialist republicans. The two were never, for this reason, ostracized for their anti-democratic violence (under the pretext of anti-communism) by the major imperialist powers. Washington rehabilitated them after 1945 (Salazar was a founding member of NATO and Spain consented to U.S. military bases), followed by the European Community—guarantor by nature of the reactionary capitalist order. After the Carnation Revolution (1974) and the death of Franco (1980), these two systems joined the camp of the new low-intensity 'democracies' of our era.

(3) The fascism of defeated powers.

These include France's Vichy government, as well as Belgium's Léon Degrelle and the 'Flemish' pseudo-government supported by the Nazis. In France, the upper class chose 'Hitler rather than the Popular Front' (see Annie Lacroix-Riz's books on this subject). This type of fascism, connected with defeat and submission to 'German Europe', was forced to retreat into the background following the defeat of the Nazis. In France, it gave way to the Resistance Councils that, for a time, united Communists with other Resistance fighters

(Charles de Gaulle in particular). Its further evolution had to wait (with the initiation of European construction and France's joining the Marshall Plan and NATO, i.e., the willing submission to U.S. hegemony) for the conservative right and anti-communist, social-democratic right to break permanently with the radical left that came out of the anti-fascist and potentially anti-capitalist Resistance.

(4) Fascism in the dependent societies of Eastern Europe.

We move down several degrees more when we come to examine the capitalist societies of Eastern Europe (Poland, the Baltic states, Romania, Hungary, Yugoslavia, Greece, and western Ukraine during the Polish era). We should here speak of backward and, consequently, dependent capitalism. In the interwar period, the reactionary ruling classes of these countries supported Nazi Germany. It is, nevertheless, necessary to examine on a case-by-case basis their political articulation with Hitler's project.

In Poland, the old hostility to Russian domination (Tsarist Russia), which became hostility to the communist Soviet Union, encouraged by the popularity of the Catholic Papacy, would normally have made this country into Germany's vassal, on the Vichy model. But Hitler did not understand it that way: the Poles, like the Russians, Ukrainians, and Serbs, were people destined for extermination, along with Jews, the Roma, and several others. There was, then, no place for a Polish fascism allied with Berlin.

Horthy's Hungary and Antonescu's Romania were, in contrast, treated as subaltern allies of Nazi Germany. Fascism in these two countries was itself the result of social crises specific to each of them: fear of 'communism' after the Béla Kun period in Hungary and the national chauvinist mobilization against Hungarians and Ruthenians in Romania.

In Yugoslavia, Hitler's Germany (followed by Mussolini's Italy) supported an 'independent' Croatia, entrusted to the management of the anti-Serb Ustashi with the decisive support of the Catholic Church, while the Serbs were marked for extermination.

The Russian Revolution had obviously changed the situation with regard to the prospects of working-class struggles and the response of the reactionary propertied classes, not only in the territory of the pre-1939 Soviet Union, but also in the lost territories—the Baltic states and Poland. Following the Treaty of Riga in 1921, Poland annexed the western parts of Belarus (Volhynia) and Ukraine (southern Galicia, which was previously an Austrian Crownland; and northern Galicia, which had been a province of the Tsarist Empire).

In this whole region, two camps took form from 1917 (and even from 1905 with the first Russian Revolution): pro-socialist (which became pro-Bolshevik), popular in large parts of the peasantry (which aspired to a radical agrarian reform for their benefit) and in intellectual circles (Jews in particular); and anti-socialist (and consequently complaisant with regard to anti-democratic governments under fascist influence) in all the landowning classes. The reintegration of the Baltic states, Belarus, and western Ukraine into the Soviet Union in 1939 emphasized this contrast.

The political map of the conflicts between 'pro-fascists' and 'anti-fascists' in this part of Eastern Europe was blurred, on the one hand, by the conflict between Polish chauvinism (which persisted in its project of 'Polonizing' the annexed Belarussian and Ukrainian regions by settler colonies) and the victimized peoples; and, on the other hand, by the conflict between the Ukrainian 'nationalists', who were both anti-Polish and anti-Russian (because of anti-communism) and Hitler's project, which envisaged no Ukrainian state as a subaltern ally, since its people were simply marked for extermination.

I here refer the reader to Olha Ostriitchouk's authoritative work

Les Ukrainiens face à leur passé.[1] Ostriitchouk's rigorous analysis of the contemporary history of this region (Austrian Galicia, Polish Ukraine, Little Russia, which became Soviet Ukraine) will provide the reader with an understanding of the issues at stake in the still ongoing conflicts as well as the place occupied by local fascism.

THE WESTERN RIGHT'S COMPLAISANT VIEW OF PAST AND PRESENT FASCISM

The right in European parliaments between the two world wars was always complaisant about fascism and even about the more repugnant Nazism. Churchill himself, regardless of his extreme 'Britishness', never hid his sympathy for Mussolini. U.S. presidents, and the establishment Democratic and Republican parties, only discovered belatedly the danger presented by Hitler's Germany and, above all, imperial/fascist Japan. With all the cynicism characteristic of the U.S. establishment, Truman openly avowed what others thought quietly: allow the war to wear out its protagonists—Germany, Soviet Russia, and the defeated Europeans—and intervene as late as possible to reap the benefits. That is not at all the expression of a principled anti-fascist position. No hesitation was shown in the rehabilitation of Salazar and Franco in 1945. Furthermore, connivance with European fascism was a constant in the policy of the Catholic Church. It would not strain credibility to describe Pius XII as a collaborator with Mussolini and Hitler.

Hitler's anti-Semitism itself aroused opprobrium only much later, when it reached the ultimate stage of its murderous insanity. The emphasis on hate for 'Judeo-Bolshevism' stirred up by Hitler's speeches was common to many politicians. It was only after the defeat of Nazism that it was necessary to condemn anti-Semitism

[1] Olha Ostriitchouk, *Les Ukrainiens face à leur passé* [Ukrainians Faced with Their Past], Brussels: P.I.E. Lang, 2013.

in principle. The task was made easier because the self-proclaimed heirs to the title of 'victims of the Shoah' had become the Zionists of Israel, allies of Western imperialism against the Palestinians and the Arab people—who, however, had never been involved in the horrors of European anti-Semitism!

Obviously, the collapse of the Nazis and Mussolini's Italy obliged rightist political forces in Western Europe (west of the 'curtain') to distinguish themselves from those who—within their own groups—had been accomplices and allies of fascism. Yet, fascist movements were only forced to retreat into the background and hide behind the scenes, without really disappearing.

In West Germany, in the name of 'reconciliation', the local government and its patrons (the United States, and secondarily Great Britain and France) left in place nearly all those who had committed war crimes and crimes against humanity. In France, legal proceedings were initiated against the Resistance for 'abusive executions for collaboration' when the Vichyists reappeared on the political scene with Antoine Pinay. In Italy, fascism became silent, but was still present in the ranks of Christian Democracy and the Catholic Church. In Spain, the 'reconciliation' compromise imposed in 1980 by the European Community (which later became the European Union) purely and simply prohibited any reminder of Francoist crimes.

The support of the socialist and social-democratic parties of Western and Central Europe for the anti-communist campaigns undertaken by the conservative right shares responsibility for the later return of fascism. These parties of the 'moderate' left had, however, been authentically and resolutely anti-fascist. Yet all of that was forgotten. With the conversion of these parties to social liberalism, their unconditional support for European construction—systematically devised as a guarantee for the reactionary capitalist order—and their no less unconditional submission to U.S. hegemony (through NATO, among other means), a reactionary bloc combining the classic right and the social liberals has been consolidated; one that could, if necessary, accommodate the new extreme right.

Subsequently, the rehabilitation of East European fascism was quickly undertaken beginning in 1990. All of the fascist movements of the countries concerned had been faithful allies or collaborators to varying degrees with Hitlerism. With the approaching defeat, a large number of their active leaders had been redeployed to the West and could, consequently, 'surrender' to the U.S. armed forces. None of them were returned to Soviet, Yugoslav, or other governments in the new people's democracies to be tried for their crimes (in violation of Allied agreements). They all found refuge in the United States and Canada. And they were all pampered by the authorities for their fierce anti-communism!

In *Les Ukrainiens face à leur passé*, Ostriitchouk provides everything necessary to establish irrefutably the collusion between the objectives of U.S. policy (and behind it of Europe) and those of the local fascists of Eastern Europe (specifically, Ukraine). For example, 'Professor' Dmytro Dontsov, up to his death (in 1975), published all his works in Canada, which are not only violently anti-communist (the term 'Judeo-Bolshevism' is customary with him), but also even fundamentally anti-democratic. The governments of the so-called democratic states of the West supported, and even financed and organized, the 'Orange Revolution' (i.e., the fascist counter-revolution) in Ukraine. And all that is continuing. Earlier, in Yugoslavia, Canada had also paved the way for the Croatian Ustashis.

The clever way in which the 'moderate' media (which cannot openly acknowledge that they support avowed fascists) hide their support for these fascists is simple: they substitute the term 'nationalist' for fascist. Professor Dontsov is no longer a fascist, he is a Ukrainian 'nationalist', just like Marine Le Pen is no longer a fascist, but a nationalist (as *Le Monde*, for example, has written)!

Are these authentic fascists really 'nationalists', simply because they say so? That is doubtful. Nationalists today deserve this label only if they call into question the power of the actually dominant forces in the contemporary world, i.e., that of the monopolies of the United States and Europe. These so-called 'nationalists' are friends of Washington, Brussels, and NATO. Their 'nationalism' amounts to chauvinistic hatred of largely innocent neighbouring people who were never responsible for their misfortunes: for Ukrainians, it is Russians (and not the Tsar); for Croatians, it is the Serbs; for the new extreme right in France, Austria, Switzerland, Greece, and elsewhere, it is 'immigrants'.

The danger represented by the collusion between major political forces in the United States (Republicans and Democrats) and Europe (the parliamentary right and the social liberals), on one side, and the fascists of the East, on the other, should not be underestimated. Hillary Clinton has set herself up as leading spokeswoman of this collusion and pushes war hysteria to the limit. Even more than George W. Bush, if that is possible, she calls for preventive war with a vengeance (and not only for repetition of the Cold War) against Russia—with even more open intervention in Ukraine, Georgia, and Moldova, among other places—against China, and against people in revolt in Asia, Africa, and Latin America. Unfortunately, this headlong flight of the United States in response to its decline could find sufficient support to allow Hillary Clinton to become 'the first woman president of the United States!' Let's not forget what hides behind this false feminist.

Undoubtedly, the fascist danger might still appear today to be no threat to the 'democratic' order in the United States and Europe west of the old 'Curtain'. The collusion between the classic parliamentary right and the social liberals makes it unnecessary for dominant capital to resort to the services of an extreme right that follows in the wake of the historical fascist movements. But then what should we conclude about the electoral successes of the extreme right over the last decade? Europeans are clearly also victims of the spread of generalized-monopoly capitalism.[2] We can see why, then, when confronted with collusion between the right and the so-called socialist left, they take refuge in electoral abstention or in voting for the extreme right. The responsibility of the potentially radical left is, in this context, huge: if this left had the audacity to propose real advances beyond current capitalism, it would gain the credibility that it lacks. An audacious radical left is necessary to provide the coherence that the current piecemeal protest movements and defensive struggles still lack. The 'movement' could, then, reverse the social balance of power in favour of the working classes and make progressive advances possible. The successes won by the popular movements in South America are proof of that.

In the current state of things, the electoral successes of the extreme right stem from contemporary capitalism itself. These successes allow the media to throw together, with the same opprobrium, the 'populists of the extreme right and those of the extreme left', obscuring the fact that the former are pro-capitalist (as the term extreme *right* demonstrates) and thus possible allies for capital, while the latter are the only potentially dangerous opponents of capital's system of power.

We observe, *mutatis mutandis*, a similar conjuncture in the United States, although its extreme right is never called fascist. The McCarthyism of yesterday, just like the Tea Party fanatics and warmongers (e.g., Hillary Clinton) of today, openly defend 'liberties'—understood as exclusively belonging to the owners and managers of monopoly capital—against 'the government', suspected of acceding to the demands of the system's victims.

One last observation about fascist movements: they seem unable to know when and how to stop making their demands. The

---

[2] For a further elaboration, see Samir Amin, *The Implosion of Contemporary Capitalism*, New York: Monthly Review Press, 2013.

cult of the leader and blind obedience, the acritical and supreme valorization of pseudo-ethnic or pseudo-religious mythological constructions that convey fanaticism, and the recruitment of militias for violent actions make fascism into a force that is difficult to control. Mistakes, even beyond irrational deviations from the viewpoint of the social interests served by the fascists, are inevitable. Hitler was a truly mentally ill person, yet he could force the big capitalists who had put him in power to follow him to the end of his madness and even gained the support of a very large portion of the population. Although that is only an extreme case, and Mussolini, Franco, Salazar, and Pétain were not mentally ill, a large number of their associates and henchmen did not hesitate to perpetrate criminal acts.

FASCISM IN THE CONTEMPORARY SOUTH

The integration of Latin America into globalized capitalism in the nineteenth century was based on the exploitation of peasants reduced to the status of 'peons' and their subjection to the savage practices of large landowners. The system of Porfirio Díaz in Mexico is a good example. The furtherance of this integration in the twentieth century produced the 'modernization of poverty'. The rapid rural exodus, more pronounced and earlier in Latin America than in Asia and Africa, led to new forms of poverty in the contemporary urban favelas, which came to replace older forms of rural poverty. Concurrently, forms of political control of the masses were 'modernized' by establishing dictatorships, abolishing electoral democracy, prohibiting parties and trade unions, and conferring on 'modern' secret services all rights to arrest and torture through their intelligence techniques. Clearly, these forms of political management are visibly similar to those of fascism found in the countries of dependent capitalism in Eastern Europe. The dictatorships of twentieth-century Latin America served the local reactionary bloc (large landowners, comprador bourgeoisies, and sometimes middle classes that benefited from this type of lumpen development), but above all, they served dominant foreign capital, specifically that of the United States, which, for this reason, supported these dictatorships up to their reversal by the recent explosion of popular movements. The power of these movements and the social and democratic advances that they have imposed exclude—at least in the short term—the return of para-fascist dictatorships. But the future is uncertain: the conflict between the movement of the working classes and local and world capitalism has only begun. As with all types of fascism, the dictatorships of Latin America did not avoid mistakes, some of which were fatal to them. I am thinking, for example, of Leopoldo Fortunato Galtieri, who went to war over the Malvinas Islands to capitalize on Argentine national sentiment for his benefit.

Beginning in the 1980s, the lumpen development characteristic of the spread of generalized-monopoly capitalism took over from the national populist systems of the Bandung era (1955–1980) in Asia and Africa.[3] This lumpen development also produced forms akin both to the modernization of poverty and modernization of repressive violence. The excesses of the post-Nasserist and post-Baathist systems in the Arab world provide good examples of this. We should not lump together the national populist regimes of the Bandung era and those of their successors, which jumped on the bandwagon of globalized neoliberalism, because they were both 'non-democratic'. The Bandung regimes, despite their autocratic political practices, benefited from some popular legitimacy both because of their actual achievements, which benefited the majority of workers, and their anti-imperialist positions. The dictatorships that followed lost this legitimacy as soon as they accepted subjection to the globalized neoliberal model and accompanying lumpen development. Popular and national authority, although

---

[3] For the spread of generalized-monopoly capitalism, see *ibid*.

not democratic, gave way to police violence as such, in service of the neoliberal, anti-popular, and anti-national project.

The recent popular uprisings, beginning in 2011, have called into question the dictatorships. But the dictatorships have only been called into question. An alternative will only find the means to achieve stability if it succeeds in combining the three objectives around which the revolts have been mobilized: continuation of the democratization of society and politics, progressive social advances, and the affirmation of national sovereignty.

We are still far from that. That is why there are multiple alternatives possible in the visible short term. Can there be a possible return to the national popular model of the Bandung era, maybe with a hint of democracy? Or a more pronounced crystallization of a democratic, popular, and national front? Or a plunge into a backward-looking illusion that, in this context, takes on the form of an 'Islamization' of politics and society?

In the conflict over—in much confusion—these three possible responses to the challenge, the Western powers (the United States and its subaltern European allies) have made their choice: they have given preferential support to the Muslim Brotherhood and/ or other 'Salafist' organizations of political Islam. The reason for that is simple and obvious: these reactionary political forces accept exercising their power within globalized neoliberalism (and thus abandoning any prospect for social justice and national independence). That is the sole objective pursued by the imperialist powers.

Consequently, political Islam's programme belongs to the type of fascism found in dependent societies. In fact, it shares with all forms of fascism two fundamental characteristics: (1) the absence of a challenge to the essential aspects of the capitalist order (and in this context this amounts to not challenging the model of lumpen development connected to the spread of globalized neoliberal capitalism); and (2) the choice of anti-democratic, police-state forms of political management (such as the prohibition of parties and organizations, and forced Islamization of morals).

The anti-democratic option of the imperialist powers (which gives the lie to the pro-democratic rhetoric found in the flood of propaganda to which we are subjected), then, accepts the possible 'excesses' of the Islamic regimes in question. Like other types of fascism and for the same reasons, these excesses are inscribed in the 'genes' of their modes of thought: unquestioned submission to leaders, fanatic valorization of adherence to the state religion, and the formation of shock forces used to impose submission. In fact, and this can be seen already, the 'Islamist' programme makes progress only in the context of a civil war (between, among others, Sunnis and Shias) and results in nothing other than permanent chaos. This type of Islamist power is, then, the guarantee that the societies in question will remain absolutely incapable of asserting themselves on the world scene. It is clear that a declining United States has given up on getting something better—a stable and submissive local government—in favour of this 'second best'.

Similar developments and choices are found outside of the Arab-Muslim world, such as Hindu India, for example. The Bharatiya Janata Party (BJP), which just won the elections in India, is a reactionary Hindu religious party that accepts the inclusion of its government into globalized neoliberalism. It is the guarantor that India, under its government, will retreat from its project to be an emerging power. Describing it as fascist, then, is not really straining credibility too much.

In conclusion, fascism has returned to the West, East, and South; and this return is naturally connected with the spread of the systemic crisis of generalized, financialized, and globalized monopoly capitalism. Actual or even potential recourse to the services of the fascist movement by the dominant centres of this hard-pressed system calls for the greatest vigilance on our part. This crisis is destined to grow worse and, consequently, the threat of resorting to fascist solutions will become a real danger. Hillary Clinton's support for Washington's warmongering does not bode well for the immediate future.

September 01, 2014

CONTEMPORARY IMPERIALISM

LESSONS FROM THE TWENTIETH CENTURY

Lenin, Bukharin, Stalin, and Trotsky in Russia, as well as Mao, Zhou Enlai, and Deng Xiaoping in China, shaped the history of the two great revolutions of the twentieth century.[1] As leaders of revolutionary communist parties and then later as leaders of revolutionary states, they were confronted with the problems faced by a triumphant revolution in countries of peripheral capitalism and forced to 'revise' (I deliberately use this term, considered sacrilegious by many) the theses inherited from the historical Marxism of the Second International. Lenin and Bukharin went much further than Hobson and Hilferding in their analyses of monopoly capitalism and imperialism and drew this major political conclusion: the imperialist war of 1914–1918 (they were among the few, if not the only ones, to anticipate it) made necessary and possible a revolution led by the proletariat.

With the benefit of hindsight, I will indicate here the limitations of their analyses. Lenin and Bukharin considered imperialism to be a new stage ('the highest') of capitalism associated with the development of monopolies. I question this thesis and contend that historical capitalism has always been imperialist, in the sense that it has led to a polarization between centres and peripheries since its origin (the sixteenth century), which has only increased over the course of its later globalized development. The nineteenth-century pre-monopolist system was not less imperialist. Great Britain maintained its hegemony precisely because of its colonial

---

[1] In this article, I am limiting myself to examining the experiences of Russia and China, with no intention of ignoring the other twentieth-century socialist revolutions (North Korea, Vietnam, Cuba).

domination of India. Lenin and Bukharin thought that the revolution, begun in Russia ('the weak link'), would continue in the centres (Germany in particular). Their hope was based on an underestimate of the effects of imperialist polarization, which destroyed revolutionary prospects in the centres.

Nevertheless, Lenin, and even more Bukharin, quickly learned the necessary historical lesson. The revolution, made in the name of socialism (and communism), was, in fact, something else: mainly a peasant revolution. So what to do? How can the peasantry be linked with the construction of socialism? By making concessions to the market and by respecting newly acquired peasant property; hence by progressing slowly towards socialism? The New Economic Plan (NEP) implemented this strategy.

Yes, but . . . Lenin, Bukharin, and Stalin also understood that the imperialist powers would never accept the Revolution or even the NEP. After the hot wars of intervention, the cold war was to become permanent, from 1920 to 1990.[2] Soviet Russia, even though it was far from being able to construct socialism, was able to free itself from the straightjacket that imperialism always strives to impose on all peripheries of the world system that it dominates. In effect, Soviet Russia delinked. So what to do now? Attempt to push for peaceful coexistence, by making concessions if necessary and refraining from intervening too actively on the international stage? But at the same time, it was necessary to be armed to face new and unavoidable attacks. And that implied rapid industrialization, which, in turn, came into conflict with the interests of the peasantry and thus threatened to break the worker-

---

[2] Before the Second World War, Stalin had desperately, and unsuccessfully, sought an alliance with the Western democracies against Nazism. After the war, Washington chose to pursue the Cold War, while Stalin sought to extend friendship with the Western powers, again without success. See Geoffrey Roberts, *Stalin's Wars: From World War to Cold War, 1939–1953*, New Haven, C.T.: Yale University Press, 2007. See the important preface by Annie Lacroix-Riz to the French edition: *Les Guerres de Staline: De la Guerre Mondiale à la Guerre froide*, Paris: Les éditions Delga, 2014.

peasant alliance, the foundation of the revolutionary state.

It is possible, then, to understand the equivocations of Lenin, Bukharin, and Stalin. In theoretical terms, there were U-turns from one extreme to the other. Sometimes a determinist attitude inspired by the phased approach inherited from earlier Marxism (first the bourgeois democratic revolution, then the socialist one) predominated, sometimes a voluntarist approach (political action would make it possible to leap over stages). Finally, from 1930 to 1933, Stalin chose rapid industrialization and armament (and this choice was not without some connection to the rise of fascism). Collectivization was the price of that choice. Here again we must beware of judging too quickly: all socialists of that period (and even more the capitalists) shared Kautsky's analyses on this point and were persuaded that the future belonged to large-scale agriculture.[3] The break in the worker-peasant alliance that this choice implied lay behind the abandonment of revolutionary democracy and the autocratic turn.

In my opinion, Trotsky would certainly not have done better. His attitude towards the rebellion of the Kronstadt sailors and his later equivocations demonstrate that he was no different than the other Bolshevik leaders in government. But, after 1927, living in exile and no longer having responsibility for managing the Soviet state, he could delight in endlessly repeating the sacred principles of socialism. He became like many academic Marxists who have the luxury of asserting their attachment to principles without having to be concerned about effectiveness in transforming reality.[4]

The Chinese communists appeared later on the revolutionary

---

[3] I am alluding here to Kautsky's theses in *The Agrarian Question*, 2 vols., London: Pluto Press, 1988 (first edition, 1899).

[4] There are pleasant exceptions among Marxist intellectuals who, without having had responsibilities in the leadership of revolutionary parties or, still less, of revolutionary states, have nonetheless remained attentive to the challenges confronted by state socialisms (I am thinking here of Baran, Sweezy, Hobsbawm, and others).

stage. Mao was able to learn from Bolshevik equivocations. China was confronted with the same problems as Soviet Russia: revolution in a backward country, the necessity of including the peasantry in revolutionary transformation, and the hostility of the imperialist powers. But Mao was able to see more clearly than Lenin, Bukharin, and Stalin. Yes, the Chinese revolution was anti-imperialist and peasant (anti-feudal). But it was not bourgeois democratic; it was popular democratic. The difference is important: the latter type of revolution requires maintaining the worker-peasant alliance over a long period. China was thus able to avoid the fatal error of forced collectivization and invent another way: make all agricultural land state property, give the peasantry equal access to use of this land, and renovate family agriculture.[5]

The two revolutions had difficulty in achieving stability because they were forced to reconcile support for a socialist outlook and concessions to capitalism. Which of these two tendencies would prevail? These revolutions only achieved stability after their 'Thermidor', to use Trotsky's term. But when was the Thermidor in Russia? Was it in 1930, as Trotsky said? Or was it in the 1920s, with the NEP? Or was it the ice age of the Brezhnev period? And in China, did Mao choose Thermidor beginning in 1950? Or do we have to wait until Deng Xiaoping to speak of the Thermidor of 1980?

It is not by chance that reference is made to lessons of the French Revolution. The three great revolutions of modern times (the French, Russian, and Chinese) are great precisely because they looked forward beyond the immediate requirements of the moment. With the rise of the Mountain, led by Robespierre, in the National Convention, the French Revolution was consolidated as both popular and bourgeois and, just like the Russian and Chinese

---

[5] See Samir Amin, 'China 2013', *Monthly Review* 64, No. 10, March 2013, pp. 14–33 (also included in the present volume), in particular for analyses concerning Maoism's treatment of the agrarian question.

Revolutions—which strove to go all the way to communism even if it were not on the agenda due to the necessity of averting defeat—retained the prospect of going much further later. Thermidor is not the Restoration. The latter occurred in France, not with Napoleon, but only beginning in 1815. Still it should be remembered that the Restoration could not completely do away with the gigantic social transformation caused by the Revolution. In Russia, the restoration occurred even later in its revolutionary history, with Gorbachev and Yeltsin. It should be noted that this restoration remains fragile, as can be seen in the challenges Putin must still confront. In China, there has not been (or not yet!) a restoration.[6]

A NEW STAGE OF MONOPOLY CAPITAL

The contemporary world is still confronted with the same challenges encountered by the revolutions of the twentieth century. The continued deepening of the centre/periphery contrast, characteristic of the spread of globalized capitalism, still leads to the same major political consequence: transformation of the world begins with anti-imperialist, national, popular—and potentially anti-capitalist—revolutions, which are the only ones on the agenda for the foreseeable future. But this transformation will only be able to go beyond the first steps and proceed on the path to socialism later if and when the peoples of the centres, in turn, begin the struggle for communism, viewed as a higher stage of universal human civilization. The systemic crisis of capitalism in the centres gives a chance for this possibility to be translated into reality.

In the meantime, there is a two-fold challenge confronting the peoples and states of the South: (1) the lumpen development that contemporary capitalism forces on all peripheries of the system

---

[6] See Eric J. Hobsbawm, *Echoes of the Marseillaise: Two Centuries Look Back on the French Revolution*, London: Verso, 1990; also see the works of Florence Gauthier. These authors do not assimilate Thermidor to restoration, as the Trotskyist simplification suggests.

has nothing to offer three-quarters of humanity; in particular, it leads to the rapid destruction of peasant societies in Asia and Africa, and consequently the response given to the peasant question will largely govern the nature of future changes;[7] (2) the aggressive geostrategy of the imperialist powers, which is opposed to any attempt by the peoples and states of the periphery to get out of the impasse, forces the peoples concerned to defeat the military control of the world by the United States and its subaltern European and Japanese allies.

The first long systemic crisis of capitalism got underway in the 1870s. The version of historic capitalism's extension over the long span that I have put forward suggests a succession of three epochs: ten centuries of incubation from the year 1000 in China to the eighteenth-century revolutions in England and France, a short century of triumphal flourishing (the nineteenth century), probably a long decline comprising in itself the first long crisis (1875–1945) and then the second (begun in 1975 and still ongoing). In each of those two long crises, capital responds to the challenge by the same triple formula: concentration of capital's control, deepening of uneven globalization, financialization of the system's management.[8] Two major thinkers (Hobson and Hilferding) immediately grasped the enormous importance of capitalism's transformation into monopoly capitalism. But it was Lenin and Bukharin who drew the political conclusion from this transformation, a transformation that initiated the decline of capitalism and thus moved the socialist revolution onto the agenda.[9]

---

[7] Concerning the destruction of the Asian and African peasantry currently underway, see Samir Amin, 'Contemporary Imperialism and the Agrarian Question', *Agrarian South: Journal of Political Economy* 1, No. 1, April 2012, pp. 11–26.

[8] I discuss here only some of the major consequences of the move to generalized monopolies (financialization, decline of democracy). As for ecological questions, I refer to the remarkable works of John Bellamy Foster.

[9] Nikolai Bukharin, *Imperialism and the World Economy*, New York: Monthly

The primary formation of monopoly capitalism thus goes back to the end of the nineteenth century, but in the United States it really established itself as a system only from the 1920s, to conquer next the Western Europe and Japan of the 'thirty glorious years' following the Second World War. The concept of surplus, put forth by Baran and Sweezy in the 1950–1960 decade, allows a grasp of what is essential in the transformation of capitalism. Convinced at the moment of its publication by that work of enrichment to the Marxist critique of capitalism, I undertook as soon as the 1970s its reformulation which required, in my opinion, the transformation of the 'first' (1920–1970) monopoly capitalism into generalized-monopoly capitalism, analysed as a qualitatively new phase of the system.

In the previous forms of competition among firms producing the same use value—numerous then, and independent of each other—decisions were made by the capitalist owners of those firms on the basis of a recognized market price which imposed itself as an external datum. Baran and Sweezy observed that the new monopolies act differently: they set their prices simultaneously with the nature and volume of their outputs. So it is an end to 'fair and open competition', which remains, quite contrary to reality, at the heart of conventional economics' rhetoric! The abolition of competition—the radical transformation of that term's meaning, of its functioning and of its results—detaches the price system from its basis, the system of values, and in that very way hides from sight the referential framework which used to define capitalism's rationality. Although use values used to constitute to a great extent autonomous realities, they become, in monopoly capitalism, the object of actual fabrications produced systematically through aggressive and particularized sales strategies (advertising, brands,

....

Review Press, 1973 (written in 1915); V.I. Lenin, *Imperialism, The Highest Stage of Capitalism*, New York: International Publishers, 1969 (written in 1916), also New Delhi: LeftWord Books, 2000.

etc.). In monopoly capitalism, a coherent reproduction of the productive system is no longer possible merely by mutual adjustment of the two departments discussed in the second volume of *Capital*: it is thenceforward necessary to take into account a Department III, conceived by Baran and Sweezy. This allows for added surplus absorption promoted by the state—beyond Department I (private investment) and beyond the portion of Department II (private consumption) devoted to capitalist consumption. The classic example of Department III spending is military expenditure. However, the notion of Department III can be expanded to cover the wider array of socially unreproductive expenditures promoted by generalized-monopoly capitalism.[10]

The excrescence of Department III, in turn, favours in fact the erasure of the distinction made by Marx between productive (of surplus-value) labour and unproductive labour. All forms of wage labour can—and do—become sources of possible profits. A hairdresser sells his services to a customer who pays him out of his income. But if that hairdresser becomes the employee of a beauty parlour, the business must realize a profit for its owner. If the country at issue puts ten million wage workers to work in Departments I, II, and III, providing the equivalent of twelve million years of abstract labour, and if the wages received by those workers allow them to buy goods and services requiring merely six million years of abstract labour, the rate of exploitation for all of them, productive and unproductive confounded, is the same 100 per cent. But the six million years of abstract labour that the workers do not receive cannot all be invested in the purchase of producer goods destined to expand Departments I and II; part of

---

[10] For further discussions of the Department III analysis and its relation to Baran and Sweezy's theory of surplus absorption see Samir Amin, *Three Essays on Marx's Value Theory*, New York: Monthly Review Press, 2013, pp. 67–76; and John Bellamy Foster, 'Marxian Crisis Theory and the State', in John Bellamy Foster and Henryk Szlajfer (eds), *The Faltering Economy*, New York: Monthly Review Press, 1984, pp. 325–49.

them will be put toward the expansion of Department III.

Generalized-Monopoly Capitalism (Since 1975)

Passage from the initial monopoly capitalism to its current form (generalized-monopoly capitalism) was accomplished in a short time (between 1975 and 2000) in response to the second long crisis of declining capitalism. In fifteen years, monopoly power's centralization and its capacity for control over the entire productive system reached summits incomparable with what had until then been the case.

My first formulation of generalized-monopoly capitalism dates from 1978, when I put forward an interpretation of capital's responses to the challenge of its long systemic crisis, which opened starting from 1971–1975. In that interpretation I accentuated the three directions of this expected reply, then barely under way: strengthened centralization of control over the economy by the monopolies, deepening of globalization (and the outsourcing of the manufacturing industry to the peripheries), and financialization. The work that Andre Gunder Frank and I published together in 1978 drew no notice probably because our theses were ahead of their time. But today the three characteristics at issue have become blindingly obvious to everybody.[11]

A name had to be given to this new phase of monopoly capitalism. The adjective 'generalized' specifies what is new: the monopolies are thenceforward in a position that gives them the capability of reducing all (or nearly all) economic activities to subcontractor status. The example of family farming in the capitalist centres provides the finest example of this. These farmers are controlled upstream by the monopolies that provide their inputs and financing, and downstream by the marketing chains,

---

[11] Andre Gunder Frank and Samir Amin, 'Let's Not Wait for 1984', in Frank, *Reflections on the World Economic Crisis*, New York: Monthly Review Press, 1981.

to the point that the price structures forced on them wipe out the income from their labour. Farmers survive only thanks to public subsidies paid for by the taxpayers. This extraction is thus at the origin of the monopolies' profits! As likewise has been observed with bank failures, the new principal of economic management is summed up in a phrase: privatization of the monopolies' profits, socialization of their losses! To go on talking of 'fair and open competition' and of 'truth of the prices revealed by the markets'— that belongs in a farce.

The fragmented, and by that fact concrete, economic power of proprietary bourgeois families gives way to a centralized power exercised by the directors of the monopolies and their cohort of salaried servitors. For generalized-monopoly capitalism involves not the concentration of property, which on the contrary is more dispersed than ever, but of the power to manage it. That is why it is deceptive to attach the adjective 'patrimonial' to contemporary capitalism. It is only in appearance that 'shareholders' rule. Absolute monarchs, the top executives of the monopolies, decide everything in their name. Moreover, the deepening globalization of the system wipes out the holistic (i.e., simultaneously economic, political, and social) logic of national systems without putting in its place any global logic whatsoever. This is the empire of chaos— the title of one of my works, published in 1991 and subsequently taken up by others: in fact international political violence takes the place of economic competition.[12]

Financialization of Accumulation

The new financialization of economic life crowns this transformation in capital's power. In place of strategies set out by real owners of fragmented capital are those of the managers of ownership titles over capital. What is vulgarly called fictitious capital (the estimated value of ownership certificates) is nothing but the expression of

[12] Samir Amin, *Empire of Chaos*, New York: Monthly Review Press, 1992.

this displacement, this disconnect between the virtual and real worlds.

By its very nature capitalist accumulation has always been synonymous with disorder, in the sense that Marx gave to that term: a system moving from disequilibrium to disequilibrium (driven by class struggles and conflicts among the powers) without ever tending toward an equilibrium. But this disorder resulting from competition among fragmented capitals was kept within reasonable limits through management of the credit system carried out under the control of the national state. With contemporary financialized and globalized capitalism those frontiers disappear; the violence of the movements from disequilibrium to disequilibrium is reinforced. The successor of disorder is chaos.

Domination by the capital of the generalized monopolies is exercised on the world scale through global integration of the monetary and financial market, based henceforward on the principle of flexible exchange rates, and giving up national controls over the flow of capital. Nevertheless, this domination is called into question, to varying degrees, by state policies of the emerging countries. The conflict between these latter policies and the strategic objectives of the triad's collective imperialism becomes by that fact one of the central axes for possibly putting generalized-monopoly capitalism once more on trial.[13]

The Decline of Democracy

In the system's centres, generalized-monopoly capitalism has brought with it generalization of the wage-form. Upper managers are thenceforward employees who do not participate in the formation of surplus-value, of which they have become consumers. At the other social pole, the generalized proletarianization that the

---

[13] Concerning the challenge to financial globalization, see Samir Amin, 'From Bandung (1955) to 2015: New and Old Challenges for the Peoples and States of the South', paper presented at the World Social Forum, Tunis, March 2015, and 'The Chinese Yuan', published in Chinese, 2013.

wage-form suggests is accompanied by multiplication in forms of segmentation of the labour force. In other words, the 'proletariat' (in its forms as known in the past) disappears at the very moment when proletarianization becomes generalized. In the peripheries, the effects of domination by generalized-monopoly capital are no less visible. Above an already diverse social structure made up of local ruling classes and the subordinate classes and status groups there is placed a dominant superclass emerging in the wake of globalization. This superclass is sometimes that of 'neo-comprador insiders', sometimes that of the governing political class (or class-state-party), or a mixture of the two.

Far from being synonyms, 'market' and 'democracy' are, on the contrary, antonyms. In the centres a new political consensus-culture (only seeming, perhaps, but nevertheless active) synonymous with depolitization, has taken the place of the former political culture based on the right-left confrontation that used to give significance to bourgeois democracy and the contradictory inscription of class struggles within its framework. In the peripheries, the monopoly of power captured by the dominant local superclass likewise involves the negation of democracy. The rise of political Islam provides an example of such a regression.

THE AGGRESSIVE GEOSTRATEGY OF CONTEMPORARY IMPERIALISM

The Collective Imperialism of the Triad; the State in Contemporary Capitalism

In the 1970s, Sweezy, Magdoff and I had already advanced this thesis, formulated by Andre Gunder Frank and me in a work published in 1978. We said that monopoly capitalism was entering a new age, characterized by the gradual—but rapid—dismantling of national production systems. The production of a growing number of market goods can no longer be defined by the label 'made in France' (or the Soviet Union or the United States), but becomes 'made in the world', because its manufacture is now broken into segments, located here and there throughout the whole world.

Recognizing this fact, now a commonplace, does not imply that there is only one explanation of the major cause for the transformation in question. For my part, I explain it by the leap forward in the degree of centralization in the control of capital by the monopolies, which I have described as the move from the capitalism of monopolies to the capitalism of generalized monopolies. The information revolution, among other factors, provides the means that make possible the management of this globally dispersed production system. But for me, these means are only implemented in response to a new objective need created by the leap forward in the centralized control of capital.

The emergence of this globalized production system eliminates coherent 'national development' policies (diverse and unequally effective), but it does not substitute a new coherence, which would be that of the globalized system. The reason for that is the absence of a globalized bourgeoisie and globalized state, which I will examine later. Consequently, the globalized production system is incoherent by nature.

Another important consequence of this qualitative transformation of contemporary capitalism is the emergence of the collective imperialism of the triad, which takes the place of the historical national imperialisms (of the United States, Great Britain, Japan, Germany, France, and a few others). Collective imperialism finds its *raison d'être* in the awareness by the bourgeoisies in the triad nations of the necessity for their joint management of the world and particularly of the subjected, and yet to be subjected, societies of the peripheries.

Some draw two correlates from the thesis of the emergence of a globalized production system: the emergence of a globalized bourgeoisie and the emergence of a globalized state, both of which would find their objective foundation in this new production system. My interpretation of the current changes and crises leads me to reject these two correlates.

There is no globalized bourgeoisie (or dominant class) in the process of being formed, either on the world scale or in the countries of the imperialist triad. I am led to emphasize the fact that the centralization of control over the capital of the monopolies takes place within the nation-states of the triad (United States, each member of the European Union, Japan) much more than it does in the relations between the partners of the triad, or even between members of the European Union. The bourgeoisies (or oligopolistic groups) are in competition within nations (and the national state manages this competition, in part at least) and between nations. Thus the German oligopolies (and the German state) took on the leadership of European affairs, not for the equal benefit of everyone, but first of all for their own benefit. At the level of the triad, it is obviously the bourgeoisie of the United States that leads the alliance, once again with an unequal distribution of the benefits. The idea that the objective cause—the emergence of the globalized production system—entails ipso facto the emergence of a globalized dominant class is based on the underlying hypothesis that the system must be coherent. In reality, it is possible for it not to be coherent. In fact, it is not coherent and hence this chaotic system is not viable.

In the peripheries, the globalization of the production system occurs in conjunction with the replacement of the hegemonic blocs of earlier eras by a new hegemonic bloc dominated by the new comprador bourgeoisies, which are not constitutive elements of a globalized bourgeoisie, but only subaltern allies of the bourgeoisies of the dominant triad. Just like there is no globalized bourgeoisie in the process of formation, there is also no globalized state on the horizon. The major reason for this is that the current globalized system does not attenuate, but actually accentuates conflict (already visible or potential) between the societies of the triad and those of the rest of the world. I do indeed mean conflict between *societies* and, consequently, *potentially* conflict between states. The advantage derived from the triad's dominant position (imperialist rent) allows the hegemonic bloc formed around the generalized monopolies to benefit from a legitimacy that is expressed, in turn, by the convergence of all major electoral parties, right and left, and their equal commitment to neoliberal economic policies and continual intervention in the affairs of the peripheries. On the other hand, the neo-comprador bourgeoisies of the peripheries are neither legitimate nor credible in the eyes of their own people (because the policies they serve do not make it possible to 'catch up', and most often lead to the impasse of lumpen development). Instability of the current governments is thus the rule in this context.

Just as there is no globalized bourgeoisie even at the level of the triad or that of the European Union, there is also no globalized state at these levels. Instead, there is only an alliance of states. These states, in turn, willingly accept the hierarchy that allows that alliance to function: general leadership is taken on by Washington, and leadership in Europe by Berlin. The national state remains in place to serve globalization as it is.

There is an idea circulating in postmodernist currents that contemporary capitalism no longer needs the state to manage the world economy and thus that the state system is in the process of withering away to the benefit of the emergence of civil society. I will not go back over the arguments that I have developed elsewhere against this naive thesis, one moreover that is propagated by the dominant governments and the media clergy in their service. There is no capitalism without the state. Capitalist globalization could not be pursued without the interventions of the United States armed forces and the management of the dollar. Clearly, the armed forces and money are instruments of the state, not of the market.

But since there is no world state, the United States intends to fulfil this function. The societies of the triad consider this function to be legitimate; other societies do not. But what does that matter? The self-proclaimed 'international community', i.e., the G7 plus Saudi Arabia, which has surely become a democratic republic, does not recognize the legitimacy of the opinion of 85 per cent of the world's population!

There is thus an asymmetry between the functions of the state in the dominant imperialist centres and those of the state in the subject, or yet to be subjected, peripheries. The state in the compradorized peripheries is inherently unstable and, consequently, a potential enemy, when it is not already one.

There are enemies with which the dominant imperialist powers have been forced to coexist—at least up until now. This is the case with China because it has rejected (up until now) the neo-comprador option and is pursuing its sovereign project of integrated and coherent national development. Russia became an enemy as soon as Putin refused to align politically with the triad and wanted to block the expansionist ambitions of the latter in Ukraine, even if he does not envision (or not yet?) leaving the rut of economic liberalism. The great majority of comprador states in the South (that is, states in the service of their comprador bourgeoisies) are allies, not enemies—as long as each of these comprador states gives the appearance of being in charge of its country. But leaders in Washington, London, Berlin, and Paris know that these states are fragile. As soon as a popular movement of revolt—with or without a viable alternative strategy—threatens one of these states, the triad arrogates to itself the right to intervene. Intervention can even lead to contemplating the destruction of these states and, beyond them, of the societies concerned. This strategy is currently at work in Iraq, Syria, and elsewhere. The *raison d'être* of the strategy for military control of the world by the triad led by Washington is located entirely in this 'realist' vision, which is in direct counterpoint to the naive view—*à la* Negri—of a globalized state in the process of formation.[14]

Responses of the Peoples and States of the South

The ongoing offensive of the United States/Europe/Japan collective imperialism against all the peoples of the South walks on two legs: the economic leg—globalized neoliberalism forced as the exclusive possible economic policy; and the political leg—continuous interventions including preemptive wars against those who reject imperialist interventions. In response, some countries of the South, such as the BRICS, at best walk on only one leg: they reject the geopolitics of imperialism but accept economic neoliberalism. They remain, for that reason, vulnerable, as the current case of Russia shows.[15] Yes, they have to understand that 'trade is war', as Yash Tandon wrote.[16]

All countries of the world outside the triad are enemies or potential enemies, except those who accept complete submission to its economic and political strategy. In that frame Russia is 'an enemy'.[17] Whatever might be our assessment of what the Soviet

---

[14] 'Contra Hardt and Negri', *Monthly Review* 66, No. 6, November 2014, pp. 25–36.

[15] The choice to delink is inevitable. The extreme centralization of the surplus at the world level in the form of imperialist rent for the monopolies of the imperialist powers is unsupportable by all societies in the periphery. It is necessary to deconstruct this system with the prospect of reconstructing it later in another form of globalization compatible with communism understood as a more advanced stage of universal civilization. I have suggested, in this context, a comparison with the necessary destruction of the centralization of the Roman Empire, which opened the way to feudal decentralization.

[16] Yash Tandon, *Trade is War*, New York: OR Books, 2015.

[17] Samir Amin, 'Russia in the World System', Chapter 7 in *Global History: A View from the South*, London: Pambazuka Press, 2010; 'The Return of Fascism in Contemporary Capitalism', *Monthly Review* 66, No. 4, September 2014, pp. 1–12 (also included in the present volume).

Union was, the triad fought it simply because it was an attempt to develop independently of dominant capitalism/imperialism. After the breakdown of the Soviet system, some people (in Russia in particular) thought that the 'West' would not antagonize a 'capitalist Russia'—just as Germany and Japan had 'lost the war but won the peace'. They forgot that the Western powers supported the reconstruction of the former fascist countries precisely to face the challenge of the independent policies of the Soviet Union. Now, this challenge having disappeared, the target of the triad is complete submission, to destroy the capacity of Russia to resist. The current development of the Ukraine tragedy illustrates the reality of the strategic target of the triad. The triad organized in Kiev what ought to be called a 'Euro/Nazi putsch'. The rhetoric of the Western medias, claiming that the policies of the Triad aim at promoting democracy, is *simply a lie*. Eastern Europe has been 'integrated' in the European Union not as equal partners, but as 'semi-colonies' of major Western and Central European capitalist/ imperialist powers. The relation between West and East in the European system is in some degree similar to that which rules the relations between the United States and Latin America!

Therefore, the policy of Russia to resist the project of colonization of Ukraine must be supported. But this positive Russian 'international policy' *is bound to fail* if it is not supported by the Russian people. And this support cannot be won on the exclusive basis of 'nationalism'. The support can be won only if the internal economic and social policy pursued promotes the interests of the majority of the working people. A people-oriented policy implies therefore moving away, as much as possible, from the 'liberal' recipe and the electoral masquerade associated with it, which claims to give legitimacy to regressive social policies. I would suggest setting up in its place a brand of new state capitalism with a social dimension (I say social, not socialist). That system would open the road to eventual advances toward a socialization of the management of the economy and therefore authentic new advances toward an invention of democracy responding to the challenges of a modern economy.

Russian state power remaining within the strict limits of the neoliberal recipe annihilates the chances of success of an independent foreign policy and the chances of Russia becoming a really emerging country acting as an important international actor. Neoliberalism can produce for Russia only a tragic economic and social regression, a pattern of 'lumpen development', and a growing subordinate status in the global imperialist order. Russia would provide the triad with oil, gas, and some other natural resources; its industries would be reduced to the status of sub-contracting for the benefit of Western financial monopolies. In such a position, which is not very far from that of Russia today in the global system, attempts to act independently in the international area will remain extremely fragile, threatened by 'sanctions' which will strengthen the disastrous alignment of the ruling economic oligarchy to the demands of dominant monopolies of the triad. The current outflow of 'Russian capital' associated with the Ukraine crisis illustrates the danger. Reestablishing state control over the movements of capital is the only effective response to that danger.

Outside of China, which is implementing a national project of modern industrial development in connection with the renovation of family agriculture, the other so-called emergent countries of the South (the BRICS) still walk only on one leg: they are opposed to the depredations of militarized globalization, but remain imprisoned in the straightjacket of neoliberalism.[18]

July 01, 2015

[18] Concerning the inadequate responses of India and Brazil, see Samir Amin, *The Implosion of Capitalism*, New York: Monthly Review Press, 2013, Chapter 2, and 'Latin America Confronts the Challenge of Globalization', *Monthly Review* 66, No. 7, December 2014, pp. 1–6.

READING *CAPITAL*,
READING HISTORICAL CAPITALISMS

I

Marx's *Capital* presents a rigorous scientific analysis of the capitalist mode of production and capitalist society, and how they differ from earlier forms. Volume 1 delves into the heart of the problem. It directly clarifies the meaning of the generalization of commodity exchanges between private property owners (and this characteristic is unique to the modern world of capitalism, even if commodity exchanges had existed earlier), specifically the emergence and dominance of value and abstract social labour. From that foundation, Marx leads us to understand how the proletarian's sale of his or her labour power to the 'man with money' ensures the production of surplus value that the capitalist expropriates, and which, in turn, is the condition for the accumulation of capital. The dominance of value governs not only the reproduction of the economic system of capitalism; it governs every aspect of modern social and political life. The concept of alienation points to the ideological mechanism through which the overall unity of social reproduction is expressed.

Volume 2 demonstrates why and how capital accumulation functions, more specifically, why and how accumulation successfully integrates the exploitation of labour in its reproduction and overcomes the effects of the social contradiction that it represents. The suitable division of social labour between production of the means of production and production of consumption goods ensures the overall balance of supply and demand for goods and services produced exclusively within the context of the capitalist system of social relations. For my part, I have argued more specifically that: (1) the mechanism of accumulation requires an advance of credit the volume of which can be calculated on the basis of the rates of progress in the productivity of social labour for each of the two departments of production in question (and that was my response to Rosa Luxemburg's poorly posed question concerning the realization of surplus value); (2) the realization of a dynamic balance of growth requires the real wage (the value of labour power) itself to increase at a rate that can be calculated on the basis of growth in productivity; and (3) consequently, the model presented in volume 2 does not allow us to say anything about the tendency of the rate of profit to fall (*Law of Worldwide Value*, Chapter 1).

Taken together, volumes 1 and 2 of *Capital* do not provide specific information on the history of the emergence of the capitalism that they analyse. As Marx himself says, his aim is to offer an analysis of the essence of capitalism, its 'ideal average'. He does not consider, then, the relations between the space controlled by this capitalist mode (the only space analysed in these two volumes) and other spaces of social production, prior to or even contemporary with the existence of concrete historical capitalism, in England or elsewhere.

This focus on the capitalist mode of production allows Marx to show how that mode is the basis for an 'economic science' that proposes to outline the conditions for a general equilibrium between supply and demand in capitalist commodities, and how the capitalist mode advances that science as the newly dominant form of social thought. Commodity alienation is the secret of this triumph. It reverses the relations between the economic instance, which becomes dominant, and the political and ideological instances, which consequently lose the characteristic dominance they had in earlier societies. This is the meaning of my reading of the subtitle of *Capital* ('Critique of Political Economy'): a reading that reveals the status of economic science in modern social thought.

Volume 3 of *Capital* is different. Here Marx moves from the analysis of capitalism in its fundamental aspects (its 'ideal average') to that of the historical reality of capitalism. He does so only partially by dealing with three sets of questions. The first set concerns ground rent, that is, the right of landowners to a fraction of the surplus value produced by the capitalist exploitation of labour. We are here plunged into the heart of the question concerning the history of the emergence of historical capitalism. Capitalism did not fall from the sky onto a virgin earth. It was forged through its conflict with the feudal society of the *ancien régime*—in England, France, and a few other places in Europe. Traces of this conflict can be found in the capitalist formations (as distinct from the capitalist mode of production) that existed in Marx's era.

The second set concerns questions about the functioning of money (commodity money—the general equivalent of exchange—and credit, of which commodity money is the support). The distinction between interest on money (and its rate) and profit on capital emerges from this analysis. This is both an inseparable complement to the analysis of the capitalist mode of production (i.e., a complement to what volumes 1 and 2 contribute to this analysis) and an opening to historical considerations. In this connection, Marx offers several observations on the management of money by the Banks of England and France and on the theories advanced in this area by others.

The third set focuses on the cycles and crises of accumulation, examined within the context of the concrete history of England and Europe of that period. Here I refer the reader to what I have written about Marx's analysis of these questions, both their general theoretical dimension and their concrete historical expressions (*Law*, Chapters 2 and 3). Further, note that there is no systematic analysis in volume 3 of two sets of major questions: first, the class struggles characteristic of the capitalist mode of production and of historical capitalisms, as well as the interaction of those struggles with the process of accumulation; and second, the new international relations distinctive of historical capitalisms, including capitalism's tendency towards globalization, and the interaction of these distinctive international relations with class struggles and the accumulation process. Marx provides only scattered observations on this subject.

II

To move from the reading of *Capital* (and particularly of volumes 1 and 2) to that of historical capitalisms at successive moments of their deployment has its own requirements, even beyond reading all of Marx and Engels. Marxist theoreticians and activists have always expressed their admiration for Marx and Engels's writings, made their reading of these writings recognizable, either explicitly or implicitly, and wanted to be inspired by them as part of their response to the challenges facing them in their struggles. I have no intention here of reviewing these diverse readings, but only to formulate what, in my reading of historical capitalisms, should be retained and discussed by all those—Marxist or not—who believe that 'another, better world is necessary'.

The reading of *Capital* that I have proposed above is certainly shared by others. But it is not the one prevalent in the dominant currents of the historical Marxisms of the Second and Third Internationals. The success of Marxism in revolutionary anti-capitalist circles of the modern world necessarily involved a dose of simplification and popularization. Kautsky produced the first of what could be called a handbook of Marxism, something that Soviet Marxism popularized even more. In contrast with these abridgements, some Marxological works restore what, in my opinion, is the rightful status of *Capital*. It remains the case, though, that Marxology almost always favours exegesis to the detriment of a confrontation between theory and reality.

The recognition of this two-fold weakness—popularization and exegesis—should make it easier to understand the reasons behind the abandonment of Marxism characteristic of our era. *Capital* analyses nineteenth century English capitalism and a reading of it does not allow us to understand the nature of contemporary capitalism. Marx's work is thus described as 'outdated'. That is not my opinion—not because I make Marx into an infallible prophet, but simply because *Capital* allows us to grasp the essential foundations of capitalism beyond its historical forms and development. In this sense, reading *Capital* will continue to provide us with guidance to perceive the diversity of forms in which the history of capitalism is expressed, but nothing more. It is still necessary to interpret historical capitalism, something that is not found in *Capital*.

Will we find such an interpretation elsewhere in the other writings of Marx and Engels, perhaps partly in volume 3 of *Capital*? I believe the answer to this question is no. Certainly, Marx devoted many of his writings to analyses of the historical capitalisms of his era. He examined the complex political and social struggles that traversed them, without reducing them to the class struggle between the proletariat and bourgeoisie. He recognized the importance of the conflicts with the aristocracies of the *anciens régimes* of England and France, but also elsewhere in Europe (Germany, Russia, and others). He gave full meaning to peasant struggles and their position in the formation of historical capitalisms. He granted complete significance to the differences in the ways that political life was managed in the various nations and emphasized the nuances in their ideological expressions. He even recognized the conflicts between the emerging nations of capitalism and their colonial conquests.

In the same spirit, Marx tackled the origins and concrete historical emergence of capitalism in England, Western Europe, and the United States. Beyond that, he initiated the study of colonial capitalism in Eastern Europe and the Americas. It is precisely because he had understood better than anyone what defines the nature of capitalism (volumes 1 and 2 of *Capital*) that he was able to grasp the significance of changes in earlier societies, those that allowed the emergence of historical capitalism in some places and did not allow it in others.

Reading all of these penetrating writings is always refreshing and full of insights. But it is not sufficient for two reasons. First, because all of these propositions that can be defined as building blocks for the construction of a materialist reading of history remain—and will continue to remain—subject to successive critical readings in the light of advances in our knowledge of the past. Once again, Marx is not a prophet beyond all possible error. The second reason is even more important: historical capitalism has continually developed and been transformed, beyond Marx. The new is not written in Marx; it must be discovered.

I am certainly not the first, or the only, one to have adopted this approach to pursuing the work begun by Marx. The Social Democrats, Lenin, Mao, and many Marxist theoreticians (like Baran or Sweezy) have shared this approach. I will not mention here non-Marxist or even anti-Marxist theoreticians who also have been devoted to the objective of analysing contemporary reality, whether or not they describe it as capitalist. Once again, I will not review these various interpretations of the contemporary world, but will only express my point of view on the question.

III

The preceding analysis should allow the reader to place my reading of historical capitalism in relation to Marx and historical

Marxisms. I intend to outline my interpretation in what follows, emphasizing contemporary capitalism, its systemic crisis, and possible responses to that crisis.

I think it is helpful here to summarize briefly my interpretation of the emergence of historical capitalism (in Europe) (*Class and Nation*). I rejected the theory of the five stages of universal history (primitive communism, slavery, feudalism, capitalism, socialism) as well as the 'Asiatic mode of production' supported by various schools of historical Marxism. Having defined feudalism as an incomplete (peripheral) form from the family of tributary modes of production, I based my explanation of the early emergence of European capitalism, which then imposed itself on the world, on the concept of unequal development (the way is paved more easily for new advances in the peripheries of a system than in its centres). The most advanced (central) tributary systems also included the pre-requisites for the emergence of capitalism (contrary to the Eurocentric prejudice). The failure of the first waves of the movement in this direction (China, Near East, Italian cities) appeared to me to be the expression of a general rule in human history: the new does not emerge suddenly and miraculously; the way to the new is paved with difficulty through successive advances and retreats. The same thing is true about the necessary and possible surpassing of capitalism. I do not believe that my contention on unequal development can be found in Marx, who appears to be continually indecisive on the issue. My reading of the *Formen die der Kapitalistichen Produktion vorhergehen* (Pre-Capitalist Economic Formations) left me unsatisfied. My general view of historical materialism (note that I say 'view' and not 'theory') led me to clarify the meaning that I gave to 'under-determination' and to propose, on this basis, an interpretation of modes of articulation between the instances of the particular reality of each historical formation. The meaning that I give to the cultural instance is obviously not the same as that attributed to it by currently fashionable culturalist theories. I define communism, understood as a superior stage of civilization and not as 'civilized' capitalism or capitalism without capitalist profiteers, precisely as the dominance of the cultural instance. The titles of the chapters in *Spectres of Capitalism* demonstrate my intentions. Here I can only refer the reader to these analyses (*Spectres of Capitalism*, Chapters 3, 4, 5).

The globalized expansion of capitalism has always been polarizing at each stage of its development, in the sense that it has continually constructed the opposition between dominant imperialist centres and dominated peripheries. Primitive accumulation is continual. The dominant social thinking, which acts as an apologist for capitalism, is forced to ignore this reality so that it can promise to the peoples of the peripheries an impossible 'catching-up' in and by means of capitalism. The currently fashionable thinking today has fostered the strong resurgence of this fatal illusion. Imperialism, which the currents of contemporary postmodernism claim is in the process of disappearing, is supposedly only a parenthesis in history, one that undertakes the real and homogenizing globalization of the advanced capitalist model. The emergent countries are allegedly proof of that possibility. I have rejected this naive, apologetic view and analysed the emergent forms as a new stage of polarization (*Implosion of Contemporary Capitalism*, Chapter 2). I do not believe that Marx was ever absolutely convinced that the power of capitalist expansion would necessarily end up by homogenizing the planet, even if he seems to have suggested that view in a few scattered observations. On other occasions, he did not hesitate to denounce the impasse constructed by colonialism, outlining the possibility of socialism's emergence from the peripheries of the globalized modern system, as shown by some of his writings on Russia.

The reality of the globalized and polarizing capitalist system forces us to take into consideration local social struggles as they are articulated with major international conflicts, both those between the imperialist centres and the peripheries struggling for their liberation and those among the dominant central powers. Marx had intended to deal with this question in the two volumes of *Capital* that, in the end, were not written. To formulate a critical economic theory of the world system is, in my opinion, inherently destined to failure. This is why I have argued that, at some point, Marx would have given up this project (*Three Essays on Marx's Value Theory*, part I). Certainly, the economic science of globalized capitalism that is offered to us is nothing more than an apology for imperialist practices. Yet another merely economic theory of the world system is just as impossible. Here we must place ourselves within the broader field of historical materialism. In this way, we can articulate classes, nations, and states in a whole that makes sense and allows us to understand how the modern world system functions through all its economic, political, and ideological dimensions. What I just said about the major conflict of our time (beginning in the twentieth century) is equally valid for the conflicts between the dominant central nations in the nineteenth and twentieth centuries. Since historical capitalism was formed on the basis of the emergence of central nations (the United Kingdom, France, Germany, the United States, and a few others), the conflict among these nations cannot be reduced to their competition in a market in the process of globalizing by economic means. Marx also proposed to deal systematically with the class struggle in a volume of *Capital* that he did not write. His scattered writings on this major subject do not fill the void.

In volume 2 of *Capital*, Marx demonstrates that the process of accumulation in a society reduced to the capitalist mode of production requires an increase in wages parallel to the increase in the productivity of social labour. Otherwise, general equilibrium is impossible. There would be an excess in the production of capital goods and consumption goods in relation to insufficient demand. Capitalism carries within itself this fatal contradiction: the dominant position of the bourgeoisie and the competition between capitalist companies makes it impossible for wages to increase at the necessary rate. Capitalism cannot, then, ever overcome this permanent crisis. And yet it has succeeded in substituting for this insufficient demand its horizontal expansion into forms of production that preceded it (small agricultural and artisanal production, small landed property, small trade, etc.). External colonial conquest has produced analogous effects. Sweezy quite accurately observes that it is not the crises of capitalism that are the problem, but the moments of prosperity in which these crises are overcome. To understand why that is so, we must place ourselves beyond the economic analysis of the capitalist mode of production and in the broader field of historical materialism. The moments of prosperity are explained by wars, German and Italian unity, waves of major innovations (textile machines, railroads, electricity, the automobile and airplane, information technology). This is why I do not see capitalism as the end of history, but rather as a short parenthesis (*Ending the Crisis of Capitalism or Ending Capitalism?*). For my part, I have attempted to place social struggles in this broader context, in particular the major class struggle between the proletariat and bourgeoisie, and have offered some systematic observations on the subject concerning the effects of this struggle on capital accumulation (*Law*, Chapters 1, 4; *Three Essays*, part I).

IV

The interpretation of contemporary capitalism that I propose begins with Baran and Sweezy's observations on the necessity for a third department to absorb the surplus produced by capitalism's fatal contradiction. I have already said that this was, for me, a decisive contribution that has enriched Marx's analyses of historical capitalism (*Three Essays*, part II). I shall summarize my central contentions on the transformations of contemporary imperialist capitalism in the following two points.

1. We have moved from monopoly capitalism as developed between 1890 and 1970 to a new stage characterized by a qualitatively higher level of centralization of control over capital. Consequently, all forms of production have been reduced to sub-contract status, thereby allowing the monopolies (which I call 'generalized' for this reason) to appropriate an always increasing fraction of the surplus value in the form of monopoly rent (*Implosion*, Chapter 1). This qualitative leap, which was effected in a relatively brief period of time between 1975 and 1990, is expressed by the power assumed by an oligarchy (several thousand individuals) that monopolizes all economic and political power. We thus move from historical forms of 'concrete' capitalisms (the description that I propose to designate the operational system of a bourgeois class made up of numerous private property owners of segments of national capital) to what I will call 'abstract capitalism'. I refer here to my analysis in these terms of the transformation of the law of value and, with this development, the separation of the system of prices from that of values (*Implosion*, Chapter 1, and *Three Essays*, part I).

2. This transformation has led to the decline in the old conflict among the imperialist powers and its replacement by a new collective imperialism of the triad (United States, Europe, Japan). The imperialist powers no longer have another way to continue their domination over the immense peripheries of the system (85 per cent of the world's population), which have become zones of permanent unrest. The emergence of this collective imperialism in no way means that there has been the concomitant emergence of a 'world bourgeoisie' (even at the level of the triad or of Europe) and a 'world state' that would manage a globalized capitalism, as suggested by certain theories I have criticized (*Pambazuka*). State and bourgeoisie remain national: American, British, Japanese,

German, etc. There is no necessary agreement between the requirements for the functioning of the economic base of the system and those for the political and ideological instances that carry out its management functions. There is no over-determination of the instances. It is, on the contrary, their under-determination that characterizes the development of social life. The concept of over-determination implies a linear and determinist view of history. Under-determination—which appears much closer to Marx's view—allows us to understand possible obstacles in the evolution of societies and the various alternative responses to those challenges. A good example of this contradiction is the current crisis of the European system, which is incapable of overcoming the reality of national governments, and the foreseeable implosion of the European Union (*Implosion*, Chapter 3).

The changes that I have described here entail extremely important consequences for the forms of political management of all national systems. In the centres (the triad), the monopoly of power exercised by the new oligarchies (which are not exclusively Russian, as Western propaganda would like us to believe!) has already emptied representative electoral democracy of any relatively positive meaning that it had acquired in the past. The alignment of social democracy, which has become social liberalism, with the positions of the classical right—in other words, the contamination of everything by the liberal virus—has already undermined the credibility of and delegitimized this democracy. This tragic evolution opens the way to the rebirth of fascism in societies that are increasingly in total disarray. The absolute power of the contemporary oligarchy is a new reality in the history of capitalism. Its dictatorship has in effect even abolished the very existence of both right and left political parties, condemned trade unions to powerlessness, and enslaved a media reduced to nothing more than a clergy dedicated to serving the oligarchy exclusively. Unfortunately, this dictatorship is quite effective, at least up to now. In these conditions, the grandiloquent discourse on the emergence of 'civil society' is laughable. The civil society in question is tolerated—even encouraged—quite simply because it leaves people helpless and powerless (*Implosion*, Chapter 1).

In the peripheries, in general, the government is hardly more than the tool of local servants of domination by the imperialist monopolies of the triad. This new subaltern oligarchy, which has replaced the earlier national historical blocs, does not have sufficient legitimacy on which to base its power and can resort only to the permanent exercise of violence. This general observation, however, does not accurately describe the situation in several emergent countries (China in particular) and in countries still resisting imperialist domination (Cuba, Vietnam, some Latin American countries). It is clear that collective imperialism does not tolerate any refusal to submit completely to the requirements of the form of globalization it has constructed. The ambition of any government that wants to assert itself on the world stage as a national capitalism (I am not talking about socialist projects that want to go beyond capitalism) and become an active participant in fashioning the world system encounters the firm determination of the triad to deny it this right, as we can see in the fierce hostility towards Russia. Another globalization, based on multipolarity, is simply unacceptable for the triad. Consequently, the powers of the triad are involved in a permanent war against the rest of the world because no nation can indefinitely tolerate the unconditional submission demanded.

The current system of liberal globalization is not viable. The extreme centralization of power to the exclusive benefit of the oligarchies is manifested in the endless increase in the unequal distribution of income and wealth functioning on a stagnant economic base in the historical centres and, of course, it is also manifested in the over-exploitation of labour in the dominated peripheries and the pillage of their natural resources. This contradiction is only overcome by the endless headlong rush into more financialization of economic life. One might think that such a system is irrational. In this vein, reformers such as Joseph Stiglitz, Amartya Sen, and others claim that it would just be necessary to control financialization to get out of the impasse. They quite simply forget that the oligarchy draws its privileges from this system, which might be absurd for everyone else, but is beneficial for it.

The current crisis, then, involves centralization of control over capital. It is thus a systemic crisis. In ordinary crises, characterized by a U-shaped curve, the same economic logic that produces the recession functions, in turn, to foster the recovery after a relatively short interval of a few years during which adjustments are made through the devalorization of capital and the liquidation of uncompetitive companies. By contrast, in a systemic crisis, characterized by an L-shaped curve, the possible recovery would require major structural transformations. In the present context, this would be precisely decentralization of economic control both at the national level in the centres and at the level of the world system. Faced with the determined opposition of the oligarchy, an effective reform necessarily implies the formulation of a radical project, one that opens the way to a challenge to capitalism itself (*Implosion*, Chapter 4). Since there is nothing to indicate that such a radicalization is on the agenda, the systemic crisis, which began in the 1970s, is far from having reached its end.

The modern world experienced its first systemic crisis beginning exactly one century before the second. Capital responded to that by a leap forward in the concentration of capital (the first monopolies at the end of the nineteenth century), the deepening of colonial globalization, and financialization managed by the City of that era, exactly as it has done to deal with the current systemic crisis, and with results just as unconvincing (*Ending the Crisis*, Introduction). The *belle époque* (for capital!) of illusions (1900–1914) was quite short. The response that history gave to this first systemic crisis was: the First World War, the Russian Revolution, the 1929 crisis, Nazism, the Second World War, the Chinese Revolution, and the reconquest of independence by the people of Asia and Africa. Nothing less! These responses were thus spread out over a wide spectrum: socialist revolution, fascism, consistent reformism, and national independence. Why, then, would this second crisis we are now living through not call for responses just as varied: a second wave of socialist revolutions, but also a second wave of fascisms?

As always, it is impossible to give any definite response to the question of the future, which is always open. But we can—should, even—attempt to outline possible responses by continually analysing current social, political, and ideological struggles and their articulation with international conflicts, particularly with the major conflict between the collective imperialism of the triad and the rest of the world. We may begin by examining the gigantic transformations in the social composition of countries in the North, South, and East. Here I shall outline what I believe are the most essential points.

In the developed centres, it is said that the working class—reduced to that fraction concentrated in the large factories of the Fordist era—is in numerical and political decline. Yet at the same time, proletarian status—defined as the situation of a worker who has nothing to sell but his or her labour power—is becoming more widespread. Already more than 80 per cent of workers are wage earners, among which I think it is useful to distinguish those who produce surplus value (the great majority) from those who do not (a minority) or are even (a small minority) direct servants of the managers of capital (*Three Essays*, part III). Independent workers are also sellers of labour power. Their independence is only an appearance because, in fact, they sell their services as sub-contractors to capital.

But simultaneous with the rise in proletarianization is its extreme segmentation based on numerous criteria (women, youth, immigrants, the precariously employed and unemployed, etc.) (*Implosion*, Chapter 1). The immediate consequence of this segmentation, systematically implemented by current policies, is that the proletarianized population encounters great difficulties in its struggles to move from defending its gains to the formulation of radical reforms, which is complicated by their disinvolvement in discredited political parties. This situation results in the spread of illusions, the most serious of which encourage the rebirth of various kinds of fascism. But it also results in the naive idea advanced by postmodernist currents that civil society is capable of 'changing life', while it is not even able to 'change the government'! The centre of gravity of struggles, then, is displaced towards fields of action viewed as critical for certain aspects of social life, particularly gender and ecological challenges. Let me be clear that I do not believe that these are minor problems, far from it. Marx already included in his critique the disequilibrium produced by the logic of capitalism in the metabolism between nature and human beings, a disequilibrium that has since become extremely dangerous. What many contemporary ecologists do not understand, unfortunately, is that re-establishing the equilibrium is impossible without a radical break with the logic of capital. Furthermore, it is unfortunately true historically that socialist movements have rarely acknowledged the central importance of relations between men and women. 'First make the revolution, then deal with this problem.' No, struggles on these two fronts are inseparable. No social advance is possible without a simultaneous advance in gender relations, at each stage of humanity's movement towards emancipation. No solid advance will be possible without an articulation of all struggles in a conscious, overall movement that would then be capable of attacking and destroying the fortress of generalized-monopoly capitalism.

Unfortunately, it is clear that the current struggles in the West are occurring without any interest in what is happening elsewhere in the world. Anti-imperialist solidarity has disappeared. Wars launched by the imperialist oligarchies are even supported and there is little awareness of the lie that hides the reality of the objectives of such wars. This is not the least of the successes of the dictatorship of the oligarchies and the use they make of their media clergy.

The changes that have affected the societies of the South and the formerly socialist East in recent decades have been equally large. Although these social transformations appear to be different from one country to another, they all follow the same logic, imposed by neoliberal imperialist globalization. Consequently, these changes have been much more dramatic in their social, political, and economic effects than in the dominant centres.

The dominant major tendency has been to accelerate the processes that destroy the peasant societies that previously encompassed a large majority of the population in Asia and Africa. The peasant question immediately raises, with violent clarity, the related question of unequal relations between men and women because the destruction of rural societies always ends in more poverty and oppression of women. I have analysed the forms taken by this accelerated and extremely brutal destruction elsewhere (*Ending the Crisis*, Chapter 5). This destruction is not compensated by the necessary rate of increase in urban employment to alleviate the resulting human tragedy—and cannot be. Historical imperialist capitalism has nothing to offer other than the construction of a planet of slums. Obviously, desperate migratory pressures are also a consequence of this process of large-scale pauperization. In urban areas, pauperization is expressed in the very rapid growth of survival activities, which are described as informal employment.

The systematic policies of planned exclusion that are implemented make possible the over-exploitation of subcontract labour to the benefit of monopoly capital.

Concomitant with these tragic developments that affect the vast majority of the people in these countries—60 to 80 per cent of the population—the process of liberal globalization encourages the rapid growth of new middle classes composed of the minority that is integrated into the system of production. This minority—most often of negligible numbers 50 years ago—today sometimes encompasses around a fifth of the population in these countries. This minority is clearly aware that it is the sole beneficiary of the system. The indiscriminate praise lavished by pro-imperialist propaganda instruments (World Bank and others) on the rise of this new middle class quite simply ignores that its price is nothing less than the pauperization of the majority.

This specific form of proletarianization or pauperization creates a political situation that is difficult to manage. The dictatorship of local oligarchies subjected to the commands of the imperialist triad has, consequently, become the only way to manage this permanent crisis. The political personnel who had carried out responsibility for the national popular governments in the earlier stage—the era of Bandung and Nonalignment, between 1960 and 1980—often subsequently aligned themselves with the new globalization in the hope of remaining in power and of being tolerated by the masters of the triad, as we can see with the U-turn by Nasser's successors in Egypt, Hafez al-Assad in Syria, and Boumedienne in Algeria, or the changes in the ANC in South Africa, in the Brazilian PT, and others. But the power of the local oligarchies, even when they are supported by the middle classes that benefit from the system, remain illegitimate in the eyes of the pauperized majority, as demonstrated by the explosion of unrest in the Arab world and elsewhere. Yet these movements have not yet succeeded in going beyond the stage of angry outbursts. The viscous character of the class structure produced by the model of lumpen development in question certainly explains the structural weaknesses of the revolts. Thus the way is easily opened to the short-term triumph of backward-looking false alternatives, based on religion or ethnicity.

V

I have attempted to outline in the analyses above my interpretation of the two-fold character of the current systemic crisis: a crisis in the power of the oligarchy tied to an unviable economic model and a crisis of the majority of people who are victims, but incapable of formulating a coherent alternative. This two-fold character of the crisis eliminates for the foreseeable future the possibility of revolutionary advances that would open the way to the surpassing of obsolescent capitalism. I have presented some propositions concerning the first possible steps for a movement that wishes to go beyond capitalism (*Implosion*, Chapter 4).

Some time ago, I was struck by the analogy between our situation and that of the fall of the Western Roman Empire. I gave an evocative title to the conclusion of my book *Class and Nation* (1979): 'Revolution or Decadence?' This book dates back to the beginning of the still ongoing long systemic crisis. The Roman Empire established a system that centralized the draining and use of the tributary surplus it drew from the exploitation of the peoples who made up the empire, a surplus that surpassed the requirements for reproducing and advancing the productive forces of that time period: everything went to Rome and its Italian provinces. This over-centralized drain of surplus eliminated the possibilities for progress in the empire's provinces (Rome's 'peripheries'). To overcome this blocked progress, then, it was necessary to make the empire explode, that is, for the provinces to 'delink'. Simultaneously, the partial redistribution of the surplus to the Roman plebeians, corrupted by 'bread and circuses', eliminated any revolutionary prospect at the centre of the system. The Roman Empire thus collapsed into chaos. The feudal system, characterized precisely by the decentralization of the draining and use of the surplus, had the way paved for it only 'by force of circumstances', with barbarian invasions and political chaos occurring for centuries. This is why we do not refer to a 'feudal revolution', but to Roman decadence. It was nearly ten centuries before the new decentralized system gave rise to a renaissance of civilization in feudal clothes, based on progress disseminated across Europe.

The contemporary system also suffers from an excessive centralization of the surplus, now drained in the forms of globalized capitalism. This over-centralization weakens the aspirations of people in the imperialist centres for a radical transformation of the system and simultaneously condemns people in the peripheries to a *lumpen development* with no prospects. Meeting the challenge requires the peripheries to delink and substitute sovereign national projects for unending adjustment to the impasse entailed in the exigencies of imperialist globalization.

The analogy inspired me to work out two possible forms of transition from one system to a higher stage of civilization. The higher form, which could be called revolutionary, is produced when, faced with a mode of production that has exhausted its historical potential, the societies in question consciously and intentionally construct a possible and effective alternative. To varying degrees, the bourgeois revolutions and the first wave of socialist revolutions may be viewed in this way and thus merit their description as revolutions. But history obliges us to take the other form of transition into account, which occurs without the active and conscious intervention of social actors. The passage to European feudalism provides a good example. It is precisely the real historical existence of these two forms of possible social evolution that caused me to reject the determinist interpretation of some historical Marxist schools and emphasize the under-determination of instances.

Certainly, feudal decentralization was not the 'end of history' any more than is the one I am proposing today through a deconstruction of the current form of globalization. Feudal deconstruction was itself gradually surpassed by a reconstruction of a centralized surplus. This reconstruction occurred in two stages. In the first one, the absolute monarchies of the *ancien régime* imposed a new national centralization in close relation with the European mercantilist system, itself really a transition to complete historical capitalism. In the second stage, in the nineteenth and twentieth centuries, the construction of capitalist/imperialist globalization completed the centralization, now operating on a world scale. In a similar way, we could imagine the long transition to communism, viewed as a higher stage of civilization, occurring in two steps: first, through the deconstruction of imperialist globalization followed by the reconstruction of a truly alternate globalization based on the fundamental principle of the solidarity of individuals and peoples in place of the principle of competition between capitals and nations. I will not venture any further in a vain attempt to describe a better future and specify what would be uniform on a world scale and what would fortunately not be so. The future is open and will be what people make it. I am satisfied with tackling issues related to what the immediate, necessary, and possible responses are to the challenge, in other words, strategies for the initial steps in a possible advance in the desired direction.

Unfortunately, there is no reason to exclude the alternative of 'civilization's suicide'. History is cluttered with the corpses of societies that were not able to overcome their contradictions, which then became fatal. Marx already made that observation, resolutely choosing a non-determinist view of history. A mismatch among the instances can become fatal. This is expressed through the continual renewal of alienations that are superimposed on one another. The commodity alienation characteristic of capitalism and the alienations from earlier history mutually reinforce one another. Clarity of awareness, that is, the capacity to understand the nature of the system's contradictions and issues and on that basis formulate a coherent alternative and effective strategies of action, seems to be absent from contemporary history. The lucid social actor has disappeared. This is what happened in the Roman Empire. The people of that time paid the price by sinking into barbarism for centuries. But while the Europe of that time succeeded in surviving the disaster, would the same thing happen in our era when the established governments have incomparable means of destruction?

Perhaps between the two extreme situations outlined here (the highest possible revolutionary awareness or its total absence) there are other 'intermediate' possibilities: partial awareness emerges from particular struggles, for example, from the struggles of peasants or women for the defence of human commons or the struggle for respect of popular sovereignty. The progress of the convergence of these particular types of awareness would make it possible to advance towards the formulation of new ways to surpass capitalism. But note: it is not a question of simply evading a forced optimism. Increased awareness will not happen through successive adaptations to the requirements of capitalist accumulation, but through awareness of the necessity of breaking with those requirements. The most enlightened segments of the movement should not isolate themselves by brandishing their disdain for others. Rather, they should involve themselves in all struggles in order to help the others to advance their understanding.

POSTSCRIPT

The attentive reader will have quickly seen that this article owes much to the line of thinking to which Paul Baran, Paul Sweezy, and

Harry Magdoff made decisive contributions. The text mentions them only in passing, but always in connection with points of prime importance. As I have noted elsewhere, I have closely read and re-read *Capital* four times during my life. It was in the 1960s that I first read Baran and Sweezy's works and then met them personally. As a result, new light was shed on my second reading of *Capital*. Since then, all of my major works have followed the line of thinking pioneered by Baran and Sweezy in *Monopoly Capital*. Like them, I understood that it was necessary to move on from reading *Capital* and Marx more generally to studying capitalism; that we had to leave behind exegesis and dare to go beyond the founding texts. Here I would like to note some salient points concerning our community of thought.

- Examination of an abstract model of 'pure' capitalism demonstrates that this system is not viable. Expanded reproduction of capital requires a growth in real wages commensurate with the increase in productivity. The subjection of workers to the diktat of capital does not allow for that. That is why Sweezy was right to say (as I recall) that it is not crises that are the problem requiring an explanation, but the existence of periods of prosperity. The discovery of the reality of the surplus and its conceptualization are essential for anyone who wants to interpret reality in its historical development, i.e., to interpret capitalism. Yet this way of interpreting the history of capitalism's development is still a minority position within the variety of historical Marxisms.
- The interpretation of historical capitalism can only be that of globalized capitalism and not that of its different (national) segments examined in isolation. In the debate on the origins of capitalism, Sweezy had already clearly adopted this position, also a minority view in the schools of historical Marxism.
- The propositions that I have made to conceptualize a law

of globalized value attempt to specify the conditions for absorption of the surplus on the global scale. In this view, imperialist rent is a decisive aspect of the monopoly rent operational in the law of globalized value. I refer to this briefly in the preceding analysis and in more detail in some of my other analyses published in *Monthly Review*.

July 01, 2016

AMIN'S WORKS REFERENCED IN TEXT

Class and Nation, Historically and in the Current Crisis (Monthly Review Press, 1980)

Ending the Crisis of Capitalism or Ending Capitalism? (London: Pambazuka Press, 2010). (Introduction; Chapter 5: Peasant Agriculture and Modern Family Agriculture)

The Implosion of Contemporary Capitalism (Monthly Review Press, 2013)

The Law of Worldwide Value (New York: Monthly Review Press, 2013)

Spectres of Capitalism: A Critique of Current Intellectual Fashions (Monthly Review Press, 1988). (Chapter 3: Is Social History Marked by Over-Determination or Under-Determination; Chapter 4: Social Revolution and Cultural Revolution; Chapter 5: From the Dominance of Economics to the Dominance of Culture: The Withering Away of the Law of Value and the Transition to Communism)

Three Essays on Marx's Value Theory (Monthly Review Press, 2013). (I: Social Value and the Price-Income System; II: The Surplus in Monopoly Capitalism and the Imperialist Rent; III: Abstract Labour and the Wage-Scale)

'Is Transnational Capitalism in the Process of Emerging', *Pambazuka News*, March 23, 2011.

'Contemporary Imperialism', *Monthly Review* 67, No. 3, July–August 2015, pp. 23–36.

REVOLUTION FROM NORTH TO SOUTH

The North-South conflict between centres and peripheries is a central factor throughout the entire history of capitalist development. Historical capitalism merges with the history of the world's conquest by Europeans and their descendants, who were victorious from 1492 to 1914. This success provided the foundation for its own legitimacy. With the presumption of superiority, the European system became synonymous with modernity and progress. Eurocentrism flourished in these circumstances and the peoples of the imperialist centres were persuaded of their 'preferential' right to the world's wealth.

We have been witness to a fundamental transformation in this phase of history. The South has been slowly awakening, clearly apparent during the twentieth century, from the revolutions undertaken in the name of socialism, first in the Russian semi-periphery, then in the peripheries of China, Vietnam, and Cuba, to the national liberation movements in Asia and Africa and the advances in Latin America. The liberation struggles of peoples in the South—increasingly victorious—have been and still are closely linked with the challenge to capitalism. This conjunction is inevitable. The conflicts between capitalism and socialism and between North and South are inseparable. No socialism is imaginable outside of universalism, which implies the equality of peoples.

In the countries of the South, most people are victims of the system, whereas in the North, the majority are its beneficiaries. Both know it perfectly well, although often they are either resigned to it (in the South) or welcome it (in the North). It is not by accident, then, that radical transformation of the system is not on the agenda in the North whereas the South is still the 'zone of storms', of continual revolts, some of which are potentially revolutionary. Consequently, actions by peoples from the South have been decisive in the transformation of the world. Taking note of this fact allows us to contextualize class struggles in the North properly: they have been focused on economic demands that generally do not call the imperialist world order into question. For their part, revolts in the South, when they are radicalized, come up against the challenges of underdevelopment. Their 'socialisms', consequently, always include contradictions between initial intentions and the reality of what is possible. The possible, but difficult, conjunction between the struggles of peoples in the South with those of peoples in the North is the only way to overcome the limitations of both.

European Marxism of the Second International ignored this essential aspect of capitalist reality. It viewed capitalist expansion as homogenizing (whereas it is polarizing) and consequently attributed a positive historical function to colonialism. Lenin broke with this simplified interpretation of Marxism, which allowed him to lead a socialist revolution in a semi-periphery of that era—his 'weak link'. But Lenin thought that the revolution would rapidly spread from his country to the advanced European centres. That did not happen. Lenin had underestimated the devastating effects of imperialism in those societies. Mao went further in his conception and implemented a revolutionary strategy in a country even more peripheral than Russia.

The central reality of the imperialist character of historical capitalism implies an inescapable correlate: the long transition to socialism occurs through unequal advances, mainly originating in the peripheries of the world system. There is no 'world revolution' on the agenda whose centre of gravity would be found in the advanced centres. Lenin, Mao, Ho Chi Minh, and Castro understood that and accepted the challenge of 'constructing socialism in one country'. Trotsky never understood that. The limits of what was achievable in these conditions, beginning with the heritage of the 'backward' capitalism found in the peripheries, accounts for the later history of the twentieth century's great revolutions, including their deviations and failures.

In the other countries of the peripheries, the first victorious struggles that transformed the world were the product of the great popular anti-imperialist movements. Nevertheless, the leaders of these movements had not properly assessed the necessity of combining the objectives of national liberation with a break from the logic of capitalism. Instead, these movements fostered the myth of 'catching up' with the centres by capitalist means within globalized capitalism in the aim of building national capitalisms developed along the same lines as those found in the centres. Consequently, the changes that could have been achieved by what I have called 'national popular' governments were in reality quite limited, and their rapid exhaustion soon collapsed into chaos.

The challenge from the socialist revolutions lay behind the fascist direction taken by the counterrevolution in the imperialist centres. Fascism simultaneously sharpened inter-imperialist conflicts, particularly between Nazi Germany and Japan, on one side, and their major opponents—the United States and Great Britain—on the other. These circumstances account for the alliance of convenience between the U.S.S.R., the United States, and the United Kingdom during the Second World War. It is easy to understand, then, why this alliance was ended by the Western powers in 1945.

The exhaustion of the possibilities in the socialist and national populist transitions has not, by itself, opened the way to new advances in the East, South, or West. The important political forces behind the original successes, and *a fortiori* the peoples involved, have not properly assessed the reasons behind the limitations inherent to the advances of the twentieth century. This is why the current counterrevolution led by the historical imperialist powers (the United States, Europe, and Japan) has been able to exploit the resulting chaos. For the time being, this chaos instead encourages illusory responses adopted by projects of so-called 'emergence' on the part of some countries in the South as well as the irrational, and consequently fascist, deviations of others (as shown by the examples of reactionary political Islam and reactionary political Hinduism). In the imperialist centres themselves, the capitulation of socialist and national populist projects has not encouraged any critical analysis of capitalism, but, on the contrary, reinforces illusions on the virtues of advanced capitalism. Here the victory of the counterrevolution and the retreat from earlier accomplishments (the Welfare State) encourage, in turn, the rebirth of neofascist responses.

In this article, I will discuss the reasons behind the power-lessness of the working classes in the countries of the central imperialist triad of the United States, Europe, and Japan. This analysis emphasizes the political cultures of the peoples involved. A political culture is the product of a long history, which is always, of course, specific to each country. Perhaps the reader will consider my 'judgements' a little too harsh. They are indeed. My observations of the South are no less so. Incidentally, political cultures are not transhistorical invariants. They change, sometimes for the worse, but just as often for the better. What is more, I believe that the construction of 'convergence in diversity' within a socialist perspective requires such change.

UNITED STATES

The political culture of the United States is not the same as the one that took form in France beginning with the Enlightenment and, above all, the Revolution. The heritage of those two signal events has, to various extents, marked the history of a large part of the European continent. U.S. political culture has quite different characteristics. The particular form of Protestantism established in New England served to legitimize the new U.S. society and its conquest of the continent in terms drawn from the Bible. The genocide of the Native Americans is a natural part of the new chosen people's divine mission. Subsequently, the United States extended to the entire world the project of realizing the work that 'God' had ordered it to accomplish. The people of the United States live as the 'chosen people'.

Of course, the American ideology is not the cause of U.S. imperialist expansion. The latter follows the logic of capital accumulation and serves the interests of capital (which are quite material). But this ideology is perfectly suited to this process. It confuses the issue. The 'American Revolution' was only a war of independence without social import. In their revolt against the English monarchy, the American colonists in no way wanted to transform economic and social relations, but simply no longer wanted to share the profits from those relations with the ruling class of the mother country. Their main objective was above all westward expansion. Maintaining slavery was also, in this context, unquestioned. Many of the revolution's major leaders were slave owners, and their prejudices in this area were unshakeable.

Successive waves of immigration also played a role in reinforcing American ideology. The immigrants were certainly not responsible for the poverty and oppression that lay behind their departure for the United States. But their emigration led them to give up collective struggle to change the shared conditions of their classes or groups in their native countries, and adopt instead the ideology of individual success in their adopted home. Adopting such an ideology delayed the acquisition of class consciousness. Once it began to mature, this developing consciousness had to face a new wave of immigrants, resulting in renewed failure to achieve the requisite political consciousness. Simultaneously, this immigration encouraged the 'communitarianization' of U.S. society. 'Individual success' does not exclude inclusion in a community of origin, without which individual isolation might become insupportable. The reinforcement of this dimension of identity—which the U.S. system reclaims and encourages—is done to the detriment of class consciousness and the forming of citizens. Communitarian ideologies cannot be a substitute for the absence of a socialist ideology in the working class. This is true even of the most radical of them, that of the black community.

The specific combination of factors in the historical formation of U.S. society—dominant 'biblical' religious ideology and absence of a workers' party—has resulted in government by a *de facto* single party, the party of capital. The two segments that make up this single party share the same fundamental liberalism. Both focus their attention solely on the minority who 'participate' in the truncated and powerless democratic life on offer. Each has its supporters in the middle classes, since the working classes seldom vote, and has adapted its language to them. Each encapsulates a conglomerate of segmentary capitalist interests (the 'lobbies') and supporters from various 'communities'. American democracy is today the advanced model of what I call 'low-intensity democracy'. It operates on the basis of a complete separation between the management of political life, grounded on the practice of electoral democracy, and the management of economic life, governed by the laws of capital accumulation. Moreover, this separation is not questioned in any substantial way, but is, rather, part of what is called the general consensus. Yet that separation eliminates all the creative potential found in political democracy. It emasculates the representative institutions (parliaments and others), which are made powerless in the face of the 'market' whose dictates must be accepted. Marx thought that the construction of a 'pure' capitalism in the United States, without any pre-capitalist antecedent, was an advantage for the socialist struggle. I think, on the contrary, that the devastating effects of this 'pure' capitalism are the most serious obstacles imaginable.

The avowed objective of the United States' new hegemonic strategy is not to tolerate the existence of any power capable of resisting Washington's commands. To accomplish that, it seeks to break up all countries considered to be 'too large' and create the maximum number of rump states, easy prey for the establishment of U.S. bases to ensure their 'protection'. Only one state has the right to be 'large': the United States. Its global strategy has five objectives: neutralize and subjugate the other partners in the triad (Europe and Japan) and minimize their ability to act outside of American control; establish NATO's military control of and 'Latin Americanize' parts of the former Soviet world; assume sole control of the Middle East and Central Asia and their petroleum resources; break up China, secure the subordination of other large states (India, Brazil), and prevent the formation of regional blocs that would be able to negotiate the terms of globalization; and marginalize regions of the South with no strategic interest. The hegemonic ambitions of the United States are ultimately based more on the outsized importance of its military power than on the 'advantages' of its economic system. It can then pose as uncontested leader of the triad by making its military power and NATO, which it dominates, the 'visible fist' in charge of imposing the new imperialist order on all possible recalcitrants.

Behind this facade there is still a people, of course, despite its evident political weaknesses. Nevertheless, my intuition is that the initiative for change will not come from there, even if it is not impossible that the American drive for hegemony will subsequently come to clash with others, which could begin the movement for a fundamental transformation.

Can Canada or Australia be something other than an external province of the United States? It is difficult to imagine another Canada, despite the political traditions of English Canada and Quebec's cultural specificity. The major political forces—polarized along the linguistic dimension of their resistance—do not envision a delinking of the Canadian economy from the economy of their large neighbour to the south.

JAPAN

Japan has a dominant capitalist economy and, at the same time, a non-European cultural ancestry. The question is which of these two dimensions will gain the upper hand: solidarity with its partners in the 'triad' (United States and Europe) against the rest of the world, or the desire for independence, supported by 'Asianism'? Analyses—even wild imaginings—on this topic could fill an entire library.

A geopolitical analysis of the contemporary world leads me to conclude that Japan will continue to follow Washington, just like Germany, and for the same reasons. I note here the long-term significance of Washington's strategic choices following the Second World War. The United States had then chosen not to destroy its two enemies—the only ones to have threatened the inexorable growth of the United States toward world hegemony—but, rather, to assist their reconstruction and push them to become faithful allies. The obvious reason is that, at the time, there was a real 'communist' threat. But even today, Beijing remains an enemy as can be seen in the conflict over islands in the South China Sea.

Are there any indications of a popular and national reaction? Certainly, the slowing down of the economic miracle and the ossification of the single ruling party have barely breached the facade of conformism. But behind this is hidden, perhaps, an inferiority complex toward China, which frequently reappears. Yet, a rapprochement with China, possibly motivated by a challenge to this conformism, does not seem likely. First, because Japan's dominant imperialist capital remains what it is. Second, because the Chinese and Koreans know it, even beyond their justified suspicion toward their former enemy.

UNITED KINGDOM AND FRANCE

Is there more of a chance for a change beginning in Europe than in the United States? Intuitively, I believe so. The first reason for this relative optimism is because the nations of Europe have a rich history as the incredible accumulation of its imposing medieval vestiges indicates. My interpretation of this history is certainly not the same as dominant Eurocentrism, whose myths I have rejected. The counter-thesis I have developed is that the same contradictions characteristic of medieval society that were surpassed by the advent of modernity occur elsewhere. Yet I reject with equal determination the 'anti-European' ranting of some third world intellectuals who probably want to be convinced that their societies were more advanced than those of 'backward' medieval Europe, ignoring the fact that the myth of the backward Middle Ages is itself a product of the later perspective of European modernity. In any case, having been the first to cross the threshold of modernity, Europe has since acquired advantages that I believe would be absurd to deny. Of course, Europe is diverse, despite a certain homogenization underway and a 'European' discourse. England and France are the pioneers of modernity. This blunt assertion does not mean that modernity did not have earlier roots, particularly in Italian cities and later in the Netherlands.

England went through a very tumultuous period of its history during the birth of new capitalist (or more precisely, mercantilist) relations. It was transformed from medieval 'Merry England' into sombre puritan England, executed its king, and proclaimed a republic in the seventeenth century. Then everything was calm. It invented modern democracy, albeit with restrictions, in the eighteenth century and then in the nineteenth experienced an open-ended accumulation of capital during the Industrial Revolution without major upheavals. Certainly, this did not happen without class conflict, which culminated in the Chartist movement in the middle of the nineteenth century. But these conflicts were not politicized to the point of calling the entire system into question.

France, in contrast, crossed the same stages through an uninterrupted series of violent political conflicts. It is the French Revolution that invented the political and cultural dimensions of capitalism's contradictory modernity. The French working classes were not as clearly developed as in England, which had the only true proletarians of the time. Yet their struggles were more politicized, beginning in 1793, and then in 1848, 1871, and much later in 1936. At the latter time, they were organized around socialist objectives, in the strong sense of the term.

There have certainly been many explanations given for these different paths. Marx was quite aware of them and it is no accident that he devoted most of his attention to analysing these two societies, offering a critique of the capitalist economy from England's experience and a critique of modern politics from France's experience.

Britain's past, perhaps, explains the present, the patience with which the British people endure the degradation of their society. Perhaps this passivity is explained by the way British national pride has been shifted to the United States. The latter is not, for the British, a foreign country like others. It remains a prodigal child. Since 1945, England has chosen to align itself unconditionally with Washington. The extraordinary world domination of the English language helps the English people live this decline without, perhaps, even feeling it to the fullest extent. The English relive their past glory by proxy through the United States.

The United Kingdom remains a key power for Europe's future. Although Brexit heralds the inevitable breakdown of the absurd European construction, the political currents that lie behind its victory in the referendum do not question either liberalism's reactionary social order or alignment with the United States. Moreover, in the system of globalized liberalism, the City, Wall

Street's privileged partner, remains in a strong position, and financial capital on the continent cannot do without its services. Nevertheless, history has no more reached its end in Great Britain than elsewhere. But my feeling is that this country will be able to rejoin the path of change once it cuts the umbilical cord attaching it to the United States. Today, no sign of such a break is visible.

GERMANY

Germany and Japan are the two reliable lieutenants of the United States, forming the real triad, the G3—United States, Germany, and Japan, rather than North America, Europe, Japan.

Neither Germany nor Italy nor Russia would have succeeded in reaching capitalist modernity without the paths pioneered by England and France. That statement should not be understood to mean that the peoples of these countries would have been, for some mysterious reason, incapable of inventing capitalist modernity, solely reserved to Anglo-French genius. Rather, the possibilities for a similar invention existed only in other areas of the world—China, India, or Japan, for example. But once a people entered capitalist modernity, it shaped that people's path, leading to the creation of either a new centre or a dominated periphery.

I interpret the history of Germany using that fundamental method. In this way, I understand German nationalism, pushed by Prussian ambitions, as a compensation for the mediocrity of its bourgeoisie, deplored by Marx. The result was an autocratic form of managing the new capitalism. Yet, despite its ethnicist tone, this nationalism (in contrast with the universalist ideologies found in England and, above all, in France, and later Russia) did not succeed in uniting all Germans (hence the eternal problem of the Austrian Anschluss, still unresolved today). This, then, became a factor that favoured the criminal and demented excesses of Nazism. But there was also, after the disaster, a powerful motivation for constructing what some have called 'Rhenish capitalism', supported by the United States. This is a capitalist form that deliberately chose democratization copied from the Anglo-French-American model. But it is without deep, local historical roots, even considering the brief existence of the Weimar Republic (the only prior democratic period of German history) and the ambiguities, to say the least, of socialism in East Germany. 'Rhenish capitalism' is not a 'good capitalism' in contrast with the Anglo-American extreme liberal model or the statism of 'Jacobin' France. Each is different, but all are ill from the same illness, i.e., a capitalism that has reached a stage characterized by predominance of its destructive aspects. Moreover, the sun has now set on 'Rhenish' and 'statist' capitalisms. Globalized Anglo-American capitalism has imposed its model on all of Europe and Japan.

In the short term, Germany's position in globalization under U.S. hegemony, just like Japan's, seems to be comfortable. Resumption of expansion to the East through a type of 'Latino-Americanization' of East European countries can encourage the illusion that Berlin's choice is a lasting one. This choice is easily satisfied with low-intensity democracy and economic and social mediocrity, and is reinforced by support for the European Union and the Euro. If the political classes on the Christian Democrat and liberal right and the Social Democrat left continue in their stubborn pursuit of this dead end, we should not exclude the emergence of right-wing, even fascist-type, populisms, though that does not mean they would necessarily be remakes of Nazism. The electoral successes of the National Front in France illustrate the reality of the general danger in Europe.

In the longer term, Germany's difficulties will probably worsen, not improve. Germany's current economic assets are based on standard industrial production methods (mechanical, chemical) that modernize by increasingly incorporating software invented elsewhere. But as in other countries, there is always the possibility that the German people will become aware of the necessity of initiating a real change off the beaten track. I believe that if France (which would then carry Germany along with it) and Russia were to take more initiative, another future for Europe would be possible. This choice could also lead to a resumption of positive movements for change in Mediterranean and Nordic Europe, which have failed up to now.

SOUTHERN EUROPE

Italy was momentarily thrust into the centre of critical analysis and action during the 'long 1968' of the 1970s. The power of the movement was sufficient to influence, in a certain way, the 'centre-left' state of that time, despite the self-confinement of the Italian Communist Party. This happy phase of Italian history is over. Now we can only examine the weaknesses of the society that made it possible. The incompletely developed sense of national citizenship can, perhaps, be explained by the fact that the rulers of the Italian states were most often foreigners. The people generally saw in them only opponents to deceive as much as possible. This weakness was expressed in the emergence of a populism that fed on a rising fascism. In Italy, as in France, the struggle for liberation during the Second World War had been a quasi-civil war. Consequently, the fascists were forced to hide in the decades following 1945 without ever having really disappeared. The country's economy, despite the 'miracle' that had given Italians a good standard of living up until the current crisis, remains fragile. But unreserved support for the European choice, which completely dominates the entire Italian political space, is, I believe, the main reason for the dead end in which the country finds itself.

The same unthinking support for the European project has

strongly contributed to the failure of the popular movements that put an end to fascism in Spain, Portugal, and Greece to realize their radical potential.

This potential was limited in Spain where Francoism simply died from the quiet death of its leader while the transition had been well prepared by the same bourgeoisie that had formed the main support of Spanish fascism. The three components of the workers' and popular movement—socialist, communist, and anarchist—had been eradicated by a dictatorship that continued its bloody repression until the late 1970s, supported by the United States in exchange for anticommunism and the concession of bases to the U.S. military. In 1980, Europe set as a condition for Spain's joining the European Community that it also join NATO— i.e., that it accede to the complete formalization of its submission to Washington's hegemony! The workers' movement attempted to play a role in the transition through its 'workers' committees' formed underground in the 1970s. It was unfortunately obvious that, not having succeeded in gaining the support of other segments of the popular and intellectual classes, this radical wing of the movement could not prevent the reactionary bourgeoisie from controlling the transition.

The revolt of the armed forces in Portugal that ended Salazarism in April 1974 was followed by a huge popular explosion the backbone of which was formed by communists, both from the official Communist Party and from Maoist currents. The defeat of this tendency within the ruling group eliminated the communist leadership to the advantage of all-too-timid socialists. Since then, the political sphere has settled back into sleep.

In Greece also, the choice in favour of Europe was not obvious following the fall of the colonels. During the Second World War, the Communist Party had succeeded, just as in Yugoslavia, in forming a single anti-fascist front. Greece and Yugoslavia not only 'resisted' the German invaders, as others did; they continually fought a real war that played a decisive role in the instantaneous collapse of the Italian armies in 1943, thereby forcing the Germans to station many troops on their territories. The Greek resistance, which became a revolution in 1945, was defeated by the joint intervention of the United States and Great Britain. The Greek right is, moreover, responsible for integrating their country into NATO, within which the European project takes shape, all to the exclusive benefit of the 'cosmopolitan' comprador bourgeoisie.

The deepening of the systemic crisis of monopoly capitalism has led to an unparalleled social disaster in the fragile countries of southern Europe. It also strikes hard at the countries of Eastern Europe, reduced to little more than the semi-colonies of Western Europe, particularly Germany. It is easy to understand, then, the recent emergence of immense popular movements (Syriza in Greece, Podemos in Spain) that have won some exciting victories in their rejection of the extreme austerity policies imposed by Berlin and Brussels. Nevertheless, we must acknowledge that the general opinion in these countries does not yet envision the necessity of deconstructing the European system; most people prefer to bury their heads in the sand and convince themselves that this Europe is reformable. Consequently, their movements continue to be paralysed.

NORTHERN EUROPE

For different reasons, the Nordic countries have maintained, up to now, a suspicious attitude with regard to the European project.

Under the leadership of Olof Palme, Sweden attempted to follow a globalist, internationalist, and neutralist path. Beginning with the country's more recent European choice and the rightward drift of its social-democratic forces, the reversal has been quite abrupt. This reversal, however, forces us to look more closely at the weak points of Sweden's exceptional experience: Palme's perhaps too personal role, the illusions of the youth who, long confined to this relatively isolated country, belatedly discovered the world with a good dose of naivety after 1968, but also its somewhat tarnished, and long hidden, past during the Second World War.

Norwegian society was formed from small peasants and fishers, without the presence of an aristocratic class like that of Sweden or Denmark. Thus it is very much alive to questions of equality. This undoubtedly explains the relative power of its extreme left party and the radical proclivities of social democratic forces that, up to now, have resisted the siren's song of Europe. The Greens appeared in this country before organizing in the others. However, the country's membership in NATO and the financial affluence from North Sea oil (an affluence that is somewhat corrupting in the long term) certainly counteract these positive tendencies.

The independence that Finland gained without a struggle during the Russian Revolution (Lenin had already unhesitatingly accepted it) was less the product of a unanimous demand than is often admitted. The Grand Duchy already benefited from a large degree of autonomy in the Russian Empire, which was considered quite satisfactory by opinion at the time. Its ruling classes served the Tsar with as much sincerity as those of the Baltic countries. The working classes were not oblivious to the programme of the Russian Revolution. That is why independence did not settle the country's problems, which were dealt with only at the end of the Civil War, a conflict barely won by the reactionary forces (with the support of imperial Germany, and later the Allies). These forces later drifted toward fascism and became allies of the fascist powers during the Second World War. What is called 'Finlandization', which NATO propaganda presented as unacceptable, was in fact only a neutralism (certainly imposed originally by the peace treaty) that could have formed one of the bases for a better European reconstruction than that of the Atlanticist alliance. Will

European pressures, which have triumphed in the monetary area (with Finland's participation in the Euro), succeed in eating away at this interesting historical heritage?

Can one expect anything from Denmark with an economy that is too dependent on Germany's? This dependence is experienced neurotically, as can be seen in the ambiguous and confused series of votes on the question of the Euro. Yet I do not think that all-too-typical social democratic forces can offer a challenge to the current course. 'The red-green alliance' is, consequently, rather isolated.

It is well known that the Netherlands was the site of the original bourgeois revolution in the seventeenth century, before England and France. But the modest size of the United Provinces prevented this country from achieving what its competitor students were able to do. Although the cultural heritage of this history is not lost, today the economic and financial system of the Netherlands functions within the mark/euro environment.

WHAT FUTURE FOR EUROPE?

In the 1970s and 1980s, I thought that the formation of a North-South 'neutralist' axis in Europe, made up of Sweden, Finland, Austria, Yugoslavia, and Greece, was possible, with positive effects on the countries of both Western and Eastern Europe. It could have encouraged the former to re-think their Atlanticist alignment and might have found a favourable echo in France. Unfortunately, De Gaulle was no longer there and the Gaullists had completely forgotten the general's reservations about NATO. Such an axis might have opened possibilities for East European countries to move toward centre-left positions and thereby avoid their later fall to the right. This project might have initiated the construction of an authentic 'other Europe', truly social and thus open to the formulation of a socialism for the twenty-first century that respected its national components, which would be independent from the United States, and facilitate reform worthy of the name in Soviet bloc countries. This construction was possible, concomitant with the Europe of Brussels, at that time consisting only of a still limited economic community. I was even able to present these ideas to the leadership of the left in the countries concerned and had the impression that the idea did not displease them. But there was no follow-up.

The European lefts have not properly assessed the stakes and have supported the development of the European project led by Brussels. This has been a reactionary project from the beginning, devised by Monnet (whose fiercely anti-democratic opinions are well known, as shown in J.P. Chevènement's book *La Faute de Monsieur Monnet*).[1] The European project, along with the Marshall Plan devised by Washington, was designed to rehabilitate rightist forces (under the cover of 'Christian democracy') or even fascists, reduced to silence by the Second World War, so as to nullify any scope for the practice of political democracy. The Communist parties understood that. But at the time, the alternative of a 'Soviet' Europe was already no longer credible. Their later unconditional adherence to the project was no better, even though it was disguised as 'Eurocommunism'.

Today, not only has the European Union trapped the peoples of the continent in an impasse, consolidated by the 'liberal' and Atlanticist (NATO) choice, but has even become the instrument for the 'Americanization' of Europe, substituting the U.S. culture of 'consensus' for the European tradition's political culture of conflict. The ultimate adherence of Europe to Atlanticism is not unthinkable, based on awareness of the advantages from exploiting the planet for the benefit of the triad's collective imperialism. The 'conflict' with the United States turns around sharing the booty,

[1] Jean-Pierre Chevènement, *La Faute de Monsieur Monnet: La République et l'Europe*, Paris: Fayard, 2006.

hardly more. If ever the project were carried out against everyone, then the European institutions would become the main obstacle to the progress of Europe's peoples.

European reconstruction, then, requires the deconstruction of the current project. Is it even thinkable today to question the European-Atlanticist project such as it is and construct an alternative Europe that would be both social and non-imperialist toward the rest of the world? I think so and even think that the beginning of an alternative project originating from anywhere would find favourable echoes throughout Europe in a short time. An authentic left, in any case, should not think otherwise. If it dares to do so, then I am one of those who believe that the European peoples can demonstrate that they still have an important role to play in shaping a future world. Short of that, the strongest probability is the collapse of the European project into chaos, which would not displease Washington. Europe will be socialist, if the left forces dare to make it so, or it simply will not be.

I believe that the change can only begin if France were to take some courageous initiatives in the right direction. That would then lead Germany to move in the same direction and, consequently, the rest of Europe. The way would then be open for a rapprochement with China and Russia. Europe's status on the international political scene is condemned to insignificance by its support for Washington's project for world domination. If it were to follow the path outlined above, it could then exploit its economic power for the reconstruction of an authentic multipolar world. Failing that, the 'West' will remain American, Europe will remain German, the North-South conflict will continue to be central, and any possible advances will largely be confined to the peripheries of the global system; in other words, a 'remake' of the twentieth century.

In conclusion, I will again point out that the system of neoliberal globalization has entered its last phase; its implosion is clearly visible, as indicated by, among other things, Brexit,

Trump's election, and the rise of various forms of neofascism. The rather inglorious end of this system opens up a potentially revolutionary situation in all parts of the world. But this potential will become reality only if radical left forces know how to seize the opportunities offered and design and implement bold offensive strategies based on the reconstruction of the internationalism of workers and peoples in the face of the cosmopolitanism of the imperialist powers' financial capital. If that does not happen, then the left forces of the West, East, and South will also share responsibility for the ensuing disaster.

July 01, 2017

REVOLUTION OR DECADENCE?

Thoughts on the Transition between Modes of Production on the Occasion of the Marx Bicentennial

INTRODUCTION

Karl Marx is a giant thinker, not just for the nineteenth century, but even more for understanding our contemporary time. No other attempt to develop an understanding of society has been as fertile, provided 'Marxists' move beyond 'Marxology' (simply repeating what Marx was able to write in relation to his own time) and instead pursue his method in accordance with new developments in history. Marx himself continuously developed and revised his views throughout his lifetime.

Marx never reduced capitalism to a new mode of production. He considered all the dimensions of modern capitalist society, understanding that the law of value does not regulate only capitalist accumulation, but rules all aspects of modern civilization. That unique vision allowed him to offer the first scientific approach relating social relations to the wider realm of anthropology. In that perspective, he included in his analyses what is today called 'ecology', rediscovered a century after Marx. John Bellamy Foster, better than anybody else, has cleverly developed this early intuition of Marx.

I have given priority to another intuition of Marx, related to the future of globalization. From my PhD thesis in 1957 to my latest book, I have devoted my efforts to unequal development resulting from a globalized formulation of the law of accumulation. I derived from it an explanation for the revolutions in the name of socialism starting from the peripheries of the global system. The contribution of Paul Baran and Paul Sweezy, introducing the concept of surplus, has been decisive in my attempt.

I also share another intuition of Marx—expressed clearly as early as 1848 and further reformulated until his last writings—according to which capitalism represents only a short bracket in history; its historical function being to have created in a short time (a century) the conditions calling for moving beyond to communism, understood as a higher stage of civilization.

Marx states in the *Manifesto* (1848) that class struggle always results 'either in a revolutionary reconstitution of society at large, or in the common ruin of the contending classes'. That sentence has been at the forefront of my thinking for a long time.

For that reason I offer my reflections on 'Revolution or Decadence?', the concluding chapter of my forthcoming book for the bicentenary of the birth of Marx.

I

The workers' and socialist movement has sustained itself on a vision of a series of revolutions beginning in the advanced capitalist countries. From the criticisms which Marx and Frederick Engels made of the programmes of German social democracy to the conclusions derived by Bolshevism from the experience of the Russian Revolution, the workers' and socialist movement has never conceived of the transition to socialism on the world scale in any other way.

However, over the past seventy-five years the transformation of the world has taken other paths. The perspective of revolution has disappeared from the horizons of the advanced West, while socialist revolutions have been limited to the periphery of the system. These have inaugurated developments of sufficient ambiguity for some people to see them only as a stage in the expansion of capitalism to the world scale. An analysis of the system in terms of unequal development attempts to give a different answer. Beginning with the contemporary imperialist system, this analysis obliges us also to consider the nature and meaning of unequal development in previous historical stages.

The comparative history of the transition from one mode of production to another calls for posing the question of the mode of transition in general and theoretical terms. Thus, similarities between the current situation and the era of the end of the Roman Empire have led those historians who are not proponents of historical materialism to draw parallels between the two situations. On the other hand, a certain dogmatic interpretation of Marxism has used the terminology of historical materialism to obscure thought on this theme. Thus Soviet historians spoke of the 'decadence of Rome', while putting forward the 'socialist revolution' as the only form of substitution of new relations of production for capitalist relations. The following comparative analysis of the form and content of the ancient and the capitalist crises in relations of production addresses this issue. Do the differences between these two crises justify treating one in terms of 'decadence' and the other in terms of 'revolution'?

My central argument is that a definite parallel exists between these two crises. In both cases, the system is in crisis because the centralization of the surplus it organizes is excessive, that is, is in advance of the relations of production that underlie it. Thus the development of the productive forces in the periphery of the system necessitates the breakup of the system and the substitution of a decentralized system for collecting and utilizing the surplus.

II

The most commonly accepted thesis within historical materialism is that of the succession of three modes of production: the slave mode, the feudal mode, and the capitalist mode. In this framework, the decadence of Rome would be only the expression of the transition from slavery to serfdom. It would still remain to explain why we do not speak of a 'feudal revolution' as we speak of bourgeois and socialist revolutions.

I consider this formulation to be West-centred in its overgeneralization of the specific characteristics of the history of the West and its rejection of the history of other peoples in all its particularities. Choosing to derive the laws of historical materialism from universal experience, I have proposed an alternative formulation of one precapitalist mode, the tributary mode, toward which all class societies tend. The history of the West—the construction of Roman antiquity, its disintegration, the establishment of feudal Europe, and, finally, the crystallization of absolutist states in the mercantilist period—thus expresses in a particular form the same basic tendency that elsewhere is expressed in the less discontinuous construction of complete, tributary states, of which China is the strongest expression. The slave mode is not universal, as are the tributary and capitalist modes; it is particular and appears strictly in connection with the extension of commodity relations. In addition, the feudal mode is the primitive, incomplete form of the tributary mode.

This hypothesis views the establishment and subsequent disintegration of Rome as a premature attempt at tributary construction. The level of development of the productive forces did not require tributary centralization on the scale of the Roman Empire. This first abortive attempt was thus followed by a forced transition through feudal fragmentation, on the basis of which centralization was once again restored within the framework of the absolutist monarchies of the West. Only then did the mode of production in the West approach the complete tributary model. It was, furthermore, only beginning with this stage that the previous level of development of the productive forces in the West attained that of the complete tributary mode of imperial China; this is doubtless no coincidence.

The backwardness of the West, expressed by the abortion of Rome and by feudal fragmentation, certainly gave it its historic advantage. Indeed, the combination of specific elements of the ancient tributary mode and of barbarian communal modes characterized feudalism and gave the West its flexibility. This explains the speed with which Europe passed through the complete tributary phase, quickly surpassing the level of development of the productive forces of the West, which it overtook, and passing on to capitalism. This flexibility and speed contrasted with the relatively rigid and slow evolution of the complete tributary modes of the Orient.

Doubtless the Roman-Western case is not the only example of an abortive tributary construction. We can identify at least three other cases of this type, each with its own specific conditions: the Byzantine-Arab-Ottoman case, the Indian case, the Mongol case. In each of these instances, attempts to install tributary systems of centralization were too far ahead of the requirements of the development of the productive forces to be firmly established. In each case, the forms of centralization were probably specific combinations of state, para-feudal, and commodity means. In the Islamic state, for instance, commodity centralization played the decisive role. Successive Indian failures must be related to the contents of Hindu ideology, which I have contrasted with Confucianism. As to the centralization of the empire of Genghis Khan, it was, as we know, extremely short-lived.

III

The contemporary imperialist system is also a system of centralization of the surplus on the world scale. This centralization operates on the basis of the fundamental laws of the capitalist mode and in the conditions of its domination over the precapitalist modes of the subject periphery. I have formulated the law of the accumulation of capital on the world scale as a form of expression of the law of value operating on this scale. The imperialist system for the centralization of value is characterized by the acceleration of accumulation and by the development of the productive forces in the centre of the system, while in the periphery these latter are held back and deformed. Development and underdevelopment are two sides of the same coin.

Thus we can see that further development of the productive forces in the periphery requires the destruction of the imperialist system of centralization of the surplus. A necessary phase of decentralization, the establishment of the socialist transition within nations must precede the reunification at a higher level of development, which a planetary classless society would constitute. This central thesis has several consequences for the theory and strategy of the socialist transition.

In the periphery, the socialist transition is not distinct from national liberation. It has become clear that the latter is impossible under local bourgeois leadership, and thus becomes a democratic stage in the process of the uninterrupted revolution by stages led by the peasant and worker masses. This fusion of the goals of national liberation and socialism engenders in its turn a series of new problems that we must evaluate. For the emphasis shifts from one aspect to the other, due to which the real movement of society alternates between progress and regression, ambivalences and alienation, particularly in nationalist form. Here again we can make a comparison with the attitude of the barbarians toward the Roman Empire: they were ambivalent toward it, notably in their formal, even slavish, imitation of the Roman model against which they were revolting.

At the same time, the parasitical character of the central society intensifies. In some, imperial tribute corrupted the plebeians and paralyzed their revolt. In the societies of the imperialist centre, a growing portion of the population benefits from unproductive employment and from privileged positions, both concentrated there by the effects of the unequal international division of labour. Thus it is harder to envision disengagement from the imperialist system and formation of an anti-imperialist alliance capable of overturning the hegemonic alliance and inaugurating the transition to socialism.

IV

The introduction of new relations of production seems easier in the periphery than in the centre of the system. In the Roman Empire, feudal relations took hold rapidly in Gaul and Germany, but only slowly in Italy and the East. It is Rome which invented serfdom which replaced slavery. But feudal authority developed elsewhere and feudal relations never fully developed in Italy itself.

Today the feeling of latent revolt against capitalist relations is very strong in the centre, but it is powerless. People want to 'change their lives' but cannot even change the government. Thus progress occurs in the area of social life more than in the organization of production and the state. The silent revolution in lifestyle, the breakup of the family, the collapse of bourgeois values demonstrate this contradictory aspect of the process. In the periphery, customs and ideas are often far less advanced, but socialist states have nonetheless been established there.

Vulgar Marxist tradition has effected a mechanistic reduction of the dialectic of social change. The revolution—the objective content of which is the abolition of old relations of production and the establishment of new relations, the precondition for the further development of the productive forces—is made into a natural law: the application to the social realm of the law by which quantity becomes quality. The class struggle reveals this objective necessity:

only the vanguard—the party—is above the fray, makes and dominates history, is de-alienated. The political moment defining the revolution is that in which the vanguard seizes the state. Leninism itself is not entirely devoid of the positivist reductionism of the Marxism of the Second International.

This theory that separates the vanguard from the class is not applicable to the revolutions of the past. The bourgeois revolution did not take this form: in it the bourgeoisie co-opted the struggle of the peasants against the feudal lords. The ideology that enabled them to do this, far from being a means of manipulation, was itself alienating. In this sense, there was no 'bourgeois revolution'— the term itself is a product of bourgeois ideology—but only a class struggle led by the bourgeoisie or, at most, at times a peasant revolution co-opted by the bourgeoisie. Even less can we speak of the 'feudal revolution', where the transition was made unconsciously.

The socialist revolution will be of a different type, presupposing de-alienated consciousness, because it will aim for the first time at the abolition of all exploitation and not at the substitution of new for old forms of exploitation. But this will be possible only if the ideology animating it becomes something other than the consciousness of the requirements of the development of the productive forces. There is nothing to say, in fact, that the statist mode of production, as a new form of relations of exploitation, is not a possible response to the requirements of this development.

V

Only people make their own history. Neither animals nor inanimate objects control their own evolution; they are subject to it. The concept of praxis is proper to society, as an expression of the synthesis of determinism and human intervention. The dialectic relation of infrastructure and superstructure is also proper to society and has no equivalent in nature. This relation is not unilateral. The superstructure is not the reflection of the needs of the infrastructure. If it were, society would always be alienated and I cannot see how it could become liberated.

This is why I propose to distinguish between two qualitatively different types of transition from one mode to another. When the transition is made unconsciously or by an alienated consciousness, that is, when the ideology animating classes does not allow them to master the process of change, the latter appears to be operating like a natural change, the ideology being part of nature. For this type of transition we can apply the expression 'model of decadence'. In contrast, if and only if the ideology expresses the total and real dimension of the desired change, can we speak of revolution.

Is the socialist revolution in which our era is engaged of the decadent or the revolutionary type? Doubtless we cannot as yet answer this question definitively. In certain aspects, the transformation of the modern world incontestably has a revolutionary character as defined above. The Paris Commune and the revolutions in Russia and China (and particularly the Cultural Revolution) have been moments of intense de-alienated social consciousness. But are we not engaged in another type of transition? The difficulties that make the disengagement of the imperialist countries nearly inconceivable today and the negative impact of this on the peripheral countries following the socialist road (leading to possible capitalist restoration, evolutions toward a statist mode, regression, nationalist alienation, etc.) call into question the old Bolshevik model.

Some people are resigned to this and believe that our time is not one of socialist transition but of worldwide expansion of capitalism which, starting from this 'little corner of Europe', is just beginning to extend to the south and the east. At the end of this transfer, the imperialist phase will appear to have been not the last, the highest stage of capitalism, but a transitional phase toward universal capitalism. And even if one continues to believe that the Leninist theory of imperialism is true and that national liberation is a part of the socialist and not of the bourgeois revolution, would not exceptions, that is, the appearance of new capitalist centres, be possible? This theory emphasizes the restorations or the evolutions toward a statist mode in the Eastern countries. It characterizes as objective processes of capitalist expansion what were only pseudo-socialist revolutions. Here Marxism appears as an alienating ideology masking the true character of these developments.

Those who hold this opinion believe that we must wait until the level of development of the productive forces at the centre is capable of spreading to the entire world before the question of the abolition of classes can really be put on the agenda. Europeans should thus allow the creation of a supranational Europe so that the state superstructure can be adjusted to the productive forces. It will doubtless be necessary to await the establishment of a planetary state corresponding to the level of the productive forces on the world scale, before the objective conditions for superseding it will obtain.

Others, myself among them, see things differently. The uninterrupted revolution by stages is still on the agenda for the periphery. Restorations in the course of the socialist transition are not irrevocable. And breaks in the imperialist front are not inconceivable in the weak links of the centre.

May 01, 2018

THE COMMUNIST MANIFESTO,
170 YEARS LATER

I

There is no other text written in the mid-nineteenth century that has held up as well as *The Communist Manifesto* of 1848 by Karl Marx and Frederick Engels. Even today, entire paragraphs of the text correspond to contemporary reality better than they did to that of 1848. Starting from premises that were hardly visible in their era, Marx and Engels drew the conclusions that the developments of 170 years of history fully verified.

Were Marx and Engels inspired prophets, magicians able to gaze into a crystal ball, exceptional beings with respect to their intuition? No. They simply understood better than anybody else, in their time and ours, the essence of that which defines and characterizes capitalism. Marx devoted his entire life to deepening this analysis through the twofold examination of the new economy, beginning with the example of England, and the new politics, starting from the example of France.[1]

Marx's *Capital* presents a rigorous scientific analysis of the capitalist mode of production and capitalist society, and how they differ from earlier forms. Volume 1 delves into the heart of the problem. It directly clarifies the meaning of the generalization of commodity exchanges between private-property owners (a phenomenon that in its centrality is unique to the modern world of capitalism, though commodity exchanges existed earlier), specifically the emergence and dominance of value and abstract

[1] I wrote about this subject in Chapter 3 of my book *October 1917 Revolution: A Century Later*, Montreal: Daraja, 2017.

social labour. From that foundation, Marx leads us to understand how the proletarian's sale of his or her labour power to the 'man with money' ensures the production of surplus value that the capitalist expropriates, and which, in turn, is the condition for the accumulation of capital. The dominance of value governs not only the reproduction of the economic system of capitalism, but also every aspect of modern social and political life. The concept of commodity alienation points to the ideological mechanism through which the overall unity of social reproduction is expressed.

These intellectual and political instruments, validated by the development of Marxism, demonstrated their worth in correctly predicting the general historical evolution of capitalist reality. No attempt to think about this reality outside of Marxism—or often against it—has led to comparable results. Marx's criticisms of the limitations of bourgeois thought, and in particular of its economic science, which he rightly described as 'vulgar', is masterful. Since it is incapable of understanding what capitalism is in its essential reality, this alienated thought is also unable to imagine where capitalist societies are going. Will the future be forged by socialist revolutions that will put an end to the domination of capital? Or will capitalism succeed in prolonging its days, thus opening the way to the decadence of society? Bourgeois thought ignores this question, posed by the *Manifesto*.

Indeed, we read in the *Manifesto* that there is 'a fight that each time ended either in a revolutionary reconstitution of society at large, or in the common ruin of the contending classes'.[2]

This sentence has attracted my attention for a long time. Starting from it, I have progressively come to formulate a reading of the movement of history focused on the concept of unequal development and the possible different processes for its transformation, originating most probably from its peripheries rather than

---

[2] Karl Marx and Frederick Engels, *The Communist Manifesto*, New York: Monthly Review Press, 1998, p. 2.

its centres. I also made some attempts to clarify each of the two models of response to the challenge: the revolutionary way and the way of decadence.[3]

Choosing to derive the laws of historical materialism from the universal experience, I have proposed an alternative formulation of one unique pre-capitalist mode, that is, the tributary mode, toward which all class societies tend. The history of the West—the construction of Roman antiquity, its disintegration, the establishment of feudal Europe, and, finally, the crystallization of absolutist states of the mercantilist era—thus expresses, in a particular form, the same basic tendency presented elsewhere toward the less discontinuous construction of complete, tributary states, of which China is the strongest example. The slave mode is not universal in our reading of history, as are the tributary and capitalist modes; it is particular and appears strictly in connection to the extension of commodity relations. Furthermore, the feudal mode is the primitive, incomplete form of the tributary mode.

This hypothesis views the establishment and subsequent disintegration of Rome as a premature attempt at tributary construction. The level of development of the productive forces did not require tributary centralization on the scale of the Roman Empire. This first unavailing attempt was thus followed by a forced transition through feudal fragmentation, on the basis of which centralization was once again restored within the framework of the absolutist monarchies of the West. Only then did the mode of production in the West approach the complete tributary model. It was, furthermore, only beginning with this stage that the level of development of the productive forces in the West attained that of the complete tributary mode of imperial China; this is doubtless no coincidence.

The backwardness of the West, expressed by the abortion of

[3] I have further written about this question in the conclusion of my book *Class and Nation*, New York: Monthly Review Press, 1980.

Rome and by feudal fragmentation, certainly gave it its historic advantage. Indeed, the combination of specific elements of the ancient tributary mode and of barbarian communal modes characterized feudalism and gave the West its flexibility. This explains the speed with which Europe experienced the complete tributary phase, quickly surpassing the level of development of the productive forces of the East, which it overtook, and passed on to capitalism. This flexibility and speed contrasted with the relatively rigid and slow evolution of the complete tributary modes of the Orient.

Doubtless the Roman-Western case is not the only example of an abortive tributary construction. We can identify at least three other cases of this type, each with its own specific conditions: the Byzantine-Arab-Ottoman case, the Indian case, and the Mongol case. In each of these instances, attempts to install tributary systems of centralization were too far ahead of the requirements of the development of the productive forces to be firmly established. In each case, the forms of centralization were probably specific combinations of state, para-feudal, and commodity means. In the Islamic state, for instance, commodity centralization played the decisive role. Successive Indian failures must be related to the contents of Hindu ideology, which I have contrasted with Confucianism. As to the centralization of the empire of Genghis Khan, it was, as we know, extremely short-lived.

The contemporary imperialist system is also a system of centralization of surplus on the world scale. This centralization operated on the basis of the fundamental laws of the capitalist mode and the conditions of its domination over the pre-capitalist modes of the subject periphery. I have formulated the law of the accumulation of capital on the world scale as an expression of the law of value operating on this scale. The imperialist system for the centralization of value is characterized by the acceleration of accumulation and by the development of the productive forces in the centre of the system, while in the periphery they are held back and deformed. Development and underdevelopment are two sides of the same coin.

Only people make their own history. Neither animals nor inanimate objects control their own evolution; they are subject to it. The concept of praxis is proper to society, as an expression of the synthesis of determinism and human intervention. The dialectic relation of infrastructure and superstructure is also proper to society and has no equivalent in nature. This relation is not unilateral. The superstructure is not the reflection of the needs of the infrastructure. If this was the case, society would always be alienated and it would not be possible to see how it could succeed in liberating itself.

This is the reason why we propose to differentiate two qualitatively different types of transition from one mode of production to another. If this transition develops in unconsciousness, or with alienated consciousness, that is, if the ideology that influences classes does not allow them to control the process of change, this process appears as if it operates analogously to natural change, with ideology becoming part of this nature. For this type of transition we reserve the expression 'model of decadence'. In contrast, if the ideology captures the real dimension of the desired changes in their totality, only then can we speak of revolution.

Bourgeois thought has to ignore this question in order to be able to think of capitalism as a rational system for all of eternity, to be able to think of 'the end of history'.

II

Marx and Engels, on the contrary, strongly suggest, from the time of the *Manifesto*, that capitalism constitutes only a brief parenthesis in the history of humanity. However, the capitalist mode of production in their time did not extend beyond England, Belgium, a small region of northern France, or the western part of the Prussian Westphalia. Nothing comparable existed in other regions of Europe. In spite of this, Marx already imagined that socialist revolutions would happen in Europe 'soon'. This expectation is evident in each line of the *Manifesto*.

Marx did not know, of course, in which country the revolution would begin. Would it be England, the only country already advanced in capitalism? No. Marx did not think this was possible except if the English proletariat emancipated itself from its support of the colonization of Ireland. Would it be France, less advanced in terms of its capitalist development, but more advanced in terms of the political maturity of its people, inherited from its great revolution? Maybe, and the Paris Commune of 1871 confirmed his intuition. For the same reason, Engels expected much from 'backward' Germany: the proletarian revolution and the bourgeois revolution could here collide together. In the *Manifesto*, they note this connection:

> The Communists turn their attention chiefly to Germany, because that country is on the eve of a bourgeois revolution that is bound to be carried out under more advanced conditions of European civilization and with a more developed proletariat than existed in England in the seventeenth, and in France in the eighteenth century, and because the bourgeois revolution in Germany will be but the prelude to an immediately following proletarian revolution.[4]

This did not happen: the unification under the world-historic crook (Bismarck) of reactionary Prussia, and the cowardice and political mediocrity of the German bourgeoisie permitted nationalism to triumph and marginalized popular revolt. Toward

[4] Marx and Engels, *The Communist Manifesto*, pp. 61–62.

the end of his life, Marx turned his glance in the direction of Russia, which he expected could engage in a revolutionary path, as his correspondence with Vera Zasulich testifies.

Marx thus did have the intuition that the revolutionary transformation could begin from the periphery of the system— the 'weak links', in the later language of Lenin. Marx, however, did not draw in his time all the conclusions that imposed themselves in this respect. It was necessary to wait for history to advance into the twentieth century in order to see, with V.I. Lenin and Mao Zedong, the communists becoming able to imagine a new strategy, qualified as 'the construction of socialism in one country'. This is an inappropriate expression, to which I prefer a long paraphrase: 'Unequal advances on the long path of the socialist transition, localized in some countries, against which the strategy of the dominant imperialism is to fight continuously and seek to severely isolate.'

The debate pertaining to the long historic transition to socialism in the direction of communism, and the universal scope of this movement, poses a series of questions concerning the transformation of the proletariat from a class in itself to a class for itself, the conditions and effects of capitalist globalization, the place of the peasantry in the long transition, and the diversity of expressions of anti-capitalist thought.

III

Marx, more than anyone, understood that capitalism had the mission of conquering the world. He wrote about it at a time when this conquest was far from being completed. He considered this mission from its origins, the discovery of the Americas, which inaugurated the transition of the three centuries of mercantilism to the final full-fledged form of capitalism.

As he wrote in the *Manifesto*, 'Modern industry has established the world-market, for which the discovery of America paved the way . . . The bourgeoisie has through its exploitation of the world-market given a cosmopolitan character to production and consumption in every country.'[5]

Marx welcomed this globalization, the new phenomenon in the history of humanity. Numerous passages in the *Manifesto* testify to this. For example: 'The bourgeoisie, wherever it has got the upper hand, has put an end to all feudal, patriarchal, idyllic relations.'[6] As well as: 'The bourgeoisie has subjected the country to the rule of the towns . . . and has thus rescued a considerable part of the population from the idiocy [isolation—*Ed.*] of rural life. Just as it has made the country dependent on the towns, so it has made barbarian and semi-barbarian countries dependent on the civilized ones, nations of peasants on nations of bourgeois, the East on the West.'[7]

The words are clear. Marx was never past oriented, regretting the good old days. He always expressed a modern point of view, to the point of appearing as a Eurocentrist. He went a long way in this direction. Yet was not the barbarization of urban labour as stultifying for the proletarians? Marx did not ignore the urban poverty that had accompanied capitalist expansion.

Did the Marx of the *Manifesto* measure correctly the political consequences of the destruction of the peasantry in Europe itself and, even more, in the colonized countries? I return to these questions in direct relation to the unequal character of the worldwide deployment of capitalism.

[5] Marx and Engels, *The Communist Manifesto*, pp. 4–8.
[6] Marx and Engels, *The Communist Manifesto*, p. 5.
[7] Marx and Engels, *The Communist Manifesto*, p. 9. ['Idiocy' is a mistranslation, since in classical Greek *Idiotes* referred to isolation from the polis, a meaning carried over in the German—a fact recognized in several translations of the *Manifesto*. See Hal Draper, *The Adventures of the Communist Manifesto*, Berkeley: Center for Socialist History, 1998, p. 211.—*Ed.*]

Marx and Engels, in the *Manifesto*, still do not know that the worldwide deployment of capitalism is not the homogenizing one that they imagine, that is, giving to the conquered East its chance to get out of the deadlock in which its history has closed it and to become, in accordance with the image of the Western countries, 'civilized' nations or industrialized countries. A few texts of Marx present the colonization of India in a consoling light. But Marx later changed his mind. These allusions, rather than constituting a systematically elaborated argumentation, witness the destructive effects of the colonial conquest. Marx gradually becomes aware of what I call unequal development, in other words, the systematic construction of the contrast between the dominant centres and dominated peripheries, and, with it, the impossibility of 'catching up' within the framework of capitalist globalization (imperialistic by its nature) with the tools of capitalism.

In that respect, if it were possible to 'catch up' within capitalist globalization, no political, social, or ideological force would be able to oppose this successfully.

With respect to the question of the 'opening' of China, in the *Manifesto* Marx says that 'the cheap prices of its commodities are the heavy artillery with which it batters down all Chinese walls, with which it forces the barbarians' intensely obstinate hatred of foreigners to capitulate.'[8]

We know that this was not how this opening operated: it was the canons of the British navy that 'opened' China. Chinese products were often more competitive than Western ones. We know also that it was not more advanced English industry that permitted the successful domination of India (again, Indian textiles were of better quality than English ones). On the contrary, it was the domination of India (and the organized destruction of Indian industries) that gave Great Britain its hegemonic position in the capitalist system of the nineteenth century.

[8] Marx and Engels, *The Communist Manifesto*, p. 9.

However, an older Marx learned how to abandon the Eurocentrism of his youth. Marx knew how to change his views, in the light of the evolution of the world.

In 1848, Marx and Engels therefore imagined the strong possibility of one or more socialist revolutions in the Europe of their time, confirming that capitalism represents only a short parenthesis in history. The facts soon proved them right. The Paris Commune of 1871 was the first socialist revolution. However, it was also the last revolution accomplished in a developed capitalist country. With the establishment of the Second International, Engels did not lose hope in new revolutionary advances, in Germany in particular. History proved him wrong. However, the treason of the Second International in 1914 should not have surprised anyone. Beyond their reformist drift, the alignment of workers' parties in all of Europe at the time with the expansionist, colonialist, and imperialist politics of their bourgeoisies indicated that there was not much to expect from the parties of the Second International. The front line for the transformation of the world moved toward the East, to Russia in 1917 and then to China. Certainly Marx did not predict this, but his later texts allow us to suppose that he probably would not have been surprised by the Russian Revolution.

With respect to China, Marx thought that it was a bourgeois revolution that was on the agenda. In January 1850 Marx wrote: 'When our European reactionaries . . . finally arrive at the Great Wall of China . . . who knows if they will not find written thereon the legend: République chinoise, Liberté, Egalité, Fraternité.'[9] The Guomindang of the 1911 revolution, of Sun Yat-sen, also imagined this, like Marx, proclaiming the (bourgeois) Republic of China. However, Sun did not succeed in either defeating the forces of the old regime whose warlords regained the territory, or in pushing

---

[9] Karl Marx and Frederick Engels, *On Colonialism*, New York: International Publishers, 1972, p. 18.

away the dominance of the imperialist forces, especially Japan. The drift of the Guomindang of Chiang Kai-shek confirmed Lenin's and Mao's arguments that there is no more room for an authentic bourgeois revolution; our era is the one of the socialist revolution. Just as the Russian February Revolution of 1917 did not have a future since it was not able to triumph over the old regime, calling therefore for the October Revolution, the Chinese Revolution of 1911 called for the revolution of the Maoist Communists, who were the only ones capable of answering to the expectations of liberation, simultaneously national and social.

It was thus Russia, the 'weak link' of the system, that initiated the second socialist revolution after the Paris Commune. Yet the Russian October Revolution was not supported, but fought by the European workers' movement. Rosa Luxemburg used harsh expressions for the drift of the European workers' movements in this respect. She spoke of their failure, betrayal, and 'the unripeness of the German proletariat for the fulfilment of its historic tasks'.[10]

I have approached this withdrawal of the working class in the developed West, in which they abandoned their revolutionary traditions, by emphasizing the devastating effects of the imperialist expansion of capitalism and the benefits that the imperial societies as a whole (and not only their bourgeoisies) drew from their dominant positions. I have therefore considered it necessary to dedicate an entire chapter in my reading of the universal importance of the October Revolution to the analysis of the development that led the European working classes to renounce their historic tasks, to use the terms of Luxemburg. I refer the reader to Chapter 4 of my book *October 1917 Revolution*.

---

[10] Rosa Luxemburg, *The Russian Revolution*, 1918, available at www.marxists. org.

IV

Revolutionary advances on the long road of the socialist or communist transition will therefore no doubt originate exclusively in the societies of the periphery of the world system, precisely in the countries in which an avant-garde would understand that it is not possible to 'catch up' by integrating into capitalist globalization, and that for this reason something else should be done, that is, to go ahead within a transition of a socialist nature. Lenin and Mao expressed this conviction, proclaiming that our time is no longer the epoch of bourgeois revolutions but instead, from then on, the epoch of socialist revolutions.

This conclusion calls for another: socialist transitions will happen necessarily in one country, which will additionally remain fatally isolated through the counter-attack of world imperialism. There is no alternative; there will be no simultaneous world revolution. Therefore, the nations and states engaged on this road will be confronted with the double challenge: (1) resist the permanent war (hot or cold) conducted by the imperialist forces; and (2) associate successfully with the peasant majority in advancing on the new road to socialism. Neither the *Manifesto*, nor Marx and Engels subsequently, were in a position to say something on these questions; it is the responsibility of living Marxism to do so instead.

These reflections lead me to assess the views that Marx and Engels developed in the *Manifesto* concerning peasants. Marx situates himself within his time, which was still the time of bourgeois unfinished revolutions in Europe itself. In this context, the *Manifesto* reads: 'At this stage, therefore, the proletarians do not fight their enemies, but the enemies of their enemies, the remnants of absolute monarchy, the landowners . . . every victory so obtained is a victory for the bourgeoisie.'[11]

[11] Marx and Engels, *The Communist Manifesto*, p. 17.

But the bourgeois revolution gave the land to the peasants, as shown particularly in the exemplary case of France. Therefore, the peasantry in its great majority becomes the ally of the bourgeoisie within the camp of the defenders of the sacred character of private property and becomes the adversary of the proletariat.

However, the transfer of the centre of gravity of the socialist transformation of the world, emigrating from dominant imperialist centres to dominated peripheries, radically modifies the peasant question. Revolutionary advances become possible in the conditions of societies that still remain, in great part, peasant, only if socialist vanguards are able to implement strategies that integrate the majority of the peasantry into the fighting block against imperialist capitalism.

V

Marx and Engels never believed, neither in the editing of the *Manifesto* nor later, in the spontaneous revolutionary potential of the working classes, since 'the ruling ideas of each age have ever been the ideas of its ruling class'.[12] Due to this fact, workers, like others, subscribe to the ideology of competition, a cornerstone of the functioning of capitalist society, and, hence, the 'organization of the proletarians into a class, and consequently into a political party, is continually being upset again by the competition between the workers themselves'.[13]

Therefore the transformation of the proletariat from a class in itself into a class for itself requires the active intervention of a communist vanguard: 'The Communists . . . are on the one hand practically the most advanced and resolute section of the working-class parties of every country, that section which pushes forward all others; on the other hand, theoretically, they have over the great

[12] Marx and Engels, *The Communist Manifesto*, p. 37.
[13] Marx and Engels, *The Communist Manifesto*, pp. 18–19.

mass of the proletariat the advantage of clearly understanding the line of march, the conditions, and the ultimate general results of the proletarian movement.'[14]

The affirmation of the unavoidable role of the vanguards does not mean for Marx an advocacy in favour of the single party. As he writes in the *Manifesto*, 'the Communists do not form a separate party opposed to other working-class parties. . . . They do not set up any sectarian principles of their own, by which to shape and mould the proletarian movement.'[15]

And later, in his conception of what should be a Proletarian International, Marx considered it necessary to integrate into it all the parties and currents of thought and action that benefit from a real popular and worker audience. The First International included in its membership the French Blanquists, the German Lasallians, English trade unionists, Proudhon, anarchists, Bakunin. Marx certainly did not spare his criticisms, often harsh, of many of his partners. And one might say that probably the violence of these conflictual debates is at the root of the brief life of this International. Let it be as it may. This organization nevertheless was the first school for the education of the future cadres engaged in the fight against capitalism.

Two observations lead to the question of the role of the party and the communists.

The first is related to the relationship between the communist movement and the nation. As we can read in the *Manifesto*: 'The working men have no country. We cannot take from them what they have not got. Since the proletariat must first of all acquire political supremacy, must rise to be the leading class of the nation, must constitute itself the nation, it is, so far, itself national, though not in the bourgeois sense of the word.'[16] And, 'though not in

[14] Marx and Engels, *The Communist Manifesto*, pp. 25–26.
[15] Marx and Engels, *The Communist Manifesto*, p. 25.
[16] Marx and Engels, *The Communist Manifesto*, pp. 35–36.

substance, yet in form, the struggle of the proletariat with the bourgeoisie is at first a national struggle'.[17]

In the capitalist world the proletarians do not share the nationalism of their country; they do not belong to that nation. The reason is that in the bourgeois world the only function of nationalism is to give legitimacy, on the one hand, to the exploitation of workers of the given country and, on the other hand, to the fight of the bourgeoisie against its foreign competitors and its fulfilment of its imperialistic ambitions. However, with the triumph of eventual socialist revolution, all would change.

The foregoing relates to the first long stages of the socialist transition in the societies of the peripheries. It also expresses respect for the necessary diversity of the roads taken. Additionally, the concept of the final objective of communism strengthens the importance of this national diversity of the proletarian nations. The *Manifesto* already formulated the idea that communism is built on diversity of individuals, collectives, and nations. Solidarity does not exclude but implies the free development of all. Communism is the antithesis of capitalism, which, in spite of its praise of 'individualism', produces in fact, through competition, clones formatted by the domination of capital.

In this connection I shall quote what I recently wrote in *October 1917 Revolution*:

The support or the rejection of national sovereignty gives rise to severe misunderstandings as long as the class content of the strategy in the frame of which it operates is not identified. The dominant social bloc in capitalist societies always conceives national sovereignty as an instrument to promote its class interests, i.e., the capitalist exploitation of home labour and simultaneously the consolidation of its position in the global system. Today, in the context of the globalized liberal system dominated by the financialized monopolies of the

---

[17] Marx and Engels, *The Communist Manifesto*, p. 22.

Triad (U.S.A., Europe, Japan) national sovereignty is the instrument which permits ruling classes to maintain their competitive positions within the system. The government of the U.S.A. offers the clearest example of that constant practice: sovereignty is conceived as the exclusive preserve of U.S. monopoly capital and to that effect the U.S. national law is given priority above international law. That was also the practice of the European imperialist powers in the past and it continues to be the practice of the major European states within the European Union.[18]

Keeping that in mind, one understands why the national discourse in praise of the virtues of sovereignty, hiding the class interests in the service of which it operates, has always been unacceptable for all those who defend the labouring classes.

Yet we should not reduce the defence of sovereignty to that modality of bourgeois nationalism. The defence of sovereignty is no less decisive for the protection of the popular alternative on the long road to socialism. It even constitutes an inescapable condition for advances in that direction. The reason is that the global order (as well as its sub-global European order) will never be transformed from above through the collective decisions of the ruling classes. Progress in that respect is always the result of the unequal advance of struggles from one country to another. The transformation of the global system (or the subsystem of the European Union) is the product of those changes operating within the framework of the various states, which, in their turn, modify the international balance of forces between them. The nation-state remains the only framework for the deployment of the decisive struggles that ultimately transform the world.

The peoples of the peripheries of the system, which is

[18] Amin, *October 1917*, pp. 83–85. I have discussed this question specific to Europe in Chapter 4 of my book *The Implosion of Contemporary Capitalism*, New York: Monthly Review Press, 2013.

polarizing by nature, have a long experience of positive, progressive nationalism, which is anti-imperialist, and rejects the global order imposed by the centres, and therefore is potentially anti-capitalist. I say only potentially because this nationalism may also inspire the illusion of a possible building of a national capitalist order that is able to catch up with the national capitalisms ruling the centres. In other words, nationalism in the peripheries is progressive only on the condition that it remains anti-imperialist, conflicting with the global liberal order. Any other nationalism (which in this case is only a facade) that accepts the global liberal order is the instrument of local ruling classes aiming to participate in the exploitation of their peoples and eventually of other weaker partners, operating therefore as sub-imperialist powers.

The confusion between these two antonymic concepts of national sovereignty, and therefore the rejection of any nationalism, annihilates the possibility of moving out of the global liberal order. Unfortunately, the left—in Europe and elsewhere—often falls prey to such confusion.

The second point concerns the segmentation of the working classes, in spite of the simplification of the society connected with the advancement of capitalism, evoked in the *Manifesto*: 'Our epoch, the epoch of the bourgeoisie, possesses, however, this distinctive feature: it has simplified the class antagonisms. Society as a whole is more and more splitting up into two great hostile camps, into two great classes directly facing each other: Bourgeoisie and Proletariat.'[19]

This double movement—of the generalization of the proletarian position and simultaneously the segmentation of the world of workers—is today considerably more visible than it was in 1848, when it was barely appearing.

We have witnessed during the prolonged twentieth century, up to our days, a generalization without precedent of the proletarian

[19] Marx and Engels, *The Communist Manifesto*, p. 3.

condition. Today, in the capitalist centres, almost the totality of the population is reduced to the status of employees selling their labour power. And, in the peripheries, the peasants are integrated more than ever before into commercial nets that have annihilated their status as independent producers, making them dominated subcontractors, reduced in fact to the status of sellers of their labour power.

This movement is associated with the pauperization processes: the individual 'becomes a pauper, and pauperism develops more rapidly than population and wealth'.[20] This pauperization thesis, retaken and amplified in *Capital*, was the object of sarcastic critiques by the vulgar economists. And still, at the level of the world capitalist system—the only level that gives the full scope to the analysis of the reality—this pauperization is considerably more visible and real than Marx imagined. Yet, parallel to this, capitalist forces have succeeded in weakening the danger that generalized proletarianization represents by implementing systematic strategies aimed at segmenting the working classes on all levels, nationally and internationally.

VI

The third section of the *Manifesto*, entitled 'Socialist and Communist Literature', could appear to a contemporary reader to belong truly to the past. Marx and Engels offer us here commentaries concerning historical subjects and their intellectual production that belong to their time. Long forgotten, these questions seem today to be the concern exclusively of archivists.

However, I am struck by the persistent analogies with more recent, in fact contemporary, movements and discourses. Marx denounces reformists of all forms, who had understood nothing of the logics of capitalist deployment. Have these disappeared

[20] Marx and Engels, *The Communist Manifesto*, p. 23.

from the scene? Marx denounced the lies of those who condemn the wrongdoings of capitalism, but nevertheless, 'in political practice . . . they join in all coercive measures against the working class'.[21] Are the fascists of the twentieth century and of today, or the allegedly religious movements (the Muslim Brothers, the fanatics of Hinduism and Buddhism), any different?

Marx's criticisms of the competitors of Marxism and their ideologies, as well as his efforts to identify the social milieus for which they are spokespeople, does not imply that for Marx, and for us, authentic anti-capitalist movements should not be necessarily diversified in their sources of inspiration. I point the reader to some of my recent writings on this subject, conceived from the perspective of the reconstruction of a new International as a condition for the efficacy of the popular struggles and visions of the future.[22]

VII

I shall conclude with words that follow my reading of the *Manifesto*.

The *Manifesto* is the hymn to the glory of capitalist modernity, of the dynamism which it inspires, having no parallel during the long history of civilization. But it is at the same time the swan song of this system, whose own movement is nothing more than a generation of chaos, as Marx always understood and reminded us. The historical rationality of capitalism does not extend beyond its production in a brief time of all the conditions—material, political, ideological, and moral—that will lead to its supersession.

I have always shared that point of view, which I believe to be that of Marx, from the *Manifesto* to the first epoch of the Second

---

[21] Marx and Engels, *The Communist Manifesto*, p. 44.

[22] See 'Unité et Diversité des Mouvements Populaires au Socialisme' in the book *Egypte, Nassérisme et Communisme*; and 'L'Indispensable Reconstruction de l'Internationale des Travailleurs et des Peuples', in Investig'Action blog, www.investigaction.net/fr.

International lived by Engels. The analyses that I have proposed concern the long ripening of capitalism—ten centuries—and the contributions of the different regions of the world to this maturation (China, the Islamic East, Italian cities, and finally Atlantic Europe), its short zenith (the nineteenth century), and finally its long decline that manifests itself through two long systemic crises (the first from 1890 to 1945, the second from 1975 to our days). These analyses have the objective of deepening that which was in Marx only an intuition.[23] This vision of the place of capitalism in history was abandoned by the reformist currents within Marxism of the Second International and then developed outside of Marxism. It was replaced by a vision according to which capitalism will have accomplished its task only when it will have succeeded in homogenizing the planet according to the model of its developed centres. Against this persistent vision of the globalized development of capitalism, which is simply unrealistic since capitalism is in its nature polarizing, we put forward the vision of the transformation of the world through revolutionary processes—breaking with the submission to the deadly vicissitudes of the decadence of civilization.

October 01, 2018

---

[23] See Samir Amin, *The Implosion of Contemporary Capitalism.*